Literature in context

RENAISSANCE LATIN POETRY

Literature in context series

General editor
DOUGLAS BROOKS-DAVIES

Renaissance views of man
STEVIE DAVIES

Jonathan Swift: the contemporary background
CLIVE T. PROBYN

In preparation

Petrarch and his followers: the English and French traditions
STEPHEN MINTA

English Romantic Hellenism, 1700–1824
TIMOTHY WEBB

Further titles in prospect

RENAISSANCE LATIN POETRY

I. D. McFARLANE

*Literature
in context*

**Manchester
University Press**

BARNES & NOBLE BOOKS · NEW YORK
(a division of Harper & Row Publishers Inc.)

MANCHESTER UNIVERSITY PRESS 1980

First published 1980
by Manchester University Press
Oxford Road, Manchester M13 9PL

British Library cataloguing in publication data

Renaissance Latin Poetry. – (Literature in context).
1. Latin poetry, Medieval and modern
I. McFarlane, Ian Dalrymple
II. Series
871'.04'08   PA8123

ISBN 0-7190-0741-0

Published in the U.S.A. 1980 by
HARPER & ROW PUBLISHERS, INC.
BARNES & NOBLE IMPORT DIVISION

ISBN 0-06-494702-5

LC 79 : 55022

Computerised Phototypesetting
by G C Typeset Ltd., Bolton, Greater Manchester

Printed and bound in Great Britain
at The Pitman Press, Bath

Contents

General editor's preface—viii

Introduction—1

The elegy

The ode

Religious poetry

Didactic poetry

Court and celebratory poetry

The eclogue

General editor's preface

One of the basic problems in reading literature is that of establishing a context for it. In the end the context of any work is infinite and unknowable. But if we approach the problem more simple-mindedly (and ignore questions posed by biography) we can say that a work's context is to a large extent definable by the ideas —theological, philosophical, political, and so on—current in the period in which it was written, and by the literary forms and genres that a period fosters and prefers. It is the ultimate aim of this series to try to help the student of English literature place works of all periods in their various contexts by providing volumes containing annotated selections of important background texts on the assumption that it is through contact with original texts only that true understanding may develop. Some of the volumes will be wide-ranging within a given period, containing a variety of texts (some in full, some extracts) illustrating dominant ideas and themes or forms; others will be more specialised, offering background material to the ideas and forms embodied in individual works of a particular author or concentrating on one or two thematic obsessions of a period. Although the emphasis is on English literature, much of the background material adduced will be of European origin. This will be presented in translation and, in appropriate cases (usually verse), the original will be printed with a translation on the facing page. The series should thus be of use to students pursuing comparative literature courses as well as interdisciplinary courses involving literature. In each volume there will be a substantial introduction, explanatory headnotes to the texts, and a bibliography of suggested further reading.

Douglas Brooks-Davies

Introduction

GENERAL OBSERVATIONS

Since the literature of the Renaissance is thoroughly grounded in the culture of the ancient world, it is hardly surprising that its awakening should express itself to a great extent in Latin, and that for poetry Latin should be just as important a vehicle of expression as the vernacular. In a curious way Neo-latin literature helps to fill the gap that opens up between a fading medieval culture and the gradual emergence of a new world. Very often, Neo-latin acts as a sort of John the Baptist to the vernacular literature that is about to take wing on its own. Not of course that this is always the case, but Neo-latin undoubtedly flourishes before the vernacular has established its claims in the eyes of the best qualified contemporaries. At the same time, the conditions in which Neo-latin can achieve its most interesting work are very delicate. It must have attained a certain linguistic and stylistic maturity, its practitioners must be in close touch with the most vital currents of their time, and scholarly considerations of an unduly purist nature must not gain so firm a grip that the language loses its contemporary relevance and becomes antiquarian in outlook.

Neo-latin literature benefited from a number of important factors. On the one hand, the suspicion died hard that the vernacular was not yet ready to express a wider range of inspiration, especially in the more elevated registers. With this was coupled the very different fear: that it was developing so rapidly that it would in all likelihood become unintelligible to succeeding generations, unlike Latin, which had withstood with signal success the onslaughts of time. On the other hand, Latin remained the linguistic instrument of important vested interests : the Church, the legal profession, the world of medicine, though encroachments were gradually to be made. Another telling argument was that

Latin by definition was the most effective channel for international communication, a point that did not escape the notice of men of letters who wished to establish their reputations beyond the frontiers of their own country. Moreover, in the sixteenth century, and particularly during the wars of religion, Latin verse was to become a substantial part of national propaganda machines. There were naturally counter-arguments in favour of the vernacular: Rome, though it had imitated Greek models in many ways, had created its own vernacular literature with conspicuous success; if the method had worked in Rome, then why not in Italy, France, England or Germany? And there were nagging thoughts that so old a language as Latin might not be equal to the rapidly growing demands of the contemporary world. Strangely, it is not uncommon for pleas in favour of the vernacular to be written in Latin. What seems clear is that, in the eyes of many, Latin and vernacular were not seen as adversaries, but as allies in a common cultural cause. Only gradually is the position of Latin eroded; it was still a live vehicle of expression down to the eighteenth century.

Other factors undoubtedly favoured the Neo-latin cause. The new humanist educational system—in which Paris played so prominent a part—provided a training in which the Latin language formed the backbone. Almost all the teaching was done in Latin and the vernacular was to all intents and purposes forbidden—there were voices in favour of the vernacular, but they were very much in the minority. Moreover certain aspects of this classical formation—including Latin verse composition—were strongly defended on grounds of Christian morality. The links between a mastery of the classics and development of the Christian man were asserted by the most distinguished humanists, above all Erasmus; nor did the persistent misgivings about the incompatibility of the Christian and the pagan worlds cut all that much ice. Then the developing vernacular literatures throughout Europe were essentially aristocratic, contemptuous of the wider, ignorant public; such an attitude would hardly work to the detriment of Latin. Two other points are worth mentioning: it is anachronistic to talk of the Renaissance sensibility not being at home in Latin, as if humanists were writing in a foreign tongue that could not correspond to the inner workings of their mind. Until 1550 in France, it seems that more works were published in Latin than in the vernacular. Many writers were bilingual both in verse and in prose. The second point is that poetry, for the Renaissance mind, was in great measure rhetoric, with all its rules, figures, styles and conventions. These features were valid in Latin as well as in the vernacular, and one cannot be sure that many poets had a lively sense of the individual rhetorical and poetical character of their native tongue. The teaching of Latin text books left its mark on the vernacular as well; and the growing interest in translation as a poetic genre lends further colour to this view.

Of course, Neo-latin poetry suffered in the long run through its links with school and university (Italy was less affected in this respect). The Erasmian view of Latin adapting itself to the development needs of contemporary civilisation was opposed by many scholars who preferred a closer adherence to Vergil and Cicero. Much Neo-latin verse is pedantic, technical rather than imaginative, and often plain trivial. In the long run it came to appeal to a limited type of audience of professional formation. But at its best, it was fed by the richest currents of the Renaissance, and was a natural vehicle for important aspects of contemporary sensibility. Latin remained valuable for propaganda and parade, so that Neo-latin verse became established in the ceremonial activities of many lands and played an important role in the religious and political controversies of the period.

NEO-LATIN POETRY IN ITALY

Renaissance Latin poetry begins early in Italy, as one would expect; and its quality remains higher than that of other countries, though these produce here and there poets of great distinction. Its beginnings are evidently associated with the growing humanist awareness of the ancient world, but there is also at work a patriotic desire to achieve literary prominence that finds its way into Latin as well as into the vernacular, and particularly at a time when the vernacular had not yet attained its majority. After all, Petrarch believed that his posthumous fame would rest on his rather unsatisfactory *Africa* (*c.* 1338). In the fourteenth century one or two figures set Neo-latin poetry on its way—Petrarch, Boccaccio and Salutati—but its prosperity depends in the long run on the growing status of humanism, connected so closely with the *vita activa*, the accompanying phenomenon of patronage in high quarters and the establishment of groups or centres likely to give further impetus to poetic activity. There continue to appear men of letters whose livelihood will be assured by teaching, sometimes political or diplomatic involvement, or an ecclesiastical career. Among these are notably Battista Spagnuoli, who rose to become head of the Carmelite order, and Faustus Andrelinus who did much, after his *Livia* (published originally in Rome in 1481), to fashion ceremonial and political poetry in France where he ultimately became *poeta regius* (court poet). Poetry of more lasting value came from well organised foci and in particular from certain Academies which maintained a remarkable range of interests in their pursuits: philosophy, letters, ethics, political theory, scientific matters and music. Four centres flourish abundantly, and two of them are outstanding.

Under the leadership of Panormita (1394–1471) there developed a very lively academy at Naples, in spite of the political strife that afflicted the city. With this Academy were associated three Latin poets of lasting quality whose works were also read in England down to the eighteenth century: Pontano, at one time the recognised head of the Academy, Jacopo Sannazaro and Michael Marullus. These men, of very different origin—Sannazaro had Spanish blood and Marullus came from a family of Cypriot origin—produced poetry which not only reflected their differing sensibilities but attained a rare standard of range and maturity. Sannazaro, who wrote in Latin and Italian, became an European model for certain types of pastoral. Ferrara and Florence brought into being their numerous bands of poets but fewer of superior attainments, fewer too whose reputation travelled beyond the confines of the Italian peninsula. In Ferrara the most notable were the two Strozzi, whereas Florence claimed Naldi and Politiano. The richest and most lasting centre was doubtless Rome, and though one notes the presence of a number of secular patrons including Angelo Colucci, the main focus for a considerable period was the Papal Court under Leo X, the son of Lorenzo de Medici of Florence, a humanist greatly addicted to Latin verse and to its practitioners. Many of these contributed significantly to the development of vernacular literature as well; among their ranks we find poets who attain European fame: Navagero, Castiglione, Vida, Fracastor, Marcantonio Flaminio, Angeriano, Lampridio, Janus Vitalis and Molza. For some time the momentum acquired over a few decades maintained a remarkable activity right into the sixteenth century, when quantity began to overtake quality; it is in the period 1450–1550 that we shall find lasting models for later Latin and vernacular developments. Their popularity will be reflected in the influence they exerted on individual authors, in editions of their works published abroad, particularly in France, and in the numerous anthologies that form so important an aspect of the humanist landscape.

Two further points may be made. First, though poetic activity was so closely connected with certain distinguished centres, one must not think of them as discrete entities: in a world so troubled politically as was Renaissance Italy and a time when scholars tended with their humanist interests to lead a somewhat peripatetic life, it was inevitable that there should be frequent personal contacts between these centres. Second, though no doubt the most seminal Latin poetry derived from these distinguished circles, one must remember that there is a lot of rather different poetry being written which was well regarded in its time, though it has since fallen into neglect. There is an abundant vein of religious poetry whose inspiration is traditional and often late-medieval in character; and a good number of poets try their hand at extended compositions of a historical or epic nature. If one consults, for instance, the *Specimen Epithetorum* of Ravisius Textor (Paris, 1519 n.s.), one will see that their names are as frequently quoted as the familiar ones of Pontano, Politian and the Strozzi. Tito Strozzi did in fact write an epic poem, the *Borsias*, but we have had to wait until this decade for it to see print. The growing interest in historiography and the vested interests of prominent families go a long way to explain the popularity of the genre; but the epic style may also find its way into religious verse, and more especially into hagiographic compositions. If however we except Mantuan, comparatively little of this sort of writing will retain the interest of readers abroad after the beginning of the sixteenth century.

NEO-LATIN POETRY IN FRANCE

French activity can be fairly conveniently divided into three main periods. The first runs from the beginnings of printing to the end of the 1520s. At first the more interesting figures cluster round Robert Gaguin and his circle; many of them have Flemish origins, and their inspiration often has a late medieval flavour. Their background is usually ecclesiastical, and like Erasmus they see the need for the Christian man to have a sound classical training; but their range of poetic interest has clear limits. During these years, much effort is put into improving Latinity and methods of education; contacts with Italy are increasing rapidly, and poets manage to establish some footing at court. Much verse is religious in character, but a number of writers try their hand at epigrams and occasional verse; and in the reign of Louis XII, partly through the initiative of Faustus Andrelinus, now permanently settled in France, there is a sudden explosion of patriotic verse which exploits the epic formula but also develops shorter encomiastic verse.

In the early years of Francis I's reign little encouragement is given to poetry in high quarters and patrons become rarer on the ground. There are however rapid and far-ranging developments on the humanist and religious front; a literary watershed appears in 1528 when Salmon Macrin who had begun his poetic career under Louis XII—and in very conventional fashion—published his *Carminum libellus*. This little book, celebrating the poet's courtship and showing the literary presence of Pontano, not only opens up the rich possibilities of lyric metres but helps to acclimatise catullan and petrarchan themes. Here and in subsequent volumes Macrin anticipates vernacular developments in his exploitation of Horace, of literary patriotism, of nature themes; he also foresees the potential value of horatian patterns for religious verse. He had his followers, of whom some for a while coalesce to form the *sodalitium lugdunense*. This was a loosely constituted group of humanists who wrote Latin poetry much of which was published in Lyon 1536–8. Etienne Dolet was for a short while their leader and responsible for the *tombeau* of the Dauphin (1536) written in Latin and French. These writers found themselves in Lyon for a variety of reasons, but they were bound together by common humanist interests and ideals. They reveal a wider awareness of Latin poetry, of Italian humanist writers, and indeed of Greek literature; moreover they are often acutely sensitive to the winds of religious change. Though many of them remain teachers of a rather peripatetic nature, Macrin himself is appointed like his friend Clément Marot *valet de chambre du roy* and his work, less schoolmasterly than some, is affected by his experience of the court and also by wider sources of inspiration in his own life, though his later volumes, apart from his *Naeniae* (1550), tend to be rather uninspired and repetitive.

French Neo-latin poetry probably reaches its peak during the heyday of the Pléiade (1548–60), with which it attains an undoubted symbiosis. This phenomenon has remained in the penumbra, partly because of the noisy gestures of the Pléiade in favour of the vernacular, partly because the quality of the Neo-latin output was obscured by the departure of some poets abroad—Bèze left for Geneva in 1548, the year in which his *Poemata* first appeared, and Muret was obliged for rather less laudable motives, to leave the country in 1553. There is a further reason: two of the most distinguished figures were reluctant to publish their verse, except in an occasional context. Michel de l'Hôpital's dignified *Sermones* do not appear in collected form until after his death; and Buchanan, who lives in France until 1561, does not publish his sacred and profane verse before the mid 1560s. The battle for the vernacular was by no means won yet; indeed many members of the Pléiade wandered into Neo-latin paths, notably Joachim du Bellay whose *Poemata* appeared in 1558. This is the period when French classical scholarship, particularly in the field of textual criticism, reaches hitherto unknown heights and attracts many foreign humanists and students to Paris; a number of these come from the Low Countries or from the other side of the Rhine, and they often distinguish themselves in Latin verse. Shortly the wars of religion will break out, and this disaster will, paradoxically, stimulate a vast production of Neo-latin verse of a committed and inevitably ephemeral character. Neo-latin poetry, which during the reign of Francis I had followed the paths of heterodoxy or at any rate Erasmian evangelism, now becomes closely associated with the Establishment, political and religious: professors and magistrates dominate the ranks of Latin versifiers, and Jean Dorat becomes *poeta regius*. In consequence, there is an abundance of court verse;

but there are also currents of Latin poetry that express Huguenot or Ligueur sentiments. During this period, one notes too the expansion of collective verse: there are the beginnings of salon verse or similar group activities, the wars encourage the publication of *tumuli* (collections of verse in honour of someone recently deceased) which become a manifestation of solidarity by authors in favour of certain religious or political attitudes, and liminary verse (introductory poems) assumes even greater proportions in the publications of the period. These collective efforts are not usually monolingual: they tend to be written in at least two languages, Latin and French, but the claims of virtuosity encourage writing in other languages as well. However, the state of the realm stimulates not only committed verse, but poetry of escape and *divertissement*, and Latin verse benefits from this state of affairs. Latin poetry tends in these circumstances to move towards preciosity, or the extended scholarly exercise, or the ephemera of commitment. Poems of word-play or formal pattern acquire some currency: Scaliger's epigrams, Dorat's chronograms, Melissus's acrostich poems and palindromes exemplify a widespread fashion, which may not always be entirely frivolous or confined to France. Little Christian poetry emerges; we have to wait rather longer for the effects of the Counter-reformation to make themselves felt. In short, this is not a period of distinguished writing, though in quantitative terms it far exceeds anything that had gone before. Only one text leaves a durable mark on English authors: the *Pancharis* of Jean Bonefons.

OTHER COUNTRIES

The Neo-latin poetry of some countries hardly impinges upon England. This is true of the Iberian peninsula and of Poland, where Latin verse is cultivated with some distinction (Casimir Sarbiewski is the interesting exception in that he is known and appreciated in England). Germany tends also to be left in the penumbra, though there are of course some poets whose achievement is partly known: Conrad Celtis in the early days and Petrus Lotichius Secundus. There are also cases where personal relationships and travel promote some exchange: Melissus (Schede) is one example, for he travelled in England and wrote a number of compositions in honour of Queen Elizabeth. The later Italian poets are also an unknown quantity, but there may be a few exceptions, as in the case of the poets quoted in Gabriel Harvey's curious composition in four books celebrating the Queen's progress to Saffron Walden in 1578. Understandably there will be much more contact between England and the Low Countries, and in particular one may stress the links with the Leiden humanists of whom Jan Douza the elder was perhaps the most prominent. A goodly number of compositions show the connections between these humanists and the Sidney circle; and we shall find many compositions celebrating Queen Elizabeth, Lord Burleigh, Robert Dudley and Philip Sidney in life and in death. Some of the Dutch humanists had visited England at one time or another—Jan Dousa is one example and, a bit later, Daniel Heinsius travels to England in his youth. Scholarly contacts are also much in evidence; but in a strictly literary sense the major literary influence from the Low Countries remains that of Joannes Secundus.

One important factor, by the beginning of the seventeenth century, is the impact of the Counter-reformation which shows itself frequently through the literary activities of the Jesuits. The Jesuit order fitted many literary exercises into its pedagogic programmes and published in consequence a very great deal of Latin verse. In schools an important role was given to the theatre and a great number of Latin plays, often of interesting quality, were composed to this effect. The Jesuits, who were keen on inculcating a good Latinity into their pupils, wanted at the same time to avoid any paganisation of their minds; and so they harnessed classical authors to their way of thinking, thus for example the secular Ovidian idiom was adapted to religious topics. Their religious verse was also determined by the spiritual concerns of the Counter-reformation, with its stress on meditation, on the imaginative picturing of suitable religious scenes and on the emotions which they should arouse. Thus there is a renewal of hagiographic verse and much is made of pathetic effects: it is towards the end of the sixteenth century that the poetry of tears assumes significant proportions, and the Jesuits make their own contribution to these currents. They also follow the fashion of paraphrasing sacred texts, and exploit the possibilities of emblematic verse which is accompanied by the taste for sententious verse. In the schools they attached some importance to regular Latin verse composition, and wrote various manuals on the penning of epigrams; and of course they pressed into service the satiric epigram to attack their enemies. Most of this Jesuit verse has been somewhat neglected in recent times, but it was extremely popular in England in the first half of the seventeenth century, as can be seen not only from the influence certain Jesuit writers exerted on poets of some stature, but from their presence in the anthologies of the period (e.g. *Sales Epigrammatum*).

NEO-LATIN POETRY IN ENGLAND

Events take a somewhat idiosyncratic turn in England, where Latin poetry develops in rather different circumstances from those that prevailed in France. There is an initial burst of activity which we associate chiefly with Thomas More and his circle. More's epigrams show an independent spirit and skilful craftsmanship, but he is essentially an European humanist and it is significant that his poems are published abroad. After his death there comes a fallow period; the major figure, John Leland the antiquary, shows equally close affinities with foreign currents, but much of his verse is published some time after his death. In the latter half of Henry VII's reign there is little overt activity, in the sense that Latin verse is rarely printed; perhaps the upsets of the Reformation and their impact on schools and universities offer a partial explanation, but neither the activist Reformer nor the orthodox catholic seems to have been much given to the writing of Latin verse then. In the middle of the century there are a number of respectable Latin poets, such as Parkhurst, Chaloner and Walter Haddon, but they appear to have few contacts with vernacular literature and preserve a slightly old-world look.

It is during the Elizabethan age that new, fruitful attitudes begin to emerge; more modern views of the classical poets prevail, and schools and universities make a much more substantial and continuous contribution to Neo-latin activity. In addition, there is a greater awareness of fruitful literary currents abroad. Westminster, Eton, Oxford and Cambridge become important centres of Latin verse composition; and apart from these foci, there appear a number of poets of stature often writing in the vernacular as well as in Latin. As Leicester Bradner has described developments in this period so thoroughly, there is no need to go over the same ground here, except to note the main areas of activity: first, the involvement of the universities no doubt helped to further the expansion, also occurring abroad, of ceremonial and aulic (courtly) verse. Neo-latin forms part and parcel of the system of parade exploited by monarch and government; and this means also an increase in collective, anthological exercises. Second, there is a markedly antiquarian verse concerned with the history of England and analogous topics, which will include encomiastic and epic elements. Camden is not unique among historians in directing some of his energies into Latin verse of this nature. Then there is the ever increasing current of epigrammatic verse, common all over Europe in the Renaissance, but reaching maturity rather later in England. Finally, with the advent of the Counter-reformation there is quite a lot of religious verse which is indebted to foreign models, often provided by the Jesuits. The peak of Neo-latin activity is perhaps between 1570 and 1620 approximately, after which there is some loss of momentum, though further impetus will occur later in the century, with the appearance of figures such as Abraham Cowley. Most of the major writers are in fact bilingual poets (Herbert, Crashaw, Campion, Phineas Fletcher, John Milton) and they all come within the period I have mentioned. There is a vigorous evolution of Latin poetry in Scotland, partly as a result of the example set by George Buchanan whose work has little to do with England—except for the poems he wrote to the Cecil circle during his diplomatic visits to London and York; some of the Scots writers find their way abroad, where religious sympathies may encourage them to remain.

AIMS OF THIS ANTHOLOGY

The title of this anthology must be seen in the context of the series to which it belongs. It is not meant to be representative of the various currents of Renaissance poetry but to point to those authors and themes which had a ready audience in England and to the importance that certain continental currents of Neo-latin poetry had for English men of letters. This means, first that certain countries are almost completely excluded: the emphasis must inevitably be on various Italian poets, with a less prominent contribution from France. With the exception of Joannes Secundus, the Low Countries have little to offer unless personal contacts are involved—and these may be very important at a wider cultural level—or there are Jesuit authors from the region. Second, the anthology does not fulfil two traditional aims: on the one hand, to express the anthologist's personal preferences, and on the other, to give a representative view of the development of Neo-latin poetry during the Renaissance. These selections will therefore not compete with two anthologies recently come on to the market: *Musae reduces*, edited by Pierre Laurens and C. Balavoine, and that prepared by John Sparrow and Alessandro Perosa, an anthology which in any case limits its terms of reference to the period 1450–1550 approximately. There is a further point of difference: with the exception of the section on didactic verse, I have decided not to give excerpts from poems.

The anthology will thus include poems which are known to have influenced certain English authors, samples from genres that acquired popularity here, texts that illustrate various technical qualities. The section containing ceremonial verse is limited by the fact that so much of this kind of poetry quickly loses topicality and may prove obscure to the modern reader; I have therefore confined myself to matters which concerned England or France. There are a number of other poems which are included because their authors had some connection with England or wrote about it. Generally speaking, I have my eye mainly on the period up to 1640 or thereabouts; but it must not be forgotten that renewed interest in Neo-latin poetry is part of the Augustan scene, with further editions of certain poets, full entries in dictionaries and encyclopaedias, and numerous translations. One literary encyclopaedia giving an extensive list of the reading one would expect to find in any educated young gentleman did not fail to include Neo-latin poets, and even mentioned the *Sequana* of Salmon Macrin. I have included an eclogue by Battista Spagnuoli, because he figures so prominently on school-programmes; and more than one critic has expressed the opinion that, in some English schools in the first half of the seventeenth century, boys were probably exposed more to Neo-latin authors than to representatives of the Golden Age. On the other hand, I have not included any samples of Neo-latin poetry written in England. This was agreed as a matter of editorial policy, since the Neo-latin verse of English poets is relatively easily available and its inclusion would have made it difficult to give a representative selection of the continental writers; but in any case, as we have seen, it is unlikely that there was all that coming and going between the vernacular and the Neo-latin poetry in England during the greater part of the period.

The Bibliography has been kept to a working minimum, and is divided into three elements: a section of a general nature at the end of the Introduction, relevant titles for each genre, to be found at the end of the introductory remarks to each section, and bibliographical references that accompany the notes to each author or poem. Finally, I have provided a very short list of the major anthologies so important for the diffusion of Neo-latin poetry.

Where possible, the translations are taken from contemporary or eighteenth-century sources: these verse renderings range from Timothy Kendall's *Trifles* (1577) to the end of the Georgian period. In one or two cases, I have given French renderings, for specific reasons that are mentioned in the relevant notes. Some of the English versions are admittedly free and long-winded—Secundus seems to attract prolix admirers; but these are versions through which in some measure knowledge of the poets filtered to wider audiences.

The texts of the poems are taken, as far as possible, from the first editions or the last editions corrected by the authors; but I also mention modern editions if they exist. In some cases, I have not been able to lay my hand upon the first edition; and so I have had recourse to volumes that would, in all likelihood, have been available to the English poets in question. Modern editions may, from one point of view, be too scholarly if they are relying on the manuscript tradition that would usually be unknown to the English poets we have in mind. It is, for instance, almost certain that a writer like George Watson would have knowledge of characters such as Etienne Forcadel or Gervais Sepin only by way of Ranutius Gherus' *Delitiae C. Poetarum Gallorum*. Latin spelling varies a good deal from printer to printer in the Renaissance; the texts have therefore been stripped of their more glaring eccentricities. The same goes for punctuation; on reflection I have decided against wholesale modernisation in a selection of this nature, as readers may wish to gain some acquaintance with practices which (as in English texts) they will encounter later.

Finally, I should like to thank Dr Terence Cave for his comments on a draft of this anthology.

BIBLIOGRAPHY

General works

Adams, J. W. L. Ch. III (on Neo-latin poetry in Scotland), in *Scottish Poetry*, ed. J. Kinsley, London, 1955.

Arnaldi, F. (ed. with Rosa, L. G. and Sabia, L. M.). *Poete latini del Quattrocento*, Milan, 1965 (La Letteratura italiana: storia e testi, vol. 15).

Binns, J. W. (ed.). *The Latin Poetry of English Poets*, London–Boston, 1974.

Bradner, Leicester. *Musae anglicanae. A History of Anglo-Latin Poetry 1500–1925*. New York, 1940.

Budik, P. *Leben und Wirken der vorzüglichsten lateinischen Dichter des XV–XVIII Jahrhunderts*. 3 vols. Vienna, 1828.

Croce, Benedetto. 'Poesia latina del Rinascimento', *La Critica* XXX (1932), 241–60; 321–38.

Ellinger, G. *Geschichte der neulateinischen Literatur Deutschlands im XVIten Jahrhundert*. 3 vols. Vol. I, Berlin–Leipzig, 1929; vol. II, Berlin–Leipzig, 1929; vol. III. i, Leipzig, 1933 (this uncompleted work covers Italian Latin poetry, German Latin poetry in the first half of the sixteenth century, and Latin poetry in the Netherlands until the beginning of the seventeenth century).

Hausmann, Frank Rutgers. 'Untersuchungen zum neulateinischen Epigramm Italiens im Quattrocento', *Humanistica Lovaniensia* XXI (1972), 1–35.

Hermann, Max (ed.). *Lateinische Literaturdenkmäler des XV und XVI Jahrhunderts*. 19 vols., Berlin, 1891–1912.

Humanistica Lovaniensia. Periodical edited by Professor J. IJsewijn (Leuwen) and specialising in Neo-latin literature.

IJsewijn, J. *Companion to Neo-Latin Studies*, Amsterdam–New York, 1977.

Laurens, P. & Claude Balavoine. *Musae Reduces. Anthologie de la poésie latine dans l'Europe de la Renaissance.* 2 tomes, Leiden, 1975.

Mann, Wolfgang. *Lateinische Dichtung in England vom Ausgang des Frühhumanismus bis zum Regierungsantritt Elizabeths.* Halle, 1939.

Murarasu, D. *La Poésie néo-latine et la Renaissance des lettres antiques en France (1500–1549).* Paris, 1928.

Sainati, A. *La lirica latina del Rinascimento.* 2 vols., Pisa, 1919.

Scaliger, J.–C. *Poetices libri septem,* Lyon, 1561 (facsimile with introduction by A. Buck, Stuttgart–Bad Cannstatt, 1964).

Schnur, Harry C. *Lateinische Gedichte deutscher Humanisten. Lateinisch und Deutsch.* Stuttgart, 1967.

Sparrow, John. 'Latin verse of the High Renaissance', in *Italian Renaissance Studies. A Tribute to the late Cecilia M. Ady,* ed. E. F. Jacob. London, 1960, pp. 354–90.

Van Tieghem, Paul. 'La Littérature latine de la Renaissance. Etude d'histoire littéraire européenne', *Bibliothèque d'Humanisme et Renaissance* IV (1944), 177–409.

Vissac, J. A. *De la Poésie latine en France au siècle de Louis XIV.* Paris, 1862.

Wright, F. A. and Sinclair, T. A. *A History of later Latin Literature.* London, 1931.

Select list of Neo-latin anthologies

1526 *Carmina quinque Hetruscorum poetarum,* Florence.

1542 *Christianae poeseos opuscula aliquot* . . . ed. J. Oporinus, Basel.

1544 *Poemata aliquot insignia illustrium poetarum,* ed. G. Cousin (Cognatus), Basel (also 1557).
Pasquillorum Tomi duo, Oporinus, Basel.

1546 *Bucolicorum Autores XXXVIII* . . . *Farrago quidem Eclogarum CLVI* . . . Oporinus, Basel.

?1546 *Doctissimorum nostra aetate Italorum epigrammata,* ed. J. de Gagnay, Paris.

1548 *Carmina quinque illustrium Poetarum,* Venice (further eds.: 1549; Florence 1552, Venice 1558).

1555–60 *Flores epigrammatum (Farrago poematum) ex optimis authoribus excerpti,* ed. L. à Quercu. 2 vols, Paris: vol. I P. Beguin, vol. II G. Cavellat.

1556 *Davidis Psalmi aliquot, latino carmine a quatuor* (sc. quinque) *poetis* . . ., H. Stephanus, Paris.

1568 *Georgii Buchanani* . . . *Franciscanus & fratres,* followed by sections containing poems by Turnèbe, Michel de l'Hôpital, Dorat and C. Utenhove, the editor, Basel.

1576–7 *Carmina illustrium poetarum Italorum,* ed. I. Matthaeus Toscanus. 2 tomes, Paris.

1577 T. Kendall, *Trifles*, London.

1600 *Veneres Blyenburgicae sive Amorum Hortus* . . ., ed. D. Blyenburg, Dordrecht.

1602 *Aenigmatographia* . . ., ed. N. Reusner, Frankfurt.

1608 *Delitiae CC Poetarum Italorum*, ed. R. Gherus (Gruter). 2 vols, Frankfurt.

1609 *Delitiae C Poetarum Gallorum*, ed. R. Gherus. 3 vols, Frankfurt.

1612 *Delitiae Poetarum Germanorum*, ed. R. Gherus. 6 vols, Frankfurt.

1614 *Delitiae Poetarum Belgicorum*, ed. R. Gherus. 7 vols, Frankfurt.

1619 *Amphitheatrum Sapientiae Socraticae Ioco-seriosae*, ed. C. Dornavius. 2 vols., Hanover.

1627 *Delitiae Poetarum Scotorum*, ed. A. Johnston (or Scots of Scotstarvit). 2 vols., Amsterdam.

1631 *Sal Musarum* , . ., ed. F. Hermann Fleyder, Frankfurt.

1637 T. Heywood, *Pleasant Dialogues and Dramma's*, London.
   Delitiae delitiarum, ed. Ab. Wright, Oxford.

1659 *Epigrammatum delectus*, Paris (Many later editions, also London).

1663 *Sales Epigrammatum*, ed. James Wright, London.

1686 *Thesaurus Epitaphiorum* . . ., ed. Philippe Labbé, Paris.

1692 *Musae anglicanae*, London (further eds. or issues: 1699, 1714, 1721, 1741, 1761).

1740 *Selecta Poemata Italorum*. ed. A. Pope. 2 vols., London.

1747 *Selecta Patrum societatis Jesu carmina*, ed. J. B. Lertius, Genoa.

Further information will be found in J. IJsewijn, *Companion to Neo-Latin Studies*, 1977, 232–5. The extensive selection by Alessandro Perosa and John Sparrow appeared after this book had gone to press. Its title is *Renaissance Latin Poetry: An Anthology*, published by Duckworth, London, 1979.

The epigram

The genre ranges very widely: it is best defined *formally*: a short poem that originally served as an inscription (epigraph). It is therefore not automatically a satiric poem, though the example of the Roman satirist Martial makes great headway during the Renaissance. Equally important in its development is the *Greek Anthology* which became known often by means of translations into Latin verse. Formally, the unit is, in the great majority of cases, the elegiac couplet and multiples of this are common up to say, sixteen lines or so, though there comes a point when the epigram may shade into other genres (e.g. the short elegy). The brevity of the poem encourages, if not exclusively, a lightness, a superficiality even of tone and theme; hence in France the neighbouring names of *nugae, ludi*. The epigram owes its success to a variety of causes: a cumulative literary tradition, of course, but also the humanists' habit of writing to each other more or less off the cuff and, with increasing solemnity, to adorn the liminary pages of colleagues' books with encomiastic verse, the development of Latin verse composition in schools, the requirements of patronage, religious and political considerations. The development of collective volumes of verse encourages the art of the epigram too.

Several sub-genres develop in their own right. The epitaph—as opposed to more exalted exercises such as the epicedion—has a vigorous existence in the Renaissance. It may be 'genuine', or humorous, it may be part of traditional satire, anecdotic or didactic. It can take various forms: address by the poet, by the deceased who talks to the Viator (traveller) or members of the family, or by a mythical figure (e.g. Fama), or dialogue. It becomes naturally prominent in the move towards the collective *tumulus* and in this context may assume didactic or political dimensions.

A strong didactic or pedagogic impulse is often at work. Cato's distichs, so-called, were popular in schools, as was Faustus Andrelinus' *Hecatodistichon*. In schools such verse had mnemonic value and would be useful, not only in inculcating potted wisdom, but in memorising the salient features of mythological figures, kings, prominent persons of one sort or another. Reinforcement of the tradition came in the shape of Alciat's *Emblemata* (1531) where moral apophthegms in short poetic form accompanied suitable illustrations with their mottoes. The vogue of emblem-poems (sometimes without the pictures) spread through the Renaissance with great rapidity—Lyon was at one time an important centre—and took root in the Low Countries, Germany and England, though in the course of time the original short poem grew into something of more literary substance. A further impetus came from the uses to which the epigram could be put in the field of religious propaganda. In Italy, there was the tradition of the *pasquilli*, satirical epigrams affixed at the New Year to the statue of Pasquin in Rome. These compositions often attacked the Popes and the higher clergy; many were by orthodox writers, but with the progress of the Reformation, the genre passed more and more into Protestant hands; and later in the sixteenth century, the religious epigram is an important instrument. A particular instance is the *Icon* which in the hands of Boissard and Bèze serves to celebrate persons thought to have contributed substantially to the fortunes of Protestantism. In the Catholic camp, the Jesuits were not slow to incorporate the epigram into their teaching programmes; they produced treatises on its composition, they often published their own efforts, and they were sometimes responsible for important anthologies.

One further sub-genre that may be briefly mentioned is the *xenium* (*strena*); originally inspired by Martial, it acquires popularity both as a form of flattery to patrons and as an exchange of civilities on New Year's days. The practice may spread to other feast-days or dates; and though its literary value can only be slight, it is worth mentioning as part of the humanist scene.

Apart from these fairly well defined sub-genres, the epigram treads familiar paths: amatory verse, sometimes of real quality, satirical and moralising verse often following Horatian tradition in attacking general targets—though there is plenty of verse lampooning recognisable individuals—gossipy trifles to and from humanists, compositions depending on word-play for their effect. The masters are predictably Martial and Ausonius, but Juvenal enters the scene as a source of vocabulary and of theme, and the *Greek Anthology* is not only imitated widely but translated into Latin verse: by the end of the sixteenth century translation becomes a respectable genre in its own right, particularly in France.

BIBLIOGRAPHY

Hudson, Hoyt Hopewell. *The Epigram in the English Renaissance*, Princeton, 1947.

Hutton, James. *The Greek Anthology in Italy to 1800*, Ithaca, 1935.

—— *The Greek Anthology in France and in the Latin Writers of the Netherlands to 1800*, Ithaca, 1946.

Dickinson, Gladys. *Du Bellay in Rome*, Leiden, 1960 (the appendix, pp. 155–211, contains a collection of *pasquilli*).

I   ANGELI POLITIANI

In Laurentium cum ruri querna corona
fronte redimitur viderem, ex tempore

Quam bene glandifera cingis tua tempora quercu
   qui civem servas non modo, sed populum.

II   TITI STROZZAE

In Scaurum divitem et avarum

Scaurus habet villas, urbana palatia, nummos,
   pinguiaque innumeris praedia bobus arat,
huic tamen adsidue maior subcrescit habendi
   numquam divitiis exsatiata fames.   4
ditior est igitur patrio contentus agello,
   qui vivit nullo faenore Fabricius.

III   I. I. PONTANI

Tumulus Ioannis Ioviani Pontani
Viator et Fama conloquuntur

V. Dic age, quid tumulos servas, dea? F. nostra tuemur
   iura. V. deos cinerum num quoque cura tenet?
F. haec mihi prima quidem cura est. V. quid concutis alas
   usque? F. fugo tenebras, quo vigeant tumuli.   4
V. quid sibi, quae collo pendet, tuba? F. nomen amico

I   ANGELO POLITIAN

On seeing Lorenzo (dei Medici) in the country
wearing a crown of oakleaves: an extempore poem

How rightly you circle your temples with oakleaves, you who
protect not only the citizen but the people.

II   TITO STROZZI

Of Scaurus, a riche man and covetous

Scaurus hath sundrie villages,
   rich farmes and manners brave;
Much lande, fat oxen, store of coine:
   he hath what he can have.
Yet still he scrapes with tooth and naile,
   more still he doth desire:
With carkyng caryng covetousnes,
   his mynde is set on fire.
Fabritius better lives than he,
   a poor contented wight:
Whom nether greedy gatheryng,
   nor usury doth delight.

III   G. G. PONTANO

The grave of Giovanni Giovano Pontano
The traveller and Fame converse

T. Tell me, goddess, why do you watch over graves?
F. I watch over what duty bids me. T. Are the gods concerned with
the ashes of the dead also? F. This is indeed the first of my
concerns. T. Why do you keep moving your wings? F. I put to
flight the darkness so that the graves may prosper. T. Why the

dat cineri; ad tumulos hac ego gesta cano.
V. dic agedum, manes cuius hi? F. Vatis; at urnam
    officio posuit docta Minerva suo.   8
hos tumulos Iovianus habet; quae serta virescunt,
    lecta suis manibus disposuere deae.
sed manes ne quaere die: per amoena vagantur
    prata, sonat riguae sicubi murmur aquae: 12
nymphae adsunt et adest dulcis Charis; aurea cantu
    fila movent; leni concinit aura sono.
nocte illum complexa fovet nitidissima coniunx;
    fervet et a nulla parte refrixit amor;   16
haec illi comes in tenebris, quas vincit amoris
    lucida fax: gemina luce coruscat amor.

IV   I. I. PONTANI

Tumulus Gallae sterilis feminae

Galla fui, Gallo coniunx bene iuncta marito,
    verum nec pullos, ova nec ulla dedi.

V   I. I. PONTANI

Ad Musas

Nymphae, quae nemorum comas virentes
atque undas Aganippidas tenetis
et saltus gelidos virentis Haemi,
vos, o Thespiadum cohors dearum,
vestris me socium choris et antris,   5
vulgi avertite dentibus maligni;
et me Castaliae liquore lymphae
sparsum cingite laureis corollis
cantantem modo Sapphicis labellis.

trumpet that hangs from your neck? F. It confers renown on the ashes I favour; and lets me sing to the tombs of the deeds performed by those buried here. T. Tell me then whose shades are these. F. They are the shades of a poet; but learned Minerva performed her duty in placing the urn here. Giovanno lies buried here; and these flourishing wreaths were laid by the goddesses with their own hands. But do not seek out the Shades by day: they wander through pleasant fields wherever the sound of flowing water is heard. The nymphs are present, and so is the gentle Grace; they sing and pluck the golden strings; the breeze utters a gentle song in concert. By night his spouse, beautiful above all others, embraces and cherishes him; their love is aflame and nowise grown cold. She is his companion in the darkness, conquered by the clear flame of their love; their love shines brightly with a double light.

IV   G. G. PONTANO

Epitaph on Galla, a childless woman

I was Galla, and fortunate to have Gallus for a husband; but I produced neither chickens nor any eggs.

V   G. G. PONTANO

To the Muses

Nymphs, who inhabit the green leaves of the woods and the waters sacred to the Muses, and the cool valleys of verdant Haemus, you, o band of Thespian goddesses, save me, a member of your troop and a familiar of your caverns, from the teeth of the evil crowd; sprinkle Castalian water upon me and crown me with laurel wreaths as I sing now in sapphic mode.

VI BALTHASSARIS CASTILIONIS

Epitaphium Gratiae puellae

Siste, viator, ni properas, hoc aspice marmor,
  et lege; ni ploras, tu quoque marmor eris.
Gratia (namque Deas etiam mors saeva profanat)
  mortua et hoc duro est condita sub tumulo. 4
abstulit haec moriens geminas miseranda sorores,
  sic Charites uno tres periere obitu.

VII MARCANTONII FLAMINII

Lusus pastoralis

Inrigui fontes et fontibus addita vallis,
  cinctaque piniferis silva cacuminibus,
Phyllis ubi formosa dedit mihi basia prima,
  primaque cantando parta corona mihi. 4
vivite felices, nec vobis aut gravis aestas,
  aut noceat saevo frigore tristis hiems,
nec lympham quadrupes, nec silvam dura bipennis,
  nec violet teneras hic lupus acer oves. 8
et nymphae laetis celebrent loca sancta choreis,
  et Pan Arcadiae praeferat illa suae.

VIII IANI VITALIS

De Roma

Qui Romam in media quaeris novus advena Roma,
  Et Romae in Roma nil reperis media,
Aspice murorum moles, praeruptaque saxa,
  Obrutaque horrenti vasta theatra situ: 4
Haec sunt Roma. Viden velut ipsa cadavera, tantae
  Urbis adhuc spirent imperiosa minas.

VI   BALDASSARE CASTIGLIONE

Epitaph on Grace a young girl

Stay Traveller, and looke upon / This Marble ere thou part.
Read here, and if thou dropst no teares, / Thou likewise marble art.
Sweet Grace is dead, for cruell death / Takes both the faire and
   wise,
(Alas the while) and here beneath / This stone, intombed lyes,
She both her sisters tooke along, / So that we now may say
All the three graces in her death / Did perish in one day.

VII   MARCANTONIO FLAMINIO

Pastoral Lusus

Water-giving springs and, valley associated with these springs, and
forest surrounded by pine-bearing peaks where fair Phyllis gave me
her first kisses and I won my first crown in the song contest, live
happily, and may neither the heavy summer heat nor dismal winter
harm you with its cruel cold. May the four-footed creature not hurt
your clear water, nor the unfeeling axe the wood, nor the savage
wolf the tender sheep. May the nymphs celebrate the sacred places
by joyful dances, and may Pan choose them in preference to his
Arcadia.

VIII   J. VITALIS

Rome

New Stranger to the City come,
Who midst of Rome enquir'st for Rome,
And midst of Rome canst nothing spye
That looks like Rome, cast backe thine eye;
Behold of walls the ruin'd mole,
The broken stones not one left whole;

Vicit ut haec mundum, nixa est se vincere; vicit,
   A se non victum ne quid in orbe foret.   8
Nunc victa in Roma Roma illa invicta sepulta est,
   Atque eadem victrix victaque Roma fuit.
Albula Romani restat nunc nominis index,
   Quinetiam rapidis fertur in aequor aquis.   12
Disce hinc, quid possit fortuna; immota labascunt,
   Et quae perpetuo sunt agitata manent.

IX   I. SANNAZARII

De mirabili urbe Venetiis

Viderat Hadriacis Venetam Neptunus in undis
   stare urbem et toto ponere iura mari.
'nunc mihi Tarpeias quantumvis Iuppiter arces
   obiice, et illa tui moenia Martis', ait;   4
'Si pelago Tybrim praefers, urbem aspice utramque,
   illam homines dices, hanc posuisse deos.'

Vast Theatres and Structures high,
That levell with the ground now lye,
These now are Rome, and of that Towne
Th'Imperious Reliques still do frowne,
And ev'n in their demolisht seat
The Heav'ns above them seem to threat,
As she the World did once subdue,
Ev'n to her selfe she overthrew;
Her hand in her owne bloud she embru'd,
Lest she should leave ought unsubdu'd:
Vanquisht in Rome, Invict Rome now
Intombed lies, as forc'd to bow.
The same Rome (of the World the head)
In Vanquisher and Vanquished.
The river Albula's the same,
And still preserves the Roman name;
Which with a swift and speedy motion
Is hourely hurry'd to the Ocean.
Learne hence what Fortune can; what's strong
And seemeth fixt, endures not long:
But more assurance may be layd
On what is moving and unstayd.

IX   J. SANNAZARO

Of the admirable city Venice

Neptune in th'Adriatick maine saw stand
Venice whose power did all the Sea command,
And saith, now Jove show thy Tarpeian Towers
And walls of Mars, unto this scite, now ours.
If thou before the mighty Ocean dare
The petty River Tiber to compare,
Behold both Cities, there give up this doome,
The Gods built Venice, Men erected Rome.

X   ANDREAE NAUGERII

Lusus IV
Vota Damidis ad Bacchum pro vite

Hanc vitem, multa quae semper fertilis uva
   haud umquam domini fallere vota solet,
nunc etiam large florentem, consecrat ipse
   vineti cultor Damis, Iacche, tibi.   4
tu face, Dive, tua haec spem non frustretur: et huius
   exemplo fructum vinea tota ferat.

XI   ANDREAE NAUGERII

Lusus XXI
De Cupidine et Hyella

Florentes dum forte vagans mea Hyella per hortos
   texit odoratis lilia cana rosis,
ecce rosas inter latitantem invenit amorem
   et simul adnexis floribus implicuit.   4
luctatur primo et contra nitentibus alis
   indomitus tentat solvere vincla puer.
mox ubi lacteolas et dignas matre papillas
   vidit, et ora ipsos nata movere deos: 8
impositosque comae ambrosios ut sensit odores
   quosque legit diti messe beatus Arabs,
I, dixit, mea, quaere novum tibi mater amorem,
   imperio sedes haec erit apta meo.   12

XII   ANDREAE ALCIATI

Amygdalus

Cur properans foliis praemittis, Amygdale, flores?
   odi pupillos, praecocis ingenii.

X   ANDREA NAVAGERO

Lusus IV
Damis' vow to Bacchus on behalf of his vine

This vine which, ever fruitful with many bunches of grapes, has a habit of never disappointing its owner's prayers, is now consecrated, even now in its abundant prime, by the vine-dresser Damis, to thee, Bacchus. May thou, O God, ensure that this vine of yours disappoints not our hope and that the whole vineyard will fructify after its example.

XI   ANDREA NAVAGERO

Lusus XXI
Cupid and Hyella

Wandering by chance through flowering gardens my Hyella was weaving together white lilies with fragrant roses, when behold, among the roses she came upon Love hiding, and entwined him forthwith in her garland of flowers. He struggled at first; and fluttering his bright wings, the fierce boy tried to loosen his chains. Soon, when he saw her milk-white breasts, worthy of his mother, and a mouth fit to move the very gods, and as he became aware of the ambrosial perfume of her hair, of that perfume which the wealthy Arab gathers in abundant harvest, 'Go, my mother', he said, 'seek for yourself a new Love. This seat will be fit for my throne.'

XII   ANDREA ALCIAT

An almond tree

Why art thou ripe so early in the year?
I hate too early ripeness anywhere.

XIII   EURICII CORDI

In concubinarios sacerdotes

Exiit a summo mandatum Praesule, ne cui
   ulla sacerdoti serva sit aut famula.
non transgressus adhuc sacer ille paruit ordo:
   nulla sacerdoti est serva, sed est domina.   4

XIV   EURICII CORDI

De medicis

Tres medicus facies habet: unam, quando rogatur,
   angelicam; mox est, cum iuvat, ipse Deus.
post ubi curato poscit sua praemia morbo,
   horridus apparet terribilisque Satan.   4

XV   NICOLAI BORBONII

Carmen

Mortuus in parva est inventus pyxide passer,
   passer, amor pulchrae deliciumque Rosae.
longe aliter periit, quam quem tua Lesbia deflet,
   Lesbia, pars animae, docte Catulle, tuae.   4
non hunc esuries, non hunc sitis arida pressit,
   insidiae nullae, nullus acerbus odor.
cum desiderio, nimioque arderet amore
   absentis dominae, tabuit et periit.   8

XIII EURICIUS CORDUS

Against priests who live with concubines

A command was issued by the Pope to the effect that no priest should have a female servant or domestic. So far the priesthood has obeyed without transgressing: a woman is not the servant, but the mistress of a priest.

XIV EURICIUS CORDUS

On doctors

A doctor has three faces: the first is that of an angel when he is called in; when he gives succour, he soon is God himself. Later, when he asks for his fee, having cured the disease, he assumes the appearance of a frightful and terrible Satan.

XV NICOLAS BOURBON

Song

The sparrow that was beautiful Rose's love and delight was found dead in its little cage. It died for a very different reason than the sparrow mourned by your Lesbia, Lesbia your other half, o learned Catullus. It did not die from hunger, nor from a raging thirst, nor from any trap or offensive odour. It was because of its desire and excessive love for its absent mistress that it pined away and died.

XVI   NICOLAI BORBONII

In Hansum Ulbium pictorem incomparabilem

Dum divina meos vultus mens exprimit, Hansi,
    per tabulam docta praecipitante manu,
ipsum et ego interea sic uno carmine pinxi:
    Hansius me pingens maior Apelle fuit.   4

XVII   THEODORI BEZAE

Pistoris et pictoris certamen, ad Buchanani imitationem

Iudice sacrifico pictor pistorque feruntur
    artis certamen constituisse suae.
tum pictor, 'quicquid vastus complectitur orbis,
    aemula naturae pinxerit ista manus.'   4
'at mihi', pistor ait, 'Christum qui condidit orbem,
    natura potior finxerit ista manus.'
'Christum,' inquit pictor, 'paucas tu condis in horas,
    cum nostrum longo tempore perstet opus.'   8
'at tu,' inquit pistor, 'pictura ludis inani,
    cum nostrum vere corpora pascat opus.'
'ergo', pictor ait, 'tu ventri numina pinsis?'
    'vermibus', at pistor, 'numina pingis?' ait.   12
tum iudex, 'satis o satis o certastis, amici,
    quandoquidem haec multis pandere sacra nefas.
ite domum potius, concordi et pectore Christos
    iste mihi pingat, pinsat et iste mihi.'   16

XVI   NICOLAS BOURBON

To Hans Holbein painter without peer

While your divine mind gave expression to my features, Hans, and
your skilled hand hurried over the canvas, I painted you thus
meanwhile in a single line of poetry: Hans, as he did my portrait,
was greater than Apelles.

XVII   THÉODORE DE BEZE

Of a painter and a baker

A Painter and a Baker strivde / which should the other passe
To paint or bake, twixt them to judge, / a Priest ordained was.
The Painter spake (quoth he) what so / the hugy world containes,
Or what so Nature woorkes, is wrought / by Painters arte and
    paines.
(Quoth Baker) this is more then that, / Christ which the worlde did
    frame.
The Baker formes in figure fine, / that all maie see the same.
Quoth Painter then, thou makest Christe, / mennes bellies for to
    fill:
Thy Christes are chrusht with crasshing teeth, / my woorke
    continues still.
Quoth Baker then, what thou doest paint, / doeth no man good in
    deede:
What we doe forme it serves as foode, / the hungrie soule to feede.
Quoth Painter, Bakers bake their Gods, / for wormes to gnawe and
    spill.
Then quoth the Judge, ho holla here, / sufficient for this tyme:
About this waightie thyng to braule, / is sure an hainous crime.
Both to your houses now departe, / and still in peace agree:
And Painters paint, and Bakers bake, / your gods to bryng to me.

XVIII   THEODORI BEZAE

Descriptio Virtutis

Quaenam tam lacero vestita incedis amictu?
  virtus antiquis nobilitata sophis.
cur vestis tam vilis? opes contemno caducas.
   cur gemina est facies? tempus utrumque noto.   4
quid docet hoc frenum? mentis cohibere furores.
  rastros cur gestas? res mihi grata labor.
cur volucris? doceo tandem super astra volare.
  cur tibi mors premitur? nescio sola mori.   8

XIX   IOACH. BELLAII

Epitaphium cuiusdam canis

Latratu fures excepi, mutus amantes:
  sic placui domino, sic placui dominae.

XX   IOANNIS AURATI

De natura mulieris

Femina dulce malum, horis opportuna duabus:
  cum iacet in thalamo, cum iacet in tumulo.

XXI   BERNARDI BAUHUSII

Epigramma

Tot tibi sunt dotes, Virgo, quot sidera caelo.

XVIII   THÉODORE DE BEZE

Description of Virtue

What one art thou, thus in torn weed yclad?
Vertue, in price, whom auncient sages had.
Why poorely rayd? For fadyng Goodes past care.
Why doublefaced? I marke eche fortunes fare.
This bridle, what? Mindes rage to restrain.
Tooles why beare you: I love to take great pain.
Why, winges? I teach above the starres to flye.
Why tread you death? I onely cannot dye.

XIX   JOACHIM DU BELLAY

Epitaph of a dog

The Lover I let passe, the Thief did seize;
So I both Master did, and Mistresse please.

XX   JEAN DORAT

A woman's nature

Women sweet evils are, and twice good those;
Both in their wedding, and their winding cloths.

XXI   BERNHARD VAN BAUHUYSEN

Epigram

You have as many qualities, Virgin, as there are stars in the sky.

XXII GEORGII BENEDICTI

Epitaphium Memoriae Do. Philippo Sidneio

Ades viator, et volens audi et dolens
quod te docere mortui manes volunt.
nomen vide, Philippus est: eques domus
virtutis, ingenique fama nobilis.
nimis sed heu Philippus; hoc nomen fuit   5
omen sinistrum Belgicae et Britanniae.
nam dum tuetur utriusque gloriam,
turmas fugaces hostium insequens equo
letale vulnus accipit, nunc hic iacet,
luctum sui reliquit omnibus bonis.   10
i nunc viator, incluti ducis memor,
tuosque oculos huius tumuli spectaculo
puta beatos esse, te miserum puta.

XXIII I. CATSII

Motto—Mors larvae similis, tremor
hinc, nihil inde maligni

Id mors est homini trepidis quod larva puellis
    excitat ingentes frons utriusque metus.
larva fugat pueros frontem, non terga videntes
    ast aliis risum posteriora movent.   4
sensibus incurrit, cum lurida mortis imago
    (ei mihi) quam multis spes animusque cadit:
at cui terga necis melior doctrina revelat,
    clamat, ades vitae mors melioris iter.   8

XXIV I. POSTHII

Tabacum

Nulla salutifero se comparet herba Tabaco,
    viribus hoc omnes exsuperat reliquas.

XXII   G. BENEDICTI

Memory's epitaph to Sir Philip Sidney

Stand here, traveller, and hear willingly and in sorrow what the shades of the dead man wish to teach you. See his name—Philip: a knight who was the seat of valour, whose fame was that of a noble mind. But alas, too much was he Philip: this name was a sinister omen for Belgium and Britain. For while he watched over the glory of both nations, pursuing the fleeing bands of the enemy upon his horse, he sustained a fatal wound. Now he lies here and has left all good men to grieve for him. Take your leave now, traveller, remembering the famous knight and consider your eyes to be fortunate at the sight of this grave, consider yourself to be wretched.

XXIII   J. KATS

Motto—Death is like a mask, hence the fright,
though there is no harm forthcoming

Death is to man, as Visards to Girles show,
Who frighted run from what they do not know.
Behold the forehead, and th'aspect affrights:
View it behinde, and the mistake delights.
So when Deaths pallid image is presented,
How many men grow strangely discontented,
Who better consel'd, on his backe parts looke,
And cry out, welcome Death; we have mistooke.

XXIV   J. POSTHIUS

Tobacco

Let no herb be compared to the health-giving tobacco-plant; by its virtues it surpasses all others.

Love poetry

Neo-latin poets, as one would expect, wrote much amatory verse; but in some countries there are sluggish beginnings, partly because the writers, with late medieval and ecclesiastical background, show little interest, partly because there is some reluctance to exploit the resources of Horatian metres. Ovid and the Roman elegists are among the principal sources of inspiration, though the Greek Anthology brings some grist to the mill. Once Renaissance trends have established themselves in literature, contemporary fashions play their part as well. In consequence, many poets will be influenced not only by classical models, but by what the pioneering Italian Neo-latins had to offer; the neo-catullan character of love poetry will be exposed to Petrarchan trends from the vernacular and enriched by the *Basia* of Joannes Secundus (1539). The pastoral idiom, developed impressively in Italy by Sannazaro and others, will leave its mark; and when the Greek anacreontic poets are better known and their texts more widely published, they too will bring variations of tone and theme. Neo-latin poets, as for instance Bonefonius, will reflect and develop the movement towards preciosity and mannerist fashions in style. The love poetry of the Neo-latins is a branch of their activity that will command interest right into the eighteenth century.

XXV ANGELI POLITIANI

In Amicam

Adlicis, expellis, sequeris, fugis, es pia, et es trux;
 me vis, me non vis, me crucias, et amas.
promittis, promissa negas, spem mi eripis, et das.
 iam iam ego vel sortem Tantale malo tuam. 4
durum ferre sitim circum salientibus undis,
 durius in medio nectare ferre sitim.

XXVI TITI STROZZAE

De Amore dormiente sub arbore

Materna caperet dum forte sub arbore somnum
 armaque securus deposuisset Amor,
incidit in puerum, neque amico lumine vidit
 antiquum repetens Cynthia mente odium. 4
mox conata faces exstinguere, frangere tela,
 fatales perhibent id vetuisse deas.
sopito certant innectere vincula nymphae,
 ipsa leves pennas vellere diva parat. 8
excutitur somno puer, et miserabile luget.
 audit et ad vocem fert Cytherea gradum.
Mars quoque in auxilium accelerat, cum Pallade Phoebus,
 Dictynne se addit, nec bona verba sonant. 12
quod nisi funestam properasset tollere litem
 Iuppiter, exempli res erat illa mali.
solvite, ait, puerum, funestaque ponite divi
 iurgia, fungatur munere quisque suo. 16

XXV   ANGELO POLITIAN

To his Ladie beloved

In rage thou turnest me awaye, / againe thou doest me take:
Thou harde at heeles dost followe me, / yet me thou doest forsake;
Kinde art thou, courteous eke, / yet cankered, curst againe:
Thou wilt, and wilt not: me thou lovste, / and me thou putst to
     paine.
Thou promisse makst, and it forsakst: / in deepe dispaire I pine,
Yet live in hope: ah Tantal, would / my state were like to thine.
O painfull plague, in cristall streames / to bee athirst and dye:
But what a plague to be a thirste, / sweete Nectar standing by?

XXVI   TITO STROZZI

Love asleep beneath a tree

While Cupid happened to be taking a nap under his mother's tree
and had laid down his arms without a care in the world, Diana
came upon the boy and looked at him with an unfriendly eye,
recalling an old hatred. Soon she tried to extinguish his torches, to
break his arrows, but it is said that this was forbidden by the Fates.
The nymphs rival each other in casting chains around the sleeper,
the goddess herself prepares to pluck out his delicate wings. The
boy is roused from his sleep and utters wretched plaints. Venus
hears and goes towards the sound of his voice. Mars also speeds to
the rescue, Phoebus with Pallas, Dictynna joins in, and far from
agreeable words are spoken. Had Jupiter not hastened to resolve
the grievous quarrel, things would have taken an unedifying turn.
Unloose the boy, he says, and Gods, put aside your grievous
quarrels, let each of you discharge his proper duty.

XXVII   I. I. PONTANI

Ad Stellam puellam

Dum furtim mihi das negasque ocellos
opponisque manum simulque rides,
post hinc et variat color per ora
et suspiria lassa sentiuntur,
stillatim mihi corda diliquescunt,   5
sudor tempora frigidus pererrat,
et passim tremor ossibus vagatur,
ut sensus animum repente linquant,
ut fiam miser et beatus una;
sed iam plus solito nitescit aër,   10
iam lux candidior diem serenat:
cur ah, cur tenebrae repente nobis,
cur nox exoritur, nigrescit aura?
an sentis, miser, an miselle sentis?
Stella est ad speculam, refulsit in te: 15
solem lumina victa pertimescunt.
o claras medio die tenebras,
o lucem sine nube nigricantem!

XXVIII   I. I. PONTANI

Ad Fanniam

Puella molli delicatior rosa,
      quam vernus aër parturit
dulcique rore Memnonis nigri parens
      rigat suavi in hortulo,   4
quae mane primo roscidis cinctos foliis
      ornat nitentes ramulos;
ubi rubentem gemmeos scandens equos
      Phoebus peragrat aethera,   8
tunc languidi floris breve et moriens decus
      comas reflectit lassulas;
mox prona nudo decidit cacumine

XXVII   G. G. PONTANO

To Stella

While stealthily you grant and refuse me your eyes and put up your hand at the same time as you laugh, then your face changes colour and I hear languid sighs; drop by drop my heart dissolves, a cold sweat covers my brow and all over a trembling seizes my frame, so that suddenly my senses take leave of my mind and I become both wretched and happy in a breath; but now the air is brighter than usual: a whiter light brings peace to the day. Ah why, why does darkness suddenly envelop me? Why does night advance and daylight darken? Do you realise, unhappy, oh poor unhappy one what is happening? Stella is at her window and her look has dazzled you; your eyes, vanquished, take fright at her radiance. Oh bright darkness appearing in the middle of the day! Oh daylight that darkens without a cloud about!

XXVIII   G. G. PONTANO

To Fannia

The maiden is more delightful than the tender rose which the spring air brings to life and which the mother of black Memnon moistens with her gentle dew in its charming little garden, the rose which early in the morning adorns the shining twigs covered with dewy leaves when, mounting his sparkling steeds, Phoebus crosses the reddening sky. Then the brief and dying grace of the languishing flower folds back its weary petals. Soon it falls headlong from the top of its bare stalk and so brief a beauty perishes. Thus does

  honorque tam brevis perit.   12
sic forma primis floret annis; indecens
  ubi senectus advenit,
heu languet oris aurei nitens color,
  quod ruga turpis exarat,   16
perit comarum fulgor et frontis decus
  dentesque flavent candidi,
pectus papillis invenustum languidis
  sinus recondet sordidus,   20
quod nunc Eois lucidum gemmis nitet
  tenuisque vestit fascia.
nullas amantis audies maesti preces
  duram querentis ianuam,   24
non serta lentis fixa cernes postibus
  exclusi amantis munera;
sed sola noctes frigido cubans toro
  nulli petita conteres.   28
quin hoc iuventae floridum atque dulce ver
  brevemque florem carpimus?
post lustra quinque iam senectus incipit
  latensque subrepit modo.   32
quare meorum o aura suavis ignium,
  dies agamus candidos
noctesque divae conteramus integras,
  quae mane lucet Hesperus.   36

XXIX   I. I. PONTANI

De infelicitate amantium

Cantando luces peragit sub fronde cicada
  et mulcet silvas carmine laeta suo,
at tenebras sub rore levi, sub deside somno
  transigit et noctes nocte iuvante suas;   4
cantando moritur, sentit nec taedia mortis,
  quin cantu vitam ducit, et exsequias;
o felix ortu, interitu felicior. at me
  et nox nigra gravat, vexat et atra dies.   8

beauty bloom in the early years; when ugly old age advances, the bright colours of the beautiful face fade, alas, furrowed by unbecoming wrinkles; the radiance of the hair dies away, the handsome forehead and the white teeth turn yellow, a dingy vest covers the bosom no longer beautiful with its sagging breasts, now resplendent with oriental jewels and covered with fine bands. You will no longer hear the prayers of the sad lover mourning the harshness of your closed door, nor will you see the wreaths of flowers fixed to the unfeeling door-posts, wreaths brought as presents by the spurned lover; but you will while away your nights in solitude on your cold bed. Why then do we not pluck the blooming and sweet springtime of youth and its short-lived flowering? After the age of twenty-five old age is already on its way and stealthily creeps on apace. Wherefore, sweet breeze of my flames, let us spend our days without a cloud and devote our entire nights to the goddess who, at dawn, shines as the morning star.

XXIX   G. G. PONTANO

Of the infelicitie of Lovers

The grashopper in medowes grene,
    Amongst the fragrant flowers:
With chirpyng chearfull chitteryng shrill,
    doeth passe the tedious howers.
And glads the goodly garnischt groves,
    with laies and merrie tunes:
And slumberyng under dewie grasse,
    the Gladless night consumes.

ante fores iaceo gelidae sub frigora brumae
   nec pudet aetatis Pieridumque senem:
ante fores, sub sole, Leo dum fervet et ignis
   ustulat Icarius, conqueror usque senex.   12
uror amans, tabesco senex; lux omnis amara,
   nox inimica mihi est, noxque diesque nocet.
sors iuvenum miseranda, senum deflenda. cicadae
   sors felix: o iam discite, quid sit amor.   16

XXX   MICHAELIS MARULLI

Ad Neaeram

Rogas quae mea vita sit, Neaera:
qualem scilicet ipsa das amanti, est:
infelix, misera, inquies, molesta
aut si triste magis potest quid esse,
haec est, quam mihi das, Neaera, vitam.   5
qui, dicis, comites? dolor, querelae,

She syngyng dies, and never feeles
    the smart of Parcas knife:
In swete and heavenlie harmonie,
    she leads and leves her life.
O blest in life, and blest in death:
    but me aye me alas:
Bothe daie and night through girt with greef,
    my daies in dole I passe.
In Winter sharpe, in froste and snowe,
    (a crooked caitiffe old)
I lye and crie before her doores,
    quight curlde almost with cold.
Again in Sommer cingyng hotte,
    when Phebus fierce doeth raigne:
Poor selie soule before her doores,
    I (grovelyng) grone and plaine.
I burne in love, age weares me out,
    no daie I finde releef,
No night I rest: but daie and night
    still gript with gronyng greef.
Aye wretched are the yonge in love,
    thrise wretched lovyng sires.
The Grashopper still happie lives,
    oh Cupids frantick fires.

XXX   MICHELE MARULLO

To Neaera

My sweete, you aske what life I live:
Even suche a life as you me give,
Distressed, dolefull, barde from reste:
As bad as well can be expreste:
This is the life for certaintee,
That you my deare doe give to me.
You doe demaunde my deare beside,
What mates a daies with me abide:
Cares, sicknesse pale, and greef of harte,

lamentatio, lacrimae perennes,
langor, anxietas, amaritudo,
aut si triste magis potest quid esse,
hos tu das comites, Neaera, vitae.   10

XXXI   MICHAELIS MARULLI

Ad Neaeram

Ignitos quotiens tuos ocellos
in me, vita, moves, repente qualis
cera defluit impotente flamma.
aut nix vere novo calente sole,
totis artubus effluo, nec ulla   5
pars nostri subitis vacat favillis;
tum qualis tenerum caput reflectens
succumbit rosa verna liliumve
quod dono cupidae datum puellae
furtivis latuit diu papillis,   10
ad terram genibus feror remissis,
nec mens est mihi nec color superstes
et iam nox oculis oberrat atra:
donec vix gelida refectus unda,
et quod vulturio iecur resurgit,   15
adsuetis redeam ignibus cremandus.

XXXII   H. ANGERIANI

De Caelia

Ferrum flamma domat, silicem domat unda, adamantum
     sanguis, at haec ferro durior et silice;
atque adamante, meo non igne, fluente nec unda,
     nec misso e venis sanguine se domuit.   4

Paine, twitching throwes, and scalding smart.
Sighes, sobbes and teares, and great unrest,
As bad, as well can be expreste:
Companions these and mates of mine,
These you my deare to me assine.

XXXI   MICHELE MARULLO

To Neaera

Every time you turn your fiery eyes in my direction, my love, suddenly like wax that has melted in a fierce flame or like snow in early spring under the warm rays of the sun, I feel all my limbs dissolving and no part of me is free from this sudden fire. Then, just as the rose in spring, with tender drooping head, or as the lily, which was presented to the love-sick maiden and nestled hidden in her bosom, fades and dies, so I sink to the ground on feeble knees, without consciousness or colour, and black night hovers before my eyes; until, brought to my senses once again by cold water poured on me, just as Prometheus' liver grows again for the profit of the vulture, I return to be consumed by the familiar fires.

XXXII   G. ANGERIANO

Of his love Caelia

The fire doeth tame the iron harde, / harde flinte the waters pearce:
Warme bloude doeth breake the Adamant, / as sundrie bookes
    rehearse:
But she whom I doe serve (more harde / then these repeated three)
Then Iron, Flint, or Adamant, / more rockie hard is she.
For ne my fire that burnes in breast, / ne teares from eyes that fall,
Nor spinnyng bloud from sanguine vaines, / maie make her rue her
    thrall.

XXXIII   ANDREAE NAUGERII

Lusus XXII
Precatio ad noctem pro celandis amoribus

Nox bona, quae tacitis terras amplexa tenebris
   dulcia iucundae furta tegis Veneris.
dum propero in carae amplexus et mollia Hyellae
   oscula, tu nostrae sis comes una viae.   4
neve aliquis nostros possit deprendere amores,
   aëra coge atras densius in nebulas.
gaudia qui credit cuiquam sua, dignus ut umquam
   dicier illius nulla puella velit.   8
non sola occultanda cavis sunt orgia cistis
   solave Eleusinae sacra silenda deae.
ipse etiam sua celari vult furta Cupido:
   saepius et poenas garrula lingua dedit.   12
una meos, quos et miserata est, novit amores
   officiis nutrix cognita fida suis.
haec quae me foribus vigilans exspectat in ipsis,
   inque sinum dominae sedula ducit anus.   16
hanc praeter, tu sancta latent qua cuncta silentque,
   tu dea sis flammae conscia sola meae:
quaeque libens astat nostrorum testis amorum
   nobiscum tota nocte lucerna vigil.   20

XXXIV   IOANNIS SECUNDI

Basia

I

Cum Venus Ascanium super alta Cythera tulisset,
   sopitum teneris imposuit violis,
albarum nimbos circumfuditque rosarum,
   et totum liquido sparsit odore locum: 4
mox veteres animo revocavit Adonidis ignes,
   notus et inrepsit ima per ossa calor.

XXXIII   ANDREA NAVAGERO

Lusus XXII:
Prayer to Night that his love remain hidden

Kindly Night, thou who embracing earth in silent darkness, concealest the sweet thefts of delightful Venus, while I hurry to the embraces and soft kisses of my beloved Hyella, be thou my only companion on my way. Lest anyone find out about our love, condense the air more compactly into coal-black clouds; he who confides his secret joy to anyone else does not deserve any girl ever willing to be called his own. It is not only mysteries that must be secreted in hollow caskets or only the religious ceremonies of the Eleusinian goddess that must not be bruited abroad. Cupid himself also wishes his thefts to remain concealed and often punishes a talkative tongue. One only has known of my love and taken pity on it—the nurse acknowledged by her duties to be trustworthy. She waits for me at the door, the watchful old woman, and solicitously takes me to the secrecy of her mistress' bedchamber. Apart from her, thou sacred one in whom all things are hidden and silent, thou, goddess, be the sole confidant of my flame; and may the lamp that gladly stands by as witness of our love keep watch with us throughout the whole night.

XXXIV   JOANNES SECUNDUS

Basia (Kisses)

I

When Venus to Cythera's top convey'd
Sleeping Ascanius, 'mongst soft violets layd,
Showres of pale Roses on the Boy she strew'd,
And with sweet Waters all the Place bedew'd;
She then her old Adonian Fire retains,
The well-known flame steals gently through her vains;

o quotiens voluit circumdare colla nepotis?
   o quotiens talis, dixit, Adonis erat?   8
sed placidam pueri metuens turbare quietem,
   fixit vicinis basia mille rosis.
ecce calent illae cupidaeque per ora Diones
   aura, susurranti flamine, lenta subit.   12
quotque rosas tetigit, tot basia nata repente
   gaudia reddebam multiplicata deae.
at Cytherea natans niveis per nubila cycnis
   ingentis terrae coepit obire globum,   16
Triptolemique modo fecundis oscula glebis
   sparsit et ignotos ter dedit ore sonos.
inde seges felix nata est mortalibus aegris:
   inde medela meis unica nata malis.   20
salvete aeternum, miserae moderamina flammae,
   umida de gelidis basia nata rosis.
en ego sum vestri quo vate canentur honores,
   nota Medusaei dum iuga montis erunt,   24
en memor Aeneadum stirpisque disertus amatae,
   mollia Romulidum verba loquetur Amor.

XXXV   IOANNIS SECUNDI

Basia

VII

Centum basia centies,
centum basia millies,
mille basia millies
et tot milia millies.
quot guttae Siculo mari,   5
quot sunt sidera caelo,
istis purpureis genis,
istis turgidulis labris
ocellisque loquaculis
ferrem continuo impetu.   10
    o formosa Neaera!
sed dum totus inhaereo

How oft her Nephew offer'd she t'imbrace!
How often said, such my Adonis was!
But fearing to disturb his soft Repose,
Thousands of kisses on the Flowers bestows;
The breath which from her Lip the Rose receives
Whispers kinde Warmth into its glowing Leaves,
And from her quickning Touch new kisses rise,
Whose ripe Encrease her full Joy multiplies.
Then round the Earth, the Goddess by a Pair
Of milk-white Swans drawn through the fleeting Air,
Sows kisses all the way, and they fell
On the fat Glebe, thrice murmurs a Dark Spell.
Hence a kinde Harvest for sick Lovers grows,
Hence springs the onely cure of all my woes.
   Dear kisses! you that scorched Hearts renew,
Born of the Rose pregnant with sacred Dew,
Upon your Poet deathless Verse distill,
That may endure long as Medusa's Hill,
Or whilst Love, mindfull still of Romes dear Race,
Shall with his Numbers their soft Language grace.

XXXV   **JOANNES SECUNDUS**

Basia (Kisses)

VII

Kisses a hundred, hundred fold,
A hundred by a thousand told,
Thousands by thousands numbered o're,
As many thousand thousand more
As are the drops the Seas comprize,
As are the Stars that paint the Skies,
To this soft Cheek, this speaking Ey,
This swelling Lip will I apply.
But whilst on these my kisses dwell

conchatim roseis genis,
conchatim rutilis labris
ocellisque loquaculis,   15
non datur tua cernere
labra, non roseas genas
ocellosque loquaculos,
  molles nec mihi risus,
qui, velut nigra discutit   20
caelo nubila Cynthius
pacatumque per aethera
gemmatis in equis micat,
  flavo lucidus orbe,
sic nutu eminus aureo   25
et meis lacrimas genis
et curas animo meo
  et suspiria pellunt.
heu, quae sunt oculis meis
nata proelia cum labris?   30
ergo ego mihi vel Iovem
rivalem potero pati?
rivales oculi mei
  non ferunt mea labra.

XXXVI   IOANNIS SECUNDI

Basia

XIII

Languidus e dulci certamine, vita, iacebam
 exanimis, fusa per tua colla manu.
omnis in arenti consumptus spiritus ore
 flamine non poterat cor recreare novo.   4
iam Styx ante oculos et regna carentia sole,
 luridaque annosi cymba Charontis erat,
cum tu suaviolum educens pulmonis ab imo
 adflasti siccis inriguum labiis,   8
suaviolum, Stygia quod me de valle reduxit

Close as the Cockle clasps her shell,
This swelling Lip I cannot spy,
This foster Cheek, this speaking Eye:
Nor those sweet Smiles which (like the Ray
Of Cynthius driving Clouds away)
From my swoln Eyes dispel all Tears,
From my sad Heart all jealous Fears.
Alas! what Discontents arise
Betwixt my aemulous Lips and Eyes!
Can I with patience brook that Jove
Should be a partner in my Love
When my strict Eye the Rivalship
Disdains to suffer of my Lip?

XXXVI   JOANNES SECUNDUS

Basia (Kisses)

XIII

I lay of Life by thee, my Life, bereav'd.
About thy Neck my Arms were loosely weav'd.
Supplies of Breath my wafted Spirits fail,
Nor could relieve my Heart with one fresh Gale:
Styx now before my Eyes appeard, the dark
Region, and aged Caron's swarthy Bark;
When thou upon my Lip a Kiss imprest
Drawn from the depth of thy enlivening Brest;
A Kiss, that call'd me from the Stygian Lake,

et iussit vacua currere nave senem.
erravi: vacua non remigat ille carina,
    flebilis ad manes iam natat umbra mea.   12
pars animae, mea vita, tuae hoc in corpore vivit
    et dilapsuros sustinet articulos;
quae tamen impatiens in pristina iura reverti
    saepe per arcanas nititur aegra vias.   10
ac nisi dilecta per te foveatur ab aura,
    iam conlabentes deserit articulos.
ergo age, labra meis innecte tenacia labris,
    adsidueque duos spiritus unus alat,   20
donec inexpleti post taedia sera furoris
    unica de gemino corpore vita fluet.

XXXVII   NICOLAI BORBONII

Ad puellam

Prae te non duri montes, non robora dura,
    durior est glacies pectore nulla tuo.
non adamas prae te durus, non marmora dura,
    duritiem vincunt nulla metalla tuam,   4
si quam dura voles, certe moriere, cinisque
    fies, o virgo mitior ergo veni.
non sum adeo informis, quin sim te dignus, amica:
    in speculo formam cogor amare meam.   8
oscula da centum, da circum bracchia collo,
    sim tuus et mea sis; accipe daque fidem.
quem fugis? ah demens! cur membra decora iuventae,
    cur etiam sordent munera nostra tibi?   12
dura manes? aliam inveniam, quae carmine nostro
    clara erit, at sero facta dolebis anus.

And made the Ferryman go empty back:
Ah! I mistook! he went not back alone,
My mournful Shade along with him is gone;
Part of my Soul within this Body raigns,
And friendly my declining Limbs sustains;
Which of return impatient, roves about,
Ransaking every Passage to get out;
And if no kindness she from thee receive,
Ev'n now her falling Tenement will leave.
Come then, unite they melting Lip to mine,
And let one Spirit both our Breasts combine,
Till in an Extasie of wild desire
Together both our Breasts one Life expire.

XXXVII   NICOLAS BOURBON

To his mistress

Compared with thee the mountains are not hard, the oaktrees are not hard, no ice is harder than thy heart. Compared with thee the diamond is not hard, marble is not hard, no metal surpasses thee in hardness. However hard thou wishest to be, thou art certain to die and shallst turn to ashes, so behave more gently, young maiden. I am not so hideous as to be unworthy of thee, my beloved; I must perforce love as mine thy image in the mirror. Give me a hundred kisses, put thy arms around my neck, let me be thine and thou be mine; let us plight our troth. Why dost thou shun me? O foolish one! why dost thou despise my handsome young body? why dost thou despise my gifts? Must thou persist in thy hardness? I shall find another, who will acquire fame through my song, but thou shalt grieve later when thou hast become an old woman.

XXXVIII   MARCANTONII MURETI

Margaridi

Cum pluit et radios Phoebus cum subtrahit orbi,
    tum sane maestus quilibet esse solet:
ne mirere igitur, si sim, mea Margari, tristis:
    ecce pluo lacrimas, tu mihi Phoebus abes.

XXXIX   I. BELLAII

Pandorae nomen aptius fuisse Faustinae

Qui tibi Faustinae, mea lux, nomen dedit, is te
    dixisset Pandoram aptius, et melius.
munera namque deos in te omnia congessisse
    ostendunt dotes corporis, atque animi.   4
et tu etiam ex oculis, tamquam de pixide aperta,
    omnia depromis seu bona, sive mala.
at mihi te erepta, mi qua sine vivere durum est,
    spes, o me miserum, nulla mihi remanet.   8

XL   GEORGII BUCHANANI

Amor

Quis puer ales? Amor. genitor quis? blandus ocelli
    ardor. quo natus tempore? vere novo.
quis locus excepit? generosi pectoris aula.
    quae nutrix? primo flore iuventa decens.   4
quo nutrit victu? inlecebris vultuque venusto.
    qui comites? levitas, otia, luxus, opes.
cur puero belli semper furiosa cupido?
    impellunt avidae spes, trepidique metus.   8
non metuit mortem? non. quare? saepe renasci,
    saepe mori deciens hunc brevis hora videt.

XXXVIII   MARC-ANTOINE DE MURET

To Margaris

When it so raines, and Phoebus rayes
    are covered all with cloudes:
Then everythyng remainyng sad,
    in silence pensive shroudes.
Therefore muse not my Margaris,
    though sad thou dost mee see:
Behold mine eyes raine teares, and thou
    my sonne art gone from mee.

XXXIX   JOACHIM DU BELLAY

Faustina were more suitably named Pandora

He who gave thee the name Faustina, my love, would more appropriately have called thee Pandora, and more felicitously. For the qualities of thy body and thy mind are proof that the gods showered all their gifts upon thee and that thou too dispensest from thy eyes, as from Pandora's opened box, all things, good or evil. But when thou art snatched away from me, thou without whom it is hard to exist, no hope remains for me, wretched that I am.

XL   GEORGE BUCHANAN

Love

Who is this winged boy? Love. Who is his father? The eye's kindly flame. When was he born? In the freshness of spring. What place claimed him for its own? the hall of a noble-minded bosom. Who nursed him? fair youth in its prime. On what was he nurtured? On charms and comely countenance. Who were his comrades? Fickleness, leisure, luxury, wealth. Why does he, a boy, show so frenzied a desire for strife? Hungry hopes and nervous fears drive him on. Has death no fears for him? None. Why so? A short hour sees him die and be born again time after time.

XLI   PAULI MELISSI

Ex gallico Ronsardi

Indignatus Amor telis petiisse Rosinam,
   queis durae nusquam saucia corda forent;
liquerat adpensam nemoris sub fronde pharetram,
   fetus in hac esset dum generatus apum.   4
ictibus egressum iam libertatis amatrix
   fecerat e thecae mellea turba sinu,
ornabantque fugam; cum plena examina fundens
   e pharetra nymphae vertit in ora puer.   8
protinus exsiluit risu, bene se ratus ultum,
   laedere quam numquam noverat arcus iners.
aetheris at natae non solum, pungere lentae,
   non figunt roseis spicula iussa labris;   12
basia sed libant, et ab apricante Rosinae
   ore legunt flores, eliciuntque favos.

XLII   IOANNIS BONEFONII

Pancharis

I   Quo petit, ut Pancharis ipsi
     basiis animam exsugat

Nympha bellula, Nympha mollicella,
cuius in roseis latent labellis
meae deliciae, meae salutes:
nympha, quae veneres venusta tota,
omnes omnibus una surpuisti,   5
amabo mihi basium propina
quo tandem meus acquiescat ardor:
ah ne basiolum mihi propina,
nam contra magis excitatur ardor:
sed mi suge animam halitu suavi,   10
dum nil quicquam animae mihi supersit.

XLI PAUL SCHEDE

From the French by Ronsard

Amour estant marri qu'il avoit ses saigettes
   Tiré contre Marie et ne l'avoit blessée,
   Par depit dans un bois sa trousse avoit laissée
   Tant que plene elle fust d'un bel essaim d'avettes.
Já de leurs piquerons ces captives mouschettes
   Pour avoir liberté la trousse avoient persée
   Et s'enfuyoient alors qu'Amour l'a renversée
   Sur la face à Marie, et sus ses mammelettes.
Soudain, après qu'il eut son carquois dechargé,
   Tout riant sautela, pensant estre vangé
   De celle, à qui son arc n'avoit sceu faire outrage,
Mais il rioit en vain: car ces filles du ciel
   En lieu de la piquer, baisans son beau visage,
   En amassoyent les fleurs, et en faisoyent du miel.

XLII JEAN BONEFONS

Pancharis

I   He desires his Pancharilla to suck out his very
        Soul with kisses   By Mr J. Philips

Thou little pretty, little tender Maid,
In whose soft pouting Rosy Lips are laid,
My ev'ry Joy, my ev'ry Bliss, and all,
That I my very Health it self can call.
Thou Charmer Thou, so beautiful alone,
Thou robb'st all Graces, and got all in one,
For Heav'n sake, prithee pledge me in a kiss:
For Heav'n sake do, and quench the burning Bliss.
Oh! no. no, Kiss me not, the raging Thirst
Will burn but Ten Times fiercer than at first.
But suck my Soul out in thy balmy Breath,
Leave me no more than Infants after Death.

ah ne, ne mi animam puella suge:
namque exsors animae quid ipse tandem
quid sim vana nisi futurus umbra,
et errans stygiis imago ripis?   15
infaustis nimis ah nimisque ripis
quae nullam venerem et suavitatem
nullas delicias iocosque norunt.
imo tu mi animam puella suge,
suge, dum mi animae nihil supersit,   20
dumque molliculi comes Catulli,
dumque molliculi comes Tibulli,
eam pallidulas et ipse ad umbras
et errem stygiis imago ripis.
  tum vicissim ego Pancharilla sugam   25
tuae florem animae suaveolentis
dum nil quicquam animae tibi supersit
dumque Lesbiolae Catullianae,
dum comes Nemesis Tibullianae
eas pallidulas et ipsa ad umbras,   30
et erres stygiis imago ripis.
namque illic etiam suos amores
exercere piae feruntur umbrae,
et illic Nemesim suam Tibullus
et illic quoque Lesbiam Catullus   35
fertur pallidulo ore suaviari.
sic illic, mea Pancharilla, tete
pallens pallidulam suaviabor,
illi ut primi etiam duces amoris
palma iam veteri superbientes,   40
et se a me fateantur et stupescant
victos multivola osculatione.

Oh! do not suck me so,—My Girl. Oh! stay
For when at last my Soul shall flit away;
What shall I then in very Deed be made,
But a poor Nothing, and an empty Shade!
A Shadow wand'ring on the Stygian shore,
The more Unhappy as it wanders more:
There, no pale Traveller can reach Delight,
For Beauty, Joy and Mirth, lye wrapp'd in endless Night.

    Yet do, my Girl, ev'n suck my utmost Breath,
'Till I've no more than Infants after Death,
'Till I with soft Catullus sweetly lost,
With soft Tibullus, 'till a Brother Ghost,
To the pale Manes of the Deep I go,
And wander on the Stygian Banks below.

Then will I, Pancharilla, in my Turn,
Suck at thy Lips, 'till thou thy Soul return;
Exhale the florid Store of balmy Breath,
'Till you've no more than Infants after Death,
'Till with Catullus, Lesbia loving Fair,
With Nemesis to kind Tibullus dear;
Thou their Companion to the Shades shalt go,
And wander on the Stygian Banks below.

For there the pious Ghosts are said to prove
The whole loose Exercise of boundless Love;
Tibullus there his Nemesis enjoys,
And with his Lesbia there Catullus lyes.
There, there, they rifle Love of ev'ry Sweet,
And with pale Lips the springing Joy repeat:
So there will, Pancharilla, Thou and I
Join our pale Forms, and ev'ry Rapture try;
'Till those first Chiefs in Cupid's Camp renown'd,
With antique Palms of Love triumphant crown'd;
Amaz'd, Astonish'd, shall be forc'd to own,
They are, in Kisses, by my self outdone.

XLIII   IOANNIS BONEFONII

Pancharis

XVI Exaggerat felicitatem et infelicitatem in osculando

Donec pressius incubo labellis
et diduco avidus tuae, puella,
flosculos animae suaveolentes,
unus tum videor mihi deorum
seu quid altius est beatiusve.   5
    mox ut te eripis, ecce ego repente
unus qui superum mihi videbar,
seu quid altius est beatiusve
Orci mi videor relatus umbris
seu quid inferiusve tristiusve.   10

XLIV   IOANNIS BONEFONII

Pancharis

XXIV   Comparationem facit inter semetipsum,
et rosam rubentem et pallentem

En flores tibi mitto discolores
pallentemque rosam et rosam rubentem.
illam cum aspicies, miselli amantis
puta pallidulos videre vultus.
cum tueberis hanc rubore tinctam,   5
putes igne rubens cor intueri.

XLIII   JEAN BONEFONS

Pancharis

XVI

Whilst, my Chloris, I recline
Lips to Lips in pressing thine:
Whilst these Heav'nly Blessings flow,
Spices, Gums and Roses blow,
I then am Happy in a high Degree,
And Jove in Triumph seems but mean to me.

But when you my Joys detain,
Then your doating Lover's slain
I who lately soar'd above,
All the Gods in Life and Love,
Lie now desponding in a strange Surprize,
Like falling Angels from the flaming Skies.

XLIV   JEAN BONEFONS

Pancharis

XXIV   To his Mistress, comparing himself
to the Red Rose and the White. By H.B.

Behold these Flowers, with diff'rent Colours spread,
And learn what means the White Rose, and the Red:
Ah me! They represent my wretched Case,
In That, you see the paleness of my Face,
In This, which wears a bright and ruddy Hue,
My Heart you see, which flames and burns for You.

The elegy

The definitions of the elegy in Renaissance times seem to have caused perplexity, partly because the interpretations given to the theory of the genre formulated by Horace were so various. Two chief characteristics were universally recognised as the proper field of the elegy: on the one hand, there was the poetry of *querimonia*, so that its inspiration ranged from the personal to the ceremonial; and on the other there was the tradition of love poetry, including naturally the love epistle fashioned by Ovid. For some moderns, there was hesitation as to the extent to which these two elements could or should combine; there seems however to be a general tendency for the elegy to assume greater autobiographical proportions, whether one thinks of Petrus Lotichius in Neo-latin or of Pierre de Ronsard in the vernacular. There is little doubt that in the Renaissance the amatory elegy owed much to the Petrarchan tradition as well as to classical sources: a curious confirmation of this is found in the Latin versions made by Thomas Biccarton of some of Ronsard's love sonnets—even excerpts from sonnets are graced with the name of *elegiae*. There may be uncertainty where to draw the line between the amatory epigram and the elegy, but it is normally agreed that one is dealing with a poem of middle length in elegiac verse; and if the Italians provide important models, poets tend to remain faithful to the pattern set by Ovid and the Roman elegists: what may vary is the emphasis given to certain thematic developments. The elegy will remain an important vehicle for the expression of autobiographical material over an extensive range of feelings.

BIBLIOGRAPHY

Walther Ludwig. 'Petrus Lotichius Secundus and the Roman Elegists: prolegomena to a study of Neo-Latin elegy', in *Classical Influences on European Culture A.D. 1500–1700*, ed. R. R. Bolgar, Cambridge University Press, 1976, pp. 171–90.

XLV   I. I. PONTANI

Laudes Casis Fontis

Casis, Hamadryadum furtis iucunde minister
  et cupidis rupes semper amica deis,
ad quem saepe, sui linquens secreta Lycaei,
  Pan egit medios sole calente dies   4
Maenalioque tuos implevit carmine montes
  et septem cecinit fistula blanda modos,
cum passim iunctaeque manus et bracchia nexae
  ducebant placidos Naides ante choros   8
carpebantque hilares iuxta virgulta capellae
  haedus et in molli subsiliebat humo;
quin etiam defessa iugis siquando Diana
  egit praecipites per cava saxa feras,   12
hic posuitque latus viridique in margine sedit
  et vitreo flavas lavit in amne comas;
te Bacchus, te Phoebus amant, tibi carmina nymphae
  dulce canunt, tibi se comit amata Dryas,   16
Pelignosque suos siquando et rura relinquit,
  lassa subit fonti Calliopea tuo
et lenem querula carpit sub fronde quietem,
  qua cadit arguto murmure lympha fugax.   20

XLVI   IACOBI SANNAZARII

Elegia IX: Ad ruinas Cumarum, urbis vetustissimae

Hic, ubi Cumaeae surgebant incluta famae
  moenia, Tyrrheni gloria prima maris,
longinquis quo saepe hospes properabat ab oris,
  visurus tripodas, Delie magne, tuos   4
et vagus antiquos intrabat navita portus,
  quaerens Daedaleae conscia signa fugae,
(credere quis quondam potuit, dum fata manebant?)
  nunc silva agrestes occulit alta feras.   8

XLV   G. G. PONTANO

In praise of the spring Casi

Casi, indulgent accomplice of the secret loves of the Hamadryads and crag for ever friendly to love-smitten gods, near which often, leaving the hidden regions of his own Lycaeus, Pan spent the heat of the midday sun and filled your hills with song and his charming pipe sounded the seven-note melody, while all around, hands linked and arms entwined, the Naiads led their placid dances before him and the cheerful goats nearby cropped the shrubs and the kid skipped around on the soft ground. Rather, sometimes, Diana, tired of the mountain slopes, drove the wild beasts headlong from grotto to grotto, lay down here and sat on the green edge and washed her yellow hair in the crystal stream. You are loved of Bacchus, of Phoebus, to you the nymphs gently sing their songs, the Dryad loved by you combs her hair for you; and if ever Calliope forsakes her Peligni and her own fields, she comes wearied to your spring and takes a gentle rest beneath the rustling leaves, where the water falls in flight with a lively sound.

XLVI   J. SANNAZARO

The ruins of Cumae, an ancient city

Here, where there rose up the distinguished walls of famous Cumae, the foremost glory of the Tyrrhenian sea, whither hastened oft the stranger from distant shores to see your tripod, mighty Delius, and where the wandering sailor entered the ancient harbour seeking signs of the flight of Daedalus, (who could have believed this, while its fortunes lasted?) now a lofty forest conceals wild

atque ubi fatidicae latuere arcana Sibyllae,
    nunc claudit saturas vespere pastor oves.
quaeque prius sanctos cogebat curia patres,
    serpentum facta est alituumque domus;   12
plenaque tot passim generosis atria ceris,
    ipsa sua tandem subruta mole iacent.
calcanturque olim sacris onerata tropaeis
    limina distractos et tegit herba deos.   16
tot decora artificumque manus, tot nota sepulcra,
    totque pios cineres una ruina premit.
et iam, intra solasque domos disiectaque passim
    culmina, saetigeros advena figit apros.   20
nec tamen hoc Graiis cecinit deus ipse carinis,
    praevia nec lato missa columba mari.
et querimur, cito si nostrae data tempora vitae
    diffugiunt? urbes mors violenta rapit.   24
atque (utinam mea fallant oracula vatem,
    vanus et a longa posteritate ferar!)
nec tu semper eris, quae septem amplecteris arces,
    nec tu, quae mediis aemula surgis aquis.   28
et te (quis putet hoc?), altrix mea, durus arator
    vertet et 'urbs', dicet, 'haec quoque clara fuit.'
fata trahunt homines. fatis urgentibus, urbes
    et quodcumque vides auferet ipsa dies.   32

XLVII   NICOLAI BORBONII

Elegia: D. Francisci Delphini, liberum Regiorum maximi,
immaturam mortem deflet poeta

Quid portenta ferant caeli insuetique calores,
    nescimus, nos, qui carnea massa sumus,
Sequana deficiens ripas ostendit hiantes,
    sic Rhodanus, sic est nobile flumen Arar.   4
Alba humilis vix apparet, vix Matrona reptat,
    tres fratres sitiunt, Mosa, Garumna, Liger.
stagna, lacus, fontes, herbae, sunt sole perusta
    omnia, terra siti viscera pandit hians.   8

beasts; and where the secrets of the prophetic sibyl lay hidden, now a shepherd gathers his well-fed sheep into their pen at eventide. The Court that once upon a time assembled the venerable elders has become the home of serpents and birds. The halls, everywhere filled with so many wax figures of noble ancestors, themselves at last lie beneath the weight of their ruined mass. The entrances formerly laden with sacred trophies lie buried, and grass covers the uprooted statues of the gods. So many splendours, so many works of art, so many famous graves and so many revered ashes have sunk beneath the same disaster; and now among the deserted houses and the scattered roof-tops, the foreigner hunts the coarse-haired boars. Still, the God himself did not prophesy this to the Greek ships, nor did the dove sent ahead over the broad sea. And shall we complain if the time allotted to our lives disappears rapidly? a violent death snatches cities away to their doom. And (would that my prophecies would deceive me the poet and that I be held an idle liar by many generations to come!) neither you will live for ever, who embrace the seven hills, nor you who rose up in rivalry from the midst of the seas. And you (who could think this?) my mother city, will be turned over by the harsh ploughman's share, and he will say: this city was also famous in its time. The fates bear men away: under their pressure, cities and all you see will vanish on the appointed day.

XLVII   NICOLAS BOURBON

Elegy: The poet mourns the premature death of Francis the dauphin, eldest of the Royal children

The meaning of portents in the sky, or of unaccustomed heatwaves, we simply do not know, poor lumps of flesh that we are. The Seine, short of water, bares its gaping banks, like the Rhone and like the splendid Saone. The lowly Aube hardly makes its appearance, the Marne hardly crawls along its bed, and three sister-rivers—the Meuse, the Garonne and the Loire—have run dry. Ponds, lakes, springs, grassy fields have all been scorched by the sun, the earth, opening up with thirst, lays bare her entrails. Each year is famed

sunt aliis alii celebres eventibus anni,
    hic erit exhaustis nobilis annus aquis.
respice nos pater altitonans et pectora nostra
    nectareo factus mitior imbre riga. 12
haec ego dum scribo attonitus, dum talia miror
    prodigia, ignarus quid sibi fata velint:
proh dolor, ecce venit tristis mihi nuntius, orbum
    qui Regem nato rettulit esse suo. 16
heu, Francisce, iaces, natorum maxime Regis
    Francisci, quem nunc Gallia tota gemit.
te pater et gemini fratres, geminaeque sorores,
    te populus, te flent flumina, stagna, lacus. 20
omnia Delphinum crudeli funere raptum
    flent adeo, in lacrimas omnis ut humor eat.
aridus hic annus iuvenem deplorat ademptum,
    delicias iuvenum, deliciasque senum. 24
set valeat felix anima et requiescat in umbra
    Elysia: cineres marmora sacra tegant.
nulla tuum, o iuvenum clarissime, saecula nomen
    delebunt, si quid carmina nostra valent. 28
qui fata heroum referent eventaque rerum
    posthac, te plangent, te super astra ferent.

XLVIII   PETRI LOTICHII SECUNDI

Elegia II: Ad Melchiorem Zobellum compatrem

Sic igitur dulces potuisti linquere Musas
    Martiaque imprudens castra, Zobelle, sequi?
et tibi iam tanti est artes cognoscere belli,
    et fera quo soleant proelia more geri? 4
scilicet a teneris ut mercenarius annis
    vulnera consuescas servitiumque pati,
et subeas totiens manifesta pericula vitae,
    dum cava terrificis ictibus aera tonant. 8
quam bene pugnabant olim, cum moenia nondum
    turribus, aut fossis oppida cincta forent,
machina nec volucres torqueret aënea glandes,

for its own special occurrences: this one will go down in history for its drought. Look down upon us, Jove the thunderer, and with a kindlier heart let a nectar-like shower rain down upon us. While, dumbfounded, I penned these lines, while I watched such marvels, uncomprehending what the fates had in store, o grief, there came in my direction a bearer of sad news to say that the King had lost his son. Oh! Francis, there you lie, the eldest son of King Francis, lamented now by the whole of France. You are mourned by your father, two brothers and two sisters, the people, rivers, ponds and lakes. All so mourn the dauphin snatched away by a cruel death that all moisture finds its way into tears. By its drought this year bewails the departed youth, delight of young people and delight of older folk. But may your soul prosper and rest in the shades of Elysium; may sacred marble cover your ashes. The passing centuries will not destroy your memory, most distinguished of youths, if our songs have any worth. Those recounting in later times the destiny of heroes and the deeds of history will mourn and praise you beyond the stars.

XLVIII   PETER LOTICH THE YOUNGER

Elegy II: To Melchior Zobel his cousin

Could you then forsake the gentle Muses and unheeding follow the camps of war, Zobel? and was it worth your while to learn the skills of war and the way in which fierce battles are waged? Certainly you have been used from your childhood to endure, as a mercenary, wounds and military bondage, and suffer so often the evident perils of such a life while the hollow bronze cannons roar with a mighty crash. How valiantly they fought in those days, when walls did not yet have towers or towns ditches surrounding them? when bronze guns did not hurl speedy shot, but sword and spear

    sed gererent partes ensis et hasta suas!   **12**
tunc clarum tibi, magna parens Germania, nomen,
    nostraque libertas sanguine parta fuit.
nunc tua dilacerant inimicae viscera gentes.
    vendis et externis in tua damna fidem.   **16**
ante tuos oculos ferro grassatur et igni
    barbarus, et Geticis Hunnus oberrat equis.
o pereant turres fossaeque et inutile vallum;
    pax ades, aut virtus illa paterna redi!   **20**
me iuvat in studiis consumere dulcibus aevum,
    signaque Musarum prosperiora sequi,
et quae sera legat nostri non immemor aetas,
    carmina tranquillae fingere pacis opus.   **24**
sed tamen ausus eram validis quoque nuper in armis,
    magnanimi custos ad latus ire ducis.
iam caput indueram galea, frameamque gerebam,
    aptus et huic lateri quilibet ensis erat.   **28**
sed dea, Castaliis quae maxima praesidet undis,
    non tulit, et vultus constitit ante meos.
constitit, et tenerae florem miserata iuventae
    'ergo, puer, fies tu quoque miles?' ait.   **32**
'torta quid imbelles urget lorica lacertos?
    quid gravat aeratae cuspidis hasta manum?
iam populatrices inter potes ire catervas?
    iam longae patiens esse sub axe viae?   **36**
at (memini) nuper fera bella timere solebas,
    classicaque insuetis auribus horror erant.
unde novus rigor hic? unde illa ferocia venit?
    mitis honoratae pacis amator ubi es?   **40**
sed, puto, praeda iuvat spoliisque Aquilonis onustum
    sublimem niveis Fama reducet equis.
quin meliora tibi solvemus praemia Musae,
    praemia per raras ante petita manus?   **44**
longa dies regum turres consumit et aurum,
    et spolia in templis exuviaeque ruunt.
at decus ingenii durat vatumque labores:
    i nunc, et partas sanguine confer opes.   **48**
adde, quod incerto Mars proelia turbine versat,
    casus et instabiles miscet utrimque vices,

played their part? those were the days, great Mother Germany, when your name was famous and our freedom was acquired by the shedding of our blood. Nowadays hostile races tear your entrails apart, and you sell your loyalty to foreigners, causing harm and damage to yourself. Before your eyes the barbarian rages with fire and sword and the Hun roams everywhere on his Thracian steeds. O perish the useless towers, ditches and ramparts! Come hither, Peace, or return to us, valour of our forefathers! I love to devote my life to agreeable study, to follow the more rewarding banners of the Muses and to compose poems, the work of untroubled peace, which posterity, not forgetful of us, may read. But nonetheless I dared also recently to take up arms vigorously and serve in defence of my great-hearted prince. I had already donned my helmet and carried my spear, and the first suitable sword that came to hand hung by my side. But the goddess who reigns supreme over the Castalian waters suffered this not and stood before me: she stood and lamenting the flower of tender youth, she said: 'And so you too, my child, want to be a soldier? Why does the leather cuirass oppress peace-loving shoulders? Why does the lance with its bronze tip lie heavy in the hand? Can you already join the bands of men bent on destruction? Can you already endure the long marches under the open sky? But (I recall) that not so long ago you were afraid of cruel war and the trumpets grated horrifyingly on your ears. Whence comes this new resolve now? Whence this savage spirit? Where are you now who so gently loved and honoured peace? But, I think, you are attracted by booty and the thought that you will return distinguished on a snow-white horse, laden with spoils from northern parts. Why should we, Muses, not grant you finer rewards, rewards that were formerly so rarely sought after? Time, over the years, devours wealth and cities, and spoils and trophies preserved in temples perish. But the glory of the mind and the creations of poets live on: go now and gather in wealth acquired by bloodshed. Remember moreover that Mars is fickle in the uncertain tumult of war and distributes calamities and

ah teneris maius ne quis iuveniliter annis
    audeat, et vires consulat ante suas! 52
tempus erit Pindum superans cum Caesar et Haemum,
    figet in Odrysiis celsa tropaea iugis.
tunc si tantus amor belli, si tanta cupido est,
    acer in adversos ense licebit eas. 56
terribiles nunc linque tubas et castra, nec auctor
    ante diem propera funeris esse tui.'
hic ego commotus dictis vultuque monentis,
    ite statim, dixi, castra tubaeque procul. 60
rursus et Aonius calor in mea pectora venit,
    ipsaque devovi quae prius arma tuli.
difficile est tacitos naturae abscondere motus,
    ponere difficile est quae placuere diu. 64
scilicet ingenuas mansuescunt corda per artes,
    nec rigidos mores esse Thalia sinit.
at tu, quandoquidem rerum sic impetus urget,
    et novus accendit pectora laudis amor, 68
i, tua quo, Zobelle, vocat te fervida virtus,
    et grave militiae fer patienter onus.
ne tamen, ah, densos vitae contemptor in hostes
    inrue: scis quam sit dulce redire domum, 72
tunc mihi narrabis, validas quis ceperit urbes
    primus, et hostiles fregerit ultor opes.
qualiter adversis concurrant agmina signis,
    altaque tormentis moenia quassa ruant, 76
et quaecumque illis exhausta pericula terris;
    hunc celeri portet Lucifer axe diem.

inconstant vicissitudes to either side. Alas, alas that youth is not more adventurous in early years and takes stock beforehand of its powers! The time will come when Caesar, overcoming Pindus and Haemus, will establish his lofty trophies on the summits of Thrace. If you show such enthusiasm for war, if your eagerness is so great, then you will, sword in hand, march keenly against the foe. Leave now the terrifying trumpets and the camp, nor hasten to be the author of your own untimely death.' I was much disquieted by these words and the countenance of her who gave this counsel. Hence without delay, I said, camp and trumpets begone. My breast was once more filled with Aeonian ardour and I cursed the very weapons I had previously borne. Hard it is to suppress the silent movements of one's mind; hard too to put away what has given pleasure over a long time. To be sure, hearts are tamed by the arts of the mind and Thalia will not let our behaviour become rough and rude. But you, whenever you are pressed by the rush of events, and a strange love of glory inflames your breast, go then, Zobel, where your fervent virtue calls you and bear in patience the heavy burden of military service. Nevertheless, do not, I pray thee, rush headlong into the serried ranks of the enemy, careless of your life; you know how pleasant is the homecoming. Then you will recount to me who was the first to seize the strongholds and tell of the avenger who destroyed the wealth of the enemy, in what manner the armies marched, with hostile standards, upon one another, and the lofty walls, shattered by missiles, collapsed to the ground; and whatever other dangers you underwent in those parts; may the morning star bring this day speedily.

The ode

The ode enjoys much favour in Neo-latin poetry, in part because of its great flexibility. It rapidly developed in Italy where some early experiments of a rather dry and formal nature (e.g. Filelfo and Landino) were soon followed, with great success, by Sannazaro, Marullus and Flaminio, to mention only three. The ode has twin ancestry in ancient times: Pindar whose poems are known early on in Italy, though a scholarly understanding of their metrical schemes was still a long way off, and Horace whose example allowed a wide range of inspiration, generally at a more personal level than his Greek model. The ode quickly became the vehicle for encomiastic verse of a high ceremonial nature, but at the same time it allowed a wide range of lyric inspiration both in theme and in metre. In France progress was slow, partly because the 'lyric' Horace was not particularly congenial to late-medieval minds, but it was in great measure through Neo-latin experiments that he became acceptable in vernacular poetry. It is also likely that Horace's more complex metrical schemes took time to be assimilated; until Salmon Macrin's time, few writers seem to be thoroughly at home in the ode. Though Perotto's little manual on Horatian metres had been on the market for decades, it is curious how often compositions of this nature are prefaced by a description of the metre used. In the hands of Macrin the ode maintains its thematic range—love poetry, encomiastic pieces, moralising trifles, nature verse and so forth. Quite soon the distinction between hymn and ode is blurred, though in principle the hymn predictably retains its religious character. One important development is the adaptation of horatian metres to the psalm paraphrase and to other types of religious inspiration.

The poets of Macrin's generation did not take Pindar as their model, though they were aware of his work. It is, possibly, through Lampridio's example that the Pindaric formula found its way into France and was exploited in both Neo-latin and vernacular verse. It is thought that Michel de l'Hôpital, for a time an exile in Italy, alerted Jean Dorat to the potential of the Pindaric ode. Dorat, the teacher of the Pléiade, lectured in Paris on the Greek poets and himself wrote a number of Pindaric odes on matters of high public concern. Though efforts to assimilate the Pindaric ode into the vernacular, notably by Ronsard, are considered to have failed, there is no doubt that Jean Dorat's example stimulated not only French writers such as Sainte-Marthe, but foreigners who came to study in Paris in the heyday of French scholarship: among these were Féderic Jamot of Béthune, Paul Schede (Melissus), and Jean Dousa (van der Does). The two latter men had close links with England at various stages of their careers, but in England the development of the Pindaric ode was to come later (e.g. Abraham Cowley). More generally it seems that the ode was able to flourish in the climate of the Counter-reformation because of its possibilities in serious, meditative, and more narrowly religious poetry.

BIBLIOGRAPHY

Maddison, Carol. *Apollo and the Nine. A History of the Ode*, London, 1960.

XLIX   I. I. PONTANI

Patulcidem et Antinianam
nymphas adloquitur

Colle de summo nemorumque ab umbris
te voco ad litus placidum, Patulci,
teque ab hortis Pausilypi et rosetis,
      Antiniana,   4

aura dum aestivos relevat calores
et leves fluctus agitant cachinni,
dum sonant pulsae zephyris harenae
      antraque clamant.   8

antra vos poscunt querulaeque harenae;
en canunt illinc Meliseus alto
fistulam inspirans scopulo, canorus
      inde Menalcas;   12

en adest culta ad speculam et superbum
dia Mergillina iugum, en capillos
ponit unguens ambrosia, en nitentis
      oris honores   16

fingit adludens speculo. Huc, iuventus,
huc age, ut spectes oculos et illud
frontis exemplar, propera et citatos
      arripe gressus.   20

implet en carmen nitidus Palaemon,
subsident colles numerum secuti,
nympha subnectit choreas, amato
      litore Triton   24

currit exsultans. cithara Palaemon,
saltibus virgo celebrant recessus,
aequor adsultat, properant citatae e
      monte Napaeae.   28

XLIX   G. G. PONTANO

The poet speaks to the nymphs
Patulcis and Antiniana

From the top of the hill and from the shade of the groves I call you to your peaceful shore, Patulcis, and from the gardens and the rose-beds of Pausilypus I call you, Antiniana,

now that the breeze moderates the summer heat and you can hear the light plashing of the waves, and the sands sound and the caves echo with the movement of the breeze.

The caves and the plaintive sands call for you. Listen, Meliseus sings from there, playing his reed on a high rock, and so does sweet-sounding Menalcas from here.

Look, there is wonderful Mergellina, beautiful with her peak and proud ridge; look, she smoothes her hair anointing it with ambrosia, look, she arranges the radiant features of her face

as she sports in the mirror. Come, young people, come hither to look upon her eyes and her forehead, an example to all, come quickly and hasten your steps.

Listen, handsome Palaemon strikes up a song, the hills as they listen remain where they are, a nymph weaves a series of dances, a Triton leaps about

on the shore he loves so much. Palaemon with his guitar, the maiden with her dancing fill the hidden places with their sound, the water joins the dance, the Napaeae hasten from the mountain.

ecce procedunt duo ruris astra
et pedum cantu minuunt laborem;
en favent silvae numeris canentum,
      plaudit et aura.   32

accipit blande Meliseus illam,
hanc Menalcas. E specula propinqua
ipsa Mergillina canit proculque
      saxa reclamant.   36

litus o felix, modulante nympha,
cui et hi montes, cui et antra et horti
adsonantque arces procul, atque ab alto ad-
      ludit imago.   40

L   ANDREAE NAUGERII

Lusus XXXVII

Dia Tithoni senioris uxor,
quae diem vultu radiante pandis,
cum genas effers roseas rubenti
      praevia soli.   4

roscidos ut nunc per agros vagari
sub tuo adventu iuvat, et recentes,
quae tuos semper comitantur axes,
      excipere auras!   8

sicca iam saevus calor uret arva,
iam vagi aurarum levium silescent
spiritus : iam sol rapidus furentes
      exseret ignes.   12

dum licet, laeti simul ite amantes:
dum licet, molles pariter puellae
ite, flaventes vario capillos
      nectite serto.   16

Look, the two stars of the countryside advance and soften the ardours of the journey with their song. Look, the woods delight in the rhythms of the singers and the breeze applauds.

Menalcas gently accepts this maiden, Meliseus the other. From a nearby height Mergellina sings and from afar the rocks echo her song.

O happy shore, as the nymph sings her song, the mountains, the caves and the gardens respond, and also the lofty crags from afar; and the echo joins in from the sea.

L   ANDREA NAVAGERO

Lusus XXXVII

Divine spouse of aged Tithonus, thou who revealest the day with thy radiant countenance, when thou showest thy rosy cheeks, harbingers of the reddening sun,

how pleasing it is to wander now upon thy coming through the dewy fields and catch the fresh breezes that ever accompany thy chariot!

Soon the violent heat will scorch the dry fields, the wandering breath of the light breezes will fall still, and soon the fiery sun will send forth its raging fires.

Go off together, joyous lovers, while you may; gentle maidens go off as well, while you may, and bind your golden hair with garlands of different colours.

nunc simul telis positis amores
matris haerentes lateri, et decentes
Gratiae plenos referunt resecto
    flore quasillos.   20

per feros saltus, per iniqua lustra
undique occultas agitans latebras
fertur et silvas varia ferarum
    strage cruentat,   24

clara Latonae soboles: nitenti
huic comae in nodum religantur auro,
pendet aurata ex humeris pharetra,
    pendet et arcus.   28

circum eunt nymphae simul: illa cursu
gaudet effusos agitare cervos,
hanc iuvat certis iaculis fugaces
    figere lyncas.   32

nunc ab umbroso simul aesculeto
Daulias late queritur; querelas
consonum circa nemus, et iocosa
    reddit imago.   36

LI   MARCANTONII FLAMINII

Hymnus in Auroram

Ecce ab extremo veniens Eoo
roscidas Aurora refert quadrigas,
et sinu lucem roseo nitentem
    candida portat.   4

ite pallentes tenebrae sub Orcum,
ite, quae tota mihi nocte diros
manium vultus, mihi dira semper
    somnia fertis.   8

Now the Cupids put aside their arrows and cling to their mother's side, and the comely Graces return with baskets full of cut flowers.

Through the wild valleys, through the steep woods, disturbing everywhere their hiding-places, there comes, reddening the woods with the carnage of many beasts,

the shining daughter of Latona. Her hair is bound in a knot of glittering gold, a golden quiver hangs from her shoulders and so does a bow.

All around her are her nymphs: one enjoys driving the scattering deer in her path; another loves to pierce the fleeing lynx with her unerring spear.

Now from the shady oak-forest, Progne too lets her plaint sound far and wide, a cheerful echo returns her complaint around the harmonious forest.

LI   MARCANTONIO FLAMINIO

Hymn to the Dawn

Lo from the farthest East comes Aurora, returning with her dewy team of four horses and, resplendent, bearing the shining light in her rosy breast.

Go, wan shadows of darkness, to the Lower World, go you who bring me throughout the night ill-omened faces of the dead, you who always bring me dreams that bode no good.

da lyram vati, puer; ipse flores
sparge, dum canto. bona diva, salve,
quae tuo furvas radiante terras
      lumine lustras.   12

en tibi suaves violas crocumque,
en odorati calathos amomi;
surgit et nostros tibi dulcis aura
      portat odores.   16

deferat laudes utinam precesque
quas tibi supplex mea Musa fundit
iam pio sanctos bene docta divos
      tollere cantu.   20

quis tuam digne celebrare lucem
possit, o almae genetrix diei?
quis tuam formam, O Dea ante Divas
      pulchrior omnes.   24

ut genas caelo roseas, comamque
auream profers, tibi fulva cedunt
astra, decedit rutilante victa
      luna decore.   28

te sine aeterna iaceant sepulti
nocte mortales; sine te nec ullus
sit color rebus, neque vita doctas
      culta per artes.   32

tu gravem pigris oculis soporem
excutis (leti sopor est imago)
evocans tectis sua quemque laetum ad
      munia mittis.   36

exsilit stratis rapidus viator,
ad iugum fortes redeunt iuvenci,
laetus in silvas properat citato
      cum grege pastor.   40

Give the poet his lyre, boy; and scatter flowers while I sing. Good goddess, hail, who with thy dazzling light illuminatest the murky regions.

Here are sweet violets for thee and crocus flowers, here are baskets of fragrant balsam; the delightful breeze rises and wafts our perfumes to thee.

May it bring the praise and the prayers which my suppliant Muse utters to thee, already well-versed in praising with divine song the sacred Gods.

Who can sing becomingly thy light, O mother of bountiful day? who can sing thy beauty, O Goddess beautiful above all other goddesses?

When thou bringest forth from heaven thy rosy cheeks and golden hair, the golden-coloured stars make way for thee, the moon retires conquered by thy glowing beauty.

Without thee mortals would lie buried in eternal darkness, without thee there would be no colour to things, nor a life of culture embellished by the learned arts.

Thou shakest heavy sleep from slothful eyes (sleep is the image of death), calling from the roof-tops thou sendest each man happy to his appointed duty.

The hastening traveller sets out briskly, the sturdy bullocks return to the yoke, cheerfully the shepherd hurries into the woods with his herds moving at a rapid pace.

ast amans carae thalamum puellae
deserit flens, et tibi verba dicit
aspera, amplexu tenerae cupito a-
     vulsus amicae.   44

ipse amet noctis latebras dolosae,
me iuvet semper bona lux. nitentem
da mihi lucem, dea magna, longos
     cernere in annos.   48

LII   IOANNIS SALMONII MACRINI

Ad Brissam Nympham

Expultrix gravium sollicitudinum
te nunc, Brissa, canam, nulla celebrior
ut sit lympha sacris rupibus Aonum,
     aut Idae Phrygiae iugis.   4

nam seu post rapidum dulce meridiem
herbis membra super sternere, eburnea
ludentem cithara, seu vacuum iuvet
     matutina magis quies,   8

ad fontis tremuli murmur amabile,
securo innumeris picta coloribus
prata haud defuerint, nec patulae novis
     passim frondibus arbores.   12

caesum hic ales Ithym Daulias integrat
nigris ilicibus flebiliter gemens,
et turtur viduus voce tibi nemus
     vicinum querula replet.   16

spissis aura comis sibila perstrepit,
somnosque exiguo murmure pellicit;
custodes ovium rustica dulcibus
     dicunt carmina fistulis.   20

But the lover forsakes in tears the couch of his beloved maiden and speaks harsh words to thee, separated as he is from the longed for embrace of his tender mistress.

Let him love the hidden retreat of deceitful night, may the good light always please me. Grant, mighty goddess, that for long years to come I may behold thy shining light.

LII   JEAN SALMON MACRIN

To the Nymph Brissa

Thou who dispellest heavy cares, Brissa, I shall sing of thee now, so that no spring will be more famed on the sacred rocks of Aonia or on the heights of Ida the Phrygian.

For whether one likes, after the fierce midday heat, to stretch out on the grass plucking the ivory lute, or prefers in idleness the morning calm,

Near the pleasant murmurs of the trembling fountain there will be no lack of fields painted in countless colours and trees spreading their fresh leaves in all directions.

Here the Daulian bird bitterly weeping mourns again the death of Itys and you can hear the widowed turtle dove filling the nearby wood with its plaint.

A breeze sighs as it soughs through the thick foliage and invites me to sleep with its gentle murmur; the shepherds play their rustic songs upon their pleasant reeds.

hic me sub platani tegmine caelibis
captantem tenuis frigora ventuli
adflat dulcisoni pectinis arbiter
      toto numine Cynthius.   24

non ut Maeoniis cantibus audeam
Titanas memorare atque acies deum,
ut Phlegraea cohors montibus arduos
      montes imposuit minax.   28

invictis neque uti viribus Hercules
Antaeum Libyco pulvere straverit,
aureumque abstulerit victor Amazoni
      in certamine baltheum.   32

heroa haec referat Flaminius tuba
cum matura virum tempora fecerint,
mira Flaminius nobilis indole
      et centum puer artium.   36

me dulcem satis est posse Gelonidem
imbelli cithara tradere posteris,
inter Pictonicas et veterum Andium
      forma praecipuam nurus.   40

nec te, Brissa, meis non fidibus canam
puro iugis aquae gurgite fertilem,
altricem salicum valle recondita
      pratorumque virentium.   44

sic glaucam tremula semper harundine
incingare comam, perspicuas neque
sus obturbet aquas, pratave proterat
      lascivo pede bucula.   48

huc potum quotiens, huc quotiens, dea,
dormitum veniam fessus ab oppido
quod Caesar statuit Iulius, haud tuas
      vati delicias neges.   52

While here under cover of the solitary plane tree I delight in the coolth of the light breeze, the Cynthian, master of the sweet-sounding lyre, inspires me with all his might.

Not so that I should dare recall in Maonian strains the battle between the Gods and the Titans when the Phlegraean horde threateningly piled lofty mountain upon mountain,

Nor tell how Hercules with his unconquered strength floored Antaeus in the dust of Lybia and victorious in the fight removed from the Amazon her golden girdle.

Let Flaminius tell of these feats on the epic trumpet when in the fulness of time he reaches maturity, the noble Flaminius of outstanding talents, the boy endowed with countless gifts.

For my part, I am content to hand down to posterity by my peaceloving guitar the name of my sweet Gelonis who outstrips in beauty the maidens of Poitou and the young women of ancient Anjou.

Nor wilt thou, Brissa, be forgotten by my lyre, thou whose streams fertilise the fields and who in the hidden valley nourishest the willows and the verdant meadows.

Thus shall thy gleaming hair ever be encircled by a quivering reed; nor shall the pig muddy your clear waters, nor the heifer trample down thy fields with playful hoof.

Whenever I come here to drink, whenever, Goddess, I come to sleep, wearied by the town that Julius Caesar founded, do not refuse your delight to your poet.

Religious poetry

Throughout the Renaissance we find religious poetry, though the turbulence of doctrinal debate and strife ensures sharp changes of inspiration and tone. Towards the end of the fifteenth century and the beginning of the sixteenth, many humanists are in holy orders and their production is abundant rather than impressive. In the more personal poetry medieval habits are only gradually sloughed off and, at a time when the epic formula is still fashionable, it is not uncommon for poets to write religious verse in what one might call a para-epic mould. Hagiographic verse is frequent, as are prayers to saints and other religious figures; and some religious controversy may be conducted in verse. In Italy Neo-latin poetry is less affected by the Reformation, though humanists with suspected evangelical views or worse do turn up—such as Marcantonio Flaminio or the curious Palingenius. In the North the *devotio moderna* remains backward in poetic expression.

With the advent of the Reformation and the flowering of classical humanism beyond the confines of Italy, religious poetry changes its character. Epic hagiography, as in Pierre Rosset who follows in the footsteps of Mantuan, soon fades out and gives way to more religious satire, usually expressed in epigrammatic form, whether on the Protestant side (e.g. Euricius Cordus or George Buchanan) or on the Catholic, with the well-known pasquil tradition deriving from Rome. Generally Catholic poetry at this time is rather self-effacing but the impact of evangelical humanism soon makes itself felt. Religious verse acquires a more personal tone, prayers are addressed in particular to Jesus Christ rather than to the Virgin Mary, and with the development of a more inward religion as well as of Hebrew studies, the psalm paraphrase takes on a new lease of life. Some of the early attempts at complete sets of psalm paraphrases are monotonous, because they were couched exclusively in elegiac couplets, so that individual variations of tone and theme were drastically reduced—there are even examples of paraphrases written only in pentameters. Soon poets began to grasp the possibilities afforded by horatian metres; and though George Buchanan's paraphrases did not see print until the end of 1565, there were precursors such as Macrin or Nicolas Bourbon who were prepared to experiment with horatian schemes, or Jean de Gagnay whose seventy-five paraphrases, published in 1547, show a serious attempt at stylistic variety. In France at least some forms of religious verse were more acceptable in Neo-latin than in the vernacular because of orthodox censorship which however remained somewhat erratic in practice. Other sacred texts soon became subjected to paraphrase, especially during the wars of religion when Job and Jeremiah were very much in accord with the spirit of the times.

Much of the Neo-latin verse published in sixteenth-century Germany is of religious character, though of course many writers strike out on their own or under the influence of Italian models (e.g. Petrus Lotichius). Lutheran humanists tend to see an irreconcilable gap between the ancient, classical and the Christian worlds, and Latin poetry is used as a vehicle for religious militancy. The role of Wittenberg is a major one and is characterised by two different generations of poets, the first centring on Melanchthon and his circle, the other numbering in its ranks figures such as Georg Fabricius. Earlier Eobanus Hessus had done much to launch the psalm paraphrase and his versions went through many editions abroad as well as at home.

With the advent of the wars of religion, Christian verse often of a highly partisan and committed character assumes important proportions; but it does not lead to a great deal of spiritual poetry in France, though under the influence of Counter-reformation views a writer like Jacques de Billy will publish in 1575 the first volume of his *Anthologia sacra*, a reduced Latin equivalent of his very successful *Sonnets spirituels* (1573). Here the inspiration of the Church Fathers is very much to the fore. Calvinist poetry flourishes for a while in Switzerland though its quality is not particularly high.

The Counter-reformation's attitudes will appear more especially in the voluminous amount of poetry brought out by the Jesuits. They were intent, among other things, on harnessing authors such as Ovid and Martial to the Christian cause and their verse shows a close knowledge of the classics. They wrote satirical epigrams against their opponents (e.g. A. Frusius), composed much encomiastic verse on Christ, biblical figures, saints and prominent fighters for the cause nearer their time. They also paraphrased the Scriptures; their verse may range from the simple, unaffected expression of emotion to experiments of much technical sophistication. There is for instance a highly developed poetry of tears. Under James I and indeed after, these Jesuit poets find a ready audience in England.

LIII   MARCANTONII FLAMINII

Comparat animum suum flori

Ut flos tenellus in sinu
telluris almae lucidam
formosus explicat comam.
si ros et imber educat
illum, tenella mens mea   5
sic floret, almi Spiritus
dum rore dulci pascitur;
hoc illa si caret statim
languescit, ut flos arida
tellure natus, eum nisi   10
et ros et imber educat.

LIV   MARCANTONII FLAMINII

Paraphrasis Psalmi CXXVIII

Beatus ille qui piam sese Deo
      in servitutem dedicat,
semper paratus exsequi sanctissimis
      quod ille verbis imperat.   4
non is paterna rura inaniter colit;
      sed quae feraci semina
sinu recepit fundus, illa maximo
      reddit colenti faenore.   8
uxor pudica bene regit domum, et optimis
      exornat ipsam liberis,
fecunda vitis instar apta diligens
      quam curat artu vinitor.   12
proles novella crescit, ut virentibus
      oliva pulchra ramulis;
et mensa turba garrula circumdata
      cumulat parentes gaudio.   16
haec est piorum vita; eosque talibus
      remuneratur praemiis

LIII   MARCANTONIO FLAMINIO

The poet compares his soul to a flower

As the delicate flower in the bosom of the bountiful earth displays, in all its beauty, its shining foliage, if it is nurtured by dew and rain, so does my delicate soul flourish while it feeds upon the gentle dew of the bountiful Spirit. Without it, it droops forthwith like a flower that has grown in parched soil, if it is not nurtured by dew and rain.

LIV   MARCANTONIO FLAMINIO

Psalm paraphrase CXXVIII

Blessed is he who has devoted himself in holy bondage to God, who is ever ready to perform what He commands in His most holy words. He does not till his father's fields to vain purpose, but his land gives back the seed it received in its rich bosom with utmost profit to the farmer. His chaste wife runs his home well and graces it with the finest of children, like a fruitful vine which the diligent dresser tends with proper skill. New sons grow like flourishing branches on a beautiful olive tree. And the garrulous crowd assembled round the table fills the parents with joy. This is the life of devout folk, with such rewards is their existence recompensed by

summi benignitas patris; quem si coles
    urbis sacratae commodis   20
laetus frueris, usquedum vivas, tuae
    prolis beatae liberos
florere cernes; patriis felicitas
    regnabit alma finibus.   24

LV   IACOBI BILLII
                        Anthologia sacra

De tristitia spirituali 33

Quis latices oculis, capiti quis porriget undas,
    ut commissa mihi nocte dieque gemam?
ut lacrimis nostro mala quae grassantur in aevo
    prosequar, excedunt quae gravitate fidem;   4
utque hostes fidei deplorem, aciemque rebellem,
    et quibus in sancta est vita profana fide.
has etiam praeter, niveas mihi quis dabit undas,
    quam fundit patriae mens memor usque suae.   8

LVI   MARII BETTINI

Beata Virgo puellulo Iesu violas

Tu qui flosculus es campi,
    valliumque lilium,
tibi, nate, quas eburna
    unguis falce mestui,   4
mollicella rubicundas
    cape manu violas:
en diductis ut labellis
    pene risu gestiunt,   8
in eburneum serendae
    tuae manus vasculum.

the bounty of their Father on high. If you worship him, you will with a glad heart enjoy the rewards of the sacred city, you will live long enough to see the children of your blessed children prosper, and bountiful happiness will reign in the land of your fathers.

LV   JACQUES DE BILLY:
Sonnets spirituels, 1573

De la tristesse spirituelle 33

Qui me donra de l'eau pour mon chef miserable,
  De larmes pour mes yeux un ruisseau tout entier?
  Qui un bien me donra secret et à cartier,
  Pour pleurer jour et nuit mon offense execrable?   4
Pour deplorer l'estat piteux et lamentable,
  Auquel nous nous voyons, pour nous estre au bourbier
  Plongez de tous pechez, en quitant le sentier,
  Qui droict guide l'esprit au sejour perdurable.   8
Pour aussi pleurer ceux qui sont hors de l'Eglise,
  Et les enfans pervers, qui font qu'on la mesprise,
  Qu'on s'en rit, qu'on luy donne à present maint assaut   11
Outre ces pleurs encor helas, helas que n'ay-je
  Pour me baigner le coeur un torrent d'eau de neige,
  Au penser de Sion et des biens de là haut.   14

LVI   MARIUS BETTINUS

The Blessed Virgin offers violets to the Infant Jesus

Thou who art the flowerlet of the field and the lily of the valleys, take in thy most gentle hand, Child, these blooming violets which I cut with the ivory edge of my nail. See how they exult on thy lips hardly creased by a smile, ready to be twined together in the ivory vase of thy hand.

LVII BERNHARDI BAUHUSII

De amore divino

O cui cor Christus terebravit harundine amoris,
   hoc qui vulnus habet, quam leve vulnus habet!
hoc qui vulnus habet, non immedicabile et atrox
   abdita quod populet viscera, vulnus habet;   4
non tabem metuat, non hinc sibi credat ituros
   horrida praecipites mortis ad antra dies.
nam cui sunt dia praecordia fossa sagitta,
   huic via facta boni est maxima, nulla mali.   8
hoc qui vulnus habet, vitae dispendia sentit
   nulla, sed e dio vulnere robur habet.
hoc qui vulnus habet, mens huic sine nube perennis
   semper ei e nitida fronte serena dies.   12
hoc qui vulnus habet, superi! quae gaudia carpit?
   gaudia quaeque aloës, nil neque fellis habent.
hoc qui vulnus habet, Christi ut mandata facessat,
   vertere Threicias nititur ante animas.   16
praecipitat, ruit, exsilit, et volat; o bone Iesu,
   hoc qui vulnus habet, quam leve vulnus habet!

LVIII I. BIDERMANNI

Flagellum Christi sanguine purpuratum

Iratus domini cum terga secare satelles
   nodoso inciperet terque quaterque flagro,
noluit imperio refugum parere flagellum,
   mitius immiti dum cupit esse manu.   4
sed parere manus cum pergere saeva iuberet,
   iusta flagrum fecit, fecit et erubuit.

LVII   BERNHARD VAN BAUHUYSEN

Divine Love

He whose heart Christ had pierced with the reed of love, he who has this wound, how light is his wound! He who has this wound has a wound that is not incurable or cruelly destroys the hidden vitals. Let him not fear a wasting disease, let him not think on this account that the days of his life will go headlong towards the dread underworld. For to him, whose heart has been pierced by the divine arrow, the way has become the finest in the direction of good and not of evil. He who has this wound, feels no loss of life, but gains strength from the divine wound. He who has this wound has a mind that is eternally unclouded, for ever his eyes look out serenely from under his clear forehead. He who has this wound, O gods, what joys does he gather, joys that have neither wormwood nor gall! He who has this wound, so that he may execute God's commands, strives to anticipate the Orphic state of mind. He hurries, rushes, jumps for joy and flies; O blessed Jesus, he who has this wound, how light is his wound!

LVIII   J. BIDERMANN

The scourge reddened with the blood of Christ

When the guard in his wrath began to cut the Lord's back with the knotted scourge time and again, the scourge drawing back refused to obey his command, as it wished to be gentler than the harsh hand that wielded it. But when the savage hand ordered it still to obey, the scourge complied and in so doing blushed.

LIX   I. BIDERMANNI

Beata Magdalena lacrimans et ad crucem procumbens

Magdalis ut fixo moribundum in stipite vidit,
    quod quondam Assyrio laverat imbre caput,
et rigidis penetrata pedum vestigia clavis,
    perque decussatam bracchia tensa trabem;   4
stipite si ex humili penderent bracchia, dixit,
    ferrem avide palmis oscula, Christe, tuis.
scala foret, peterem terebrati pectoris antrum,
    ablueremque meas vulnera per lacrimas,   8
stans ego mulcerem madidis pia genua labellis;
    nunc possum extremos tangere flexa pedes.
malo pedes, ah malo. tui pars corporis illa
    iam didicit lacrimis ante favere meis.   12

LX   HERMANNI HUGONIS:
               Pia Desideria, III, xxxiv

Ego dilecto meo, et ad me conversio eius. Cant. 7

Maesta cupressiferi nemoris spatiabar in umbra,
    tristitiam lacrimis compositura meis:
iamque sinum tepidis submerserat imbribus unda,
    concideramque meis paene subacta malis.   4
Fors Chelys ex humeris pendebat eburnea nostris,
    maestitiae quondam certa medela chelys.
obruta tristitia, frondente sub arbore sedi,
    adsocians querulis talia verba modis: 8
ergo mihi vidui, sine lusibus, ibitis anni?
    nullus et in nostro carmine vivet amor?
ah precor! ah nostris ita torpeat hostibus aetas,
    et tolerent tanti segnia damna probri!   12
non ego pro verae numeravero tempore vitae,
    ducere si vacuos cogar amore dies.
unicus est homini, vivendi fructus, amare,
    solus amans, vixi; dicere iure potest.   16

LIX   J. BIDERMANN

The blessed Magdalene weeping and prostrate before the Cross

When Magdalene saw Him dying on the planted Cross, the head she had formerly washed in Assyrian water, the traces of the harsh nails that had pierced His feet, and His arms stretched out on the cross, she said: If Thy arms hung from a lowly Tree, I would eagerly kiss the palms of Thy hands, O Christ; were there a ladder, I would seek out the cavities of Thy pierced breast and wash Thy wounds with my tears. Standing I would soothe Thy sacred knees with my moistened lips. Now bending down I can touch the tips of Thy feet: I prize Thy feet, I do indeed. That part of Thy body has already learned to be well disposed to my tears.

LX   HERMANN HUGO:
Pia Desideria, or Divine Addresses

I am my Beloved's and his desire is towards me

A Cypress Grove (whose melancholy shade
To sute the temper of the sad was made)
I chose for my retreat, there laid me down,
Hoping my sorrows in my tears to drown.
They vainly flow'd; and now o'erwhelm'd with grief,
From Musick's charming sounds I sought relief.
This song compos'd, I strike my Lyre, and sing,
Soft notes rebounding from each silver string.
Ah! shall my wasted days no passion crown,
And must my empty years roul useless on!
So hard a fate I'd wish my greatest foes;
He lives not, who the flames of Love ne're knows:
Stupid his soul lies hid in darkest night,
Who is not chear'd with Loves transpiercing light:
He bears no Image of the God above,
Whose icy breast's insensible of Love.

qualis, in ima, suo desidit pondere tellus,
   et subit aerias, ardua flamma, vias;
nos ita fax animi, violento cogit amore,
   abripimurque leves, impete quisque suo. 20
me quoque sollicitans, ut amem, meus impetus urget,
   visque adhibet tacitas, nescio quanta, faces.
quo meus ergo suos Amor eiaculabitur ignes?
   (primitiae nostri namque caloris erunt) 24
an ferar humanae furiata Cupidine taedae,
   cognata angelicis, stirpsque sororque choris?
aut mea mortales venient in colla lacerti
   quae sum immortali sponsa creata Deo? 28
ah, super hasce hiemes, nostri rapiuntur amores,
   terra parem thalamis non habet ista meis.
nec quae Penelopen adamavit turba procorum,
   nec quibus impediunt regia sceptra manum. 32
nympha puellarum pulcherrima Romulearum
   Agnes, Ausonio sponsa petita proco;
absit, ait, iuvenis mea ne tibi foedera speres,
   iam mea caelestis foedera sponsus habet. 36
sic nostra aetherios ambit quoque fax Hymenaeos,
   inde petendus erit qui mihi sponsus erit.
hunc ego, non alium, solum hunc ego diligo sponsum,
   nemo potest uno tempore amare duos. 40
illius ante oculos mihi semper oberrat imago,
   ante oculos, quamvis longius absit, adest.
et loquor absenti momentis omnibus, absens,
   absentique sonos illius aure bibo. 44
sic ubi magnetis vim ferrea linea sensit,
   semper ad agnati vertitur alta poli.
utque hinc Sydoniis petitur cynosura carinis,
   servat et hinc Helicen cymba pelasga suam; 48

The pond'rous Earth, by'ts proper weight deprest,
Beneath all other Elements doth rest;
While pointed Flames do thro the solid mass
Force their bright way, and unresisted pass.
So thro the solid lump of Man the soul
Sends forth those fires that do the frame controul;
And his desires do hurry him away,
Where-e're those flames do guide th'obedient Clay,
And now I feel an unknown warmth all o're;
I burn, I melt, but know not from what Pow'r;
These sharp quick fires are urg'd thro ev'ry vein,
Mingling at once such Pleasure and such Pain.
Ah! Whither will this furious passion drive?
(In vain against Love's raging force we strive)
Shall my aspiring Soul, like vulgar hearts,
Complain of shameful wounds from Cupid's Darts?
If I shou'd be embrac'd by mortal arms,
They'd fade my beauties, sully all my Charms!
My rising mind soars vast degrees above
Terrestrial Charms, they're much beneath my Love:
These gross desires my purer Soul disdains;
She'll be his Spouse who ev'ry beeing frames.
Agnes, of Rome the wonder and the pride,
Her charms to an Ausonian youth deny'd,
And in these terms refus'd to be his Bride:
'If I have kindled fires within your breast,
I cannot grant, but pity your request:
Nor can you justly my refusal blame,
Since I burn with a much diviner flame;
For my Creator hath engag'd my heart,
My soul from such a Spouse can ne're depart:
His lovely Image still is in my sight,
And at this distance He's my sole delight:
In absence we converse; I speak in Pray'rs
And he in absence charms my listning ears.'
So by the Loadstones unseen wondrous force
The faithfull Needle steers the Seamans course:
Tow'rds its lov'd North it constantly doth rise,
Helping their way, to their extreme Surprize.

sic laesi sequeris studiosa pedissequa Phoebi
   dilectam Clytie; flos modo facta, facem:
bisque die quovis, verso iubar ore salutans,
   mane precaris Ave; sero precare Vale.   52
obvia fraternos ita spectas Cynthia vultus
   et reparat vultus ignibus ille tuos.
sponse, meus sol es, tua sumque ego Cynthia; vultus
   adversis oculis figere cogit amor.   56
tu mihi, sponse, Helice, Cynosuraque duplicis Arcti,
   tu volucres oculos ad tua signa rapis;
quid mirum, alterno si respondemus amori?
   magnetem sequitur linea tacta suum.   60

    LXI   FRANCISCI REMUNDI

                  Elegia II

Crudelis regio, quae te fovet usque latentem,
   illa meis facta est terra beata malis.
ah! pereat quisquis, si fas est dicere, primus
   inviti docuit terga domare salis;   4
intactum qui fregit iter, montesque subegit,
   virgineam pedibus qui violavit humum.
septeni colles et Tibridis ostia tutus
   exigui limes tunc erat Imperii.   8
tunc erat Vrbs vix nota sibi, parvoque Quiriti
   extremi Aethiopes porta Capena fuit.
dictator numerabat oves, pressoque senator
   fessus aratro, humili sub lare iura dabat.   12
nunc quoque sic utinam, clausis regionibus, esses
   mecum sub vili pauper Alexi casa!
cur fugis e patria non ullo pulsus ab hoste?
   si tibi cura mei est, o fugitive redi   16
si tibi cura mei nulla est, miserere parentum:
   quem trahis, ipse iubet spiritus esse pium.
non haec sperabant meritae solacia vitae,
   et pater infelix et miseranda parens.   20
immatura utrique paras (heu!) funera: iam iam

So doth the Flow'r of Phoebus twice a day
Turn tow'rds her Sun, and her glad leaves display.
Fair Cynthia thus regards Brother's beams,
Renews her Beauty from his borrow'd flames.
I am thy Clytie (Spouse), thou art my Sun,
I, Cynthia, always tow'rds thy light must run.
My Spouse, my Helice, with longing I
(Where-e're thou draw'st) tow'rds thee in raptures flie.
What wonder if in mutual Love we burn,
Since Steel can tow'rds the senseless Loadstone turn?

LXI   R. CRASHAW

The Third Elegie

Rich, churlish Land! that hid'st so long in thee
My treasures, rich, alas, by robbing mee.
Needs must my miseryes owe that man a Spite
Who e're he be was the first wandring Knight.
O had he nere been at that cruell cost
Nature's virginity had nere been lost.
Seas had not bin rebuk't by sawcy oares
But ly'n lockt up safe in their sacred shores.
Men had not spurn'd at mountaines; nor made warrs
With rocks; nor bold hands struck the world's strong barres,
Nor lost in too larg bounds our little Rome
Full sweetly with it selfe had dwell't at home.
My poor Alexis, then in peacefull life,
Had under some lowe roofe lov'd his plain wife.
But now, ah me, from where he has no foes
He flyes; and into willfull exile goes.
Cruell return. Or tell the reason why
Thy dearest parents have deserv'd to dy.

in tumulum tristi cum patre mater abit.
prompta tuae tu solus habes medicamina culpae;
    funera regressu sunt revocanda tuo.   24
vita veni, quid enim tandem peccavimus omnes?
    totane Roma potest esse noverca tibi?
ast ego quid merui? vel quo rea crimine dicor?
    nullum in me crimen, praeter amare, vides.   28
si tibi virginitas, iuvenis castissime, sancta est,
    virgineo possum vivere nupta toro.
vivere si possum cum coniuge virgine virgo;
    cur fugis aspectus, dure marite, meos?   32
este mihi testes superi, nil firmius opto,
    quam vita exacta caelibe posse mori.
connubii non vincla Venus, non foedera nectit,
    nec facit amplexus concubitusque virum.   36
caelicolum Regina potens et gloria terrae,
    ipsa simul coniunx, virgo, parensque fuit.
Caecilia antiquae potuit nova gloria gentis
    o quam dissimilem ducere virgo virum!   40
coniugis in thalamum prima cum nocte veniret,
    protinus exclamat, Valeriane cave;
Valeriane cave, custos fortissimus astat,
    qui mihi libati corporis ultor erit.   44
est mihi virginitas summo iurata Tonanti;
    pervigil in lectum fert sua vota sopor.
Gorgone tuta, meo caream Alite? telaque vibrans
    fingitur a vobis Pallas; inermis ero?   48
crede mihi, Paridis non est haec fabula vestri,
    cum Menelao rapta Lacaena toro est.
sum tua, tu meus es, Christum cole: sim modo virgo,
    tu pater et coniunx, et mihi frater eris.   52
sic ait. ille sacro lustratus fonte, meretur
    optato aetherii militis ore frui.
sanguis utrumque iterum fecunda in morte maritat:
    ornat utrique manum palma, corona caput.   56
noster hymen tali caleat face, taeda iugalis
    sentiet haud flammas, dire Cupido, tuas.
femina virque iugo sacri subiguntur amoris:
    o quanta exsistit vis in amore pari!   60

And I, what is my crime I cannot tell,
Unlesse it be a crime to' have lov'd too well.
If Heates of holye love and high desire
Make bigge thy fair brest with immortall fire,
What needs my virgin lord fly thus from me
Who only wish his virgin wife to be?
Wittnesse, chast heavns! no happyer vowes I know
Then to a virgin Grave untouch't to goe.
Love's truest knott by Venus is not ty'd;
Nor doe embraces onely make a bride.
The Queen of Angels (and men chast as You)
Was Maiden Wife and Maiden Mother too.
Cecilia, Glory of her name and blood
With happy gain her maiden vowes made good.
The lusty bridegroom made approach: young man,
Take heed (said she), take heed, Valerian!
My bosom's Guard, a Spirit great and strong,
Stands arm'd, to sheild me from all wanton wrong.
My Chastity is sacred; and my sleep
Wakefull, her dear vowes undefil'd to keep.
Pallas beares armes, forsooth, and should there be
No fortresse built for true Virginity?
No gaping Gorgon, this. None, like the rest
Of your learn'd lyes. Here you'l find no such jest.
I'am yours, O were my God, my Christ so too,
I'd know no name of love on earth but you.
He yeilds, and straight Baptis'd obtains the Grace
To gaze on the fair souldier's glorious face.
Both mixt at last their blood in one rich bed
Of rosy martyrdome, twice Married.
O burn our hymen bright in such high Flame.
Thy torch, terrestrial love, have here no name.
How sweet the mutuall yoke of man and wife

ast ego te rerum pulcherrime, semper amavi:
  sic placidi redeant in mea vota dies.
o quotiens cum me peteret male sana procorum
  turba, meus, dixi, solus Alexis erit!   64
altera vera fuit, fuit (heu!) vox altera mendax:
  es solus, sed non diceris esse meus.

When holy fires maintain love's Heavnly life!
But I (so help me heavn my hopes to see)
When thousands sought my love, lov'd none but Thee.
Still, as their vain teares my firm vowes did try,
Alexis, he alone is mine (said I)
Half true, alas, half false, proves that poor line.
Alexis is alone; But is not mine.

Didactic poetry

Didactic poetry is widespread in the Renaissance: at a time when educational progress was so rapid and so much in the forefront of humanist concerns, this is hardly surprising. On the one hand, we detect a fair amount of *haute vulgarisation* for college purposes—Antoine Mizault is a good example—and on the other there is a broad current of moral, exemplary poetry best illustrated by the emblem and the icon but also showing itself in the longer composition. Here the eclogue may be pressed into service—as in the case of Mantuan's compositions—and an even more extended formula will be found in the *Liber zodiacus* of Palingenius, a work that was widely read and studied in Protestant countries.

There is a further, more exalted reason to explain the growing interest in this type of poetry, the advances made in things scientific. Here the main forces at work were the willingness to maintain what had for a long time been a flourishing tradition and the humanist ideal of the scholar-poet: the Muses after all combined learning and the arts. Significantly, Buchanan's friends continued to press him to complete his *De Sphaera* in the belief that such a work would crown an already distinguished career. Poetic genres are however easier to define than to follow in practice; and the scientific poem could range widely not only in its main theme but in the variety of topics it might treat. It might remain essentially technical—this is true of certain verse treatises on astronomy, for instance; but when the question of man's destiny and place in the universe enters the stage, the composition may spill over into something approaching a religious or philosophical epic or will at least contain digressions of matters going beyond the strictly scientific, as we might interpret the term. In any case, a 'scientific' subject was much less clearly defined for the Renaissance mind: astronomy merged into astrology, alchemy had respectable status for many, and man's capacity for 'knowledge' begged certain theological questions. And an important classical model for the genre such as Lucretius' *De rerum natura* was endowed with a major philosophical infrastructure. With the introduction of the theme of man's destiny, a historical and therefore epic element might well be found. Sainte-Marthe's didactic poem may deal with the education of children, but this does not prevent his introducing a versified account of the Garden of Eden and the Fall of man. Vida's poem on the game of chess is a technical poem, in spite of some inaccuracies, but it is also a *ludus poeticus* in which fun is made of traditional epic and which may also conceal allusions to the contemporary political scene. A poem dealing with the art of hunting will easily move into the aulic, encomiastic sphere too, for hunting was the sport of kings. There is a cognate genre, the city-blason which will deal primarily with the historical fortunes, technical achievements and architectural features of a town (e.g. the poems of Germain Audebert), but circumstances will often make a composition of this nature an exercise in encomium. There is a tendency, however, for all these extended poems to be written in the hexameter but the practice is not without its exceptions: an unpublished poem by Jean Dampierre on the education of young girls is couched entirely in hendecasyllables. At all events, there is a recognisable and abundant flow of didactic poetry throughout our period, which deserves to be represented here, not only because of its important development, but because certain compositions in this vein find their way into schools and therefore play their part in forming humanists who may later turn their mind to the writing of verse. Authors like Pontano no doubt exerted influence on strictly scientific poetry dealing with astronomy or cognate subjects.

LXII I.I.PONTANI

De solis prognosticis

Ille etiam ventos tempestatesque futuras
atque imbres aestusque graves et frigora monstrat.
namque ubi caeruleo rapidum petit aequore caelum
exoriens, aperitque diem natalibus undis,
si nigram obscuro faciem variaverit ortu   5
concavus, inque atram condentur lumina nubem,
et pelago et terris violentior incubat Eurus,
turbatasque amnis in pontum devehet undas.
quin etiam ut nullae densentur in aëre nubes,
si tamen aut hebetes radii torpere videntur,   10
aut si plus nimio torrens incanduit ardor,
collige venturos imbres. at pallida quando
Aurora oceano caput exserit, horridave inter
nubila diversis rumpit sol partibus, et nunc
obliquos effert radios, nunc pallidus ore   15
delituit nimboso, heu, rupto foedere, caelum
in terras ruet, et saevum per inane rotatae
praecipitent nimborum acies, quae grandine mixtae
arboribus stragemque dabunt et vitibus almis,
vix ovium ut clausos defendant culmina fetus.   20
non mihi tum, non claustra boumve armentave equarum
ducenda a stabulis, non me extra tecta domorum
ducet iter. servanda dies, quam rite serenam
spondeat, oceani seras cum lucidus undas
intrarit, non nube comam, non turbidus ora,   25
sed qualem Hesperio Tethys suspirat in antro.
quod si tum quoque nigranti velatus amictu
occiderit, sive ipse suo quamquam emicat ore,
si tamen aut atras nubes raptaverit, aut si
palleat et maculae fundant sese undique nigrae,   30
venturam exspectes pluviam.

LXII G. G. PONTANO

Weather signs provided by the sun

The sun also gives indications of impending winds and storms, of approaching rain, and of severe heatwaves or cold spells on the way. For if, as it mounts from the blue expanse of the sea, seeks the rapidly moving sky and reveals the daylight on the waters from which it was born, dark spots appear on its face as it rises indistinctly and its rays are hidden behind dark cloud, then a rather violent south wind will oppress sea and land, and rivers will flow into the sea with muddied waters. If moreover, when no clouds thicken in the sky, the sun's rays appear to be wan and lacking in power, or if its heat rages excessively, consider this to be a sign that rain is on the way. But when Dawn rises pale from the ocean, or the sun breaks through the ugly clouds, shining forth in different directions, and at one moment emits slanting rays and at another lurks wanly behind watery clouds, then alas! the truce is broken and the sky will collapse upon the earth, the ranks of whirling clouds will rush headlong down and, mingling with the hail, will bring destruction on the trees and bountiful vines with such force that the flocks of sheep will scarcely manage to protect their offspring in the pens. This is not the moment for me to remove the bolts and let the herds of cattle and the mares out of their stalls, or to journey forth from the protection of my home. One must watch the day which the sun usually promises to be fair, when shining brightly it sinks below the evening waves, not with clouded rays or troubled face but just as Tethys longed for him in her western cave. For if then too the sun should set behind a darkening veil, or if shining brightly it has nonetheless attracted black clouds to itself, or if it turns pale and dark spots speed across its face, you may expect rain to be close at hand.

LXIII   MARCI HIERONYMI VIDAE

De Arte poetica

Nunc geminas puer huc aures, huc dirige mentem,
nam, quia non paucos parte ex utraque poetas
nostrosque Graiosque tibi se offerre videbis,
quos hic evites, quibus idem fidere tutus
evaleas, dicam, ne quis te fallere possit.   5
haud multus labor auctores tibi prodere Graios,
quos inter potitur sceptris insignis Homerus.
hunc omnes alii observant, hinc pectore numen
concipiunt vates, blandumque Heliconis amorem.
felices quos illa aetas, quos protulit illi   10
proxima, divino quanto quisque ortus Homero
vicinus magis, est tanto praestantior omnis.
degenerant adeo magis ac magis usque minores
obliti veterum praeclara inventa parentum . . .

Atque ita deinde rudes paulatim sumere versus   15
coeperunt formam insignem, penitusque Latini
agrestem exuerunt morem, liquidissima donec
tempestas veluti caeli post nubila, et imbres
extulit os sacrum soboles certissima Phoebi
Vergilius, qui mox veterum squalore, situque   20
deterso in melius mira omnia rettulit arte
vocem, animumque Deo similis. date lilia plenis

LXIII   M.-G. VIDA

The art of poetry

But now, young bard, with strict attention hear,
And drink my precepts in at either ear;
Since a vast crowd of poets you may find,
Both of the Graecian, and Ausonian kind,
Learn hence what bards to quit or to pursue,
To shun the false, and to embrace the true;
Nor is it hard to cull each noble piece,
And point out every glorious son of Greece,
Above whose numbers Homer sits on high,
And shines supreme in distant majesty;
Whom with a rev'rent eye the rest regard,
And owe their raptures to the sov'reign bard;
Thro' him the god their panting souls inspires,
Swells every breast, and warms with all his fires.
Blest were the poets with the hallow'd rage,
Train'd up in that, and the succeeding age:
As to his time each poet nearer drew,
His spreading fame in just proportion grew.
By like degrees the next degen'rate race
Sunk from the height of honour to disgrace.
And now the fame of Greece extinguisht lies,
Her ancient language with her glory dies . . .

Ausonia's bards drew off from every part
The barbrous dregs, and civilised the art,
'Till like the day all shining and serene,
That drives the clouds, and clears the gloomy scene,
Refines the air, and brightens up the skies,
See the majestick head of Virgil rise;
Phoebus' undoubted son! . . . who clears the rust
From the great Ancients, and shakes off their dust.
He on them works a nobler grace bestowed;
He thought, and spoke in every word a god.
To grace their mighty bard, ye muses, bring
Your choicest flow'rs, and rifle all the spring;

Pierides calathis, tantoque adsurgite alumno.
unus hic ingenio praestanti gentis Achivae
divinos vates longe superavit et arte,   25
aureus, immortale sonans. stupet ipsa, pavetque
quamvis ingentem miretur Graecia Homerum.

Haud alio Latium tantum se tempore iactat.
tunc linguae Ausoniae potuit quae maxima virtus
esse fuit, caeloque ingens se gloria vexit   30
Italiae, sperare nefas sit vatibus ultra,
nulla mora, ex illo in peius ruere omnia visa,
degenerare animi, atque retro res lapsa referri,
hic namque ingenio confisus posthabet artem.
ille furit strepitu, tenditque aequare tubarum   35
voce sonos, versusque tonat sine more per omnes.
dant alii cantus vacuos et inania verba
incassum, sola capti dulcedine vocis,
Pierides donec Romam, et Tiberina fluenta
deseruere Italis expulsae protinus oris.   40
tanti causa mali Latio gens aspera aperto
saepius inrumpens. sunt iussi vertere morem
Ausonidae victi, victoris vocibus usi.
cessit amor Musarum, artes subiere repente
indignae atque opibus cuncti incubuere parandis.   45
iampridem tamen Ausonios invisere rursus
coeperunt Medicum revocatae munere Musae,
Tuscorum Medicum, quos tandem protulit aetas
Europae in tantis solamen dulce ruinis.
illi etiam Graiae miserati incommoda gentis,   50
ne Danaum penitus caderet cum nomine virtus,

See! how the Grecian bards at distance thrown,
With rev'rence bow to this distinguisht son,
Immortal sounds his golden lines impart,
And nought can match his genius but his art.
Ev'n Greece turns pale, and trembles at his fame,
Which shades the lustre of her Homer's name . . .

'Twas then Ausonia saw her language rise
In all its strength, and glory to the skies;
Such glory never could she boast before,
Nor could succeeding poets make it more.
From that blest period the poetick state
Ran down the precipice of time and fate;
Degenerate souls succeed, a wretched train;
And her old fame at once drew back again.
One to his genius trusts, in ev'ry part,
And scorns the rules and disciplines of art,
While this an empty tide of sounds affords,
And roars and thunders in a storm of words.
Some, musically dull, all methods try
To win the ear with sweet stupidity;
Unruffled strains for solid wit dispense,
And give us numbers, when we call for sense.
'Till from the hesperian plains and Tyber chas'd,
From Rome the banisht sisters fled at last,
Driv'n by the barb'rous nations, who from far
Burst into Latium with a tide of war.
Hence a vast change of their old manners sprung,
And forc'd the slaves to speak their master's tongue;
No honours now were paid the sacred muse,
But all were bent on mercenary views;
'Till Latium saw with joy th'Aonian train
By the great Medici restor'd again;
Th' illustrious Medici of Tuscan race
Were born to cherish learning in disgrace,
New life in every science to bestow,
And lull the cries of Europe in her woe.
With pity they beheld those turns of fate,
And prop'd the ruins of the Grecian state;

in Latium advectos iuvenes, iuvenumque magistros
Argolicas artes quibus esset cura tueri,
securos Musas iussere atque otia amare.
illi etiam captas late misere per urbes   55
qui doctas tabulas veterum monumenta virorum
mercati pretio adveherent, quae barbarus igni
tradebat Danaum regnis, opibusque potitus.
et tentamus adhuc sceptris imponere nostris
externum, nec dum civiles condimus enses.   60
haec aetas omnis, vatum haec fortuna priorum,
ergo ipsum ante alios animo venerare Maronem,
atque unum sequere utque potes, vestigia serva.
qui si forte tibi non omnia sufficit unus,
adde illi natos eodem quoque tempore vates.   65
parce dehinc puer atque alios ne quaere doceri;
nec te discendi capiat tam dira cupido.
tempus erit, tibi mox cum firma advenerit aetas,
spectatum ut cunctos impune accedere detur.

LXIV   MARCI HIERONYMI VIDAE

Scacchia Ludus (Scacchorum Ludus)

Tum tacitus secum versat, quem ducere contra
conveniat; peditemque iubet procedere campum
in medium, qui reginam dirimebat ab hoste.
ille gradus duplices superat; cui tum arbiter ater
ipse etiam adversum recto de gente nigranti   5
tramite agit peditem, atque iubet subsistere contra
advenientem hostem, paribusque occurrere in armis.
stant ergo adversis inter se frontibus ambo

For lest her wit should perish with her fame
Their care supported still the Argive name;
They call'd th'aspiring youths from distant parts,
To plant Ausonia with the Grecian arts;
To bask in ease, and science to diffuse,
And to restore the empires of the muse.
They sent to ravag'd provinces with care,
And cities wasted by the rage of war,
To buy the ancient works, of deathless fame,
And snatch'd th'immortal labours from the flame;
To which the foes had doom'd each glorious piece,
Who reign and lord it in the realms of Greece.
(But we, ye gods, would raise a foreign lord,
As yet untaught to sheath the civil sword;)
Thro' many a period this has been the fate,
And this the list of the poetick fate.
    Hence sacred Vergil from thy soul adore
Above the rest, and to thy utmost pow'r
Pursue the glorious paths he struck before.
If he supplies not all your wants, peruse
Th'immortal strains of each Augustan muse.
There stop,—nor rashly seek to know the rest,
But drive the dire ambition from thy breast,
'Till riper years and judgement form thy thoughts
To mark their beauties, and avoid their faults.

LXIV   M.-G. VIDA

The game of chess

Awhile he ponder'd which of all his train
Should bear his first comnission on the plain
And then determined to begin the scene
With him that stood before to guard the Queen.
He took a double step; with instant care
Does the black Monarch in his turn prepare
The adverse champion, and with stern command
 ̀id him repel the charge with equal hand.

in mediis campi spatiis, ac mutua tentant
vulnera, nequiquam: neque enim vis ulla nocendi est   10
armigeris, tractu dum miscent proelia eodem.
subsidio socii dextra laevaque frequentes
hinc atque hinc subeunt, late et loca milite complent,
alternantque vices: necdum tamen horrida miscent
proelia, sed placidus mediis Mars ludit in armis: 15
excursusque breves tentant, tutique tenent se.
   Iamque pedes nigri rectoris, qui prior hostem
contra iit, obliquum laeva clam strinxerat ensem,
atque album e mediis peditem cito sustulit armis,
illiusque locum arripuit praestantibus ausis: 20
ah miser instantem lateri non viderat hostem!
ipse etiam cadit, et pugnas in morte relinquit.
tum cautus fuscae regnator gentis ab aula
subduxit sese media, penitusque repostis
castrorum latebris extrema in fauce recondit,   25
et peditum cuneis stipantibus abditus haesit.
nec mora, surgit eques bellator laevus utrimque,
et mediis hinc inde insultant coetibus ambo,
alternique ruunt, et spargunt fata per hostes.
sternuntur pedites passim miseranda iuventus,   30
quod nequeant revocare gradum: sonat ungula campo
in medio, et totis miscentur funera castris.
   Dum vero peditum intentus Latonius heros
caedibus instat atrox, equitemque per agmina versat
vastatorem alae piceae, longe Arcada maior   35
ardor agit tacitis iamdudum invadere furtis
magnum aliquid, peditumque ultro saepe obvia transit
agmina, cornipedem ducens in proelia laevum,
qui regi insidias tendens huc vertitur atque huc,
per mediosque hostes impune infrenis oberrat.   40
constitit, optataque diu statione potitus
letum intentabat pariter regique elephantique,
alae qui dextro cornu turritus in auras
attollens caput ingenti se mole tenebat.
Delius ingemuit clauso succurrere regi   45

There front to front, the midst of all the field,
With furious threats their shining arms they wield;
Yet vain the conflict, neither can prevail
While in one path each other they assail.
On ev'ry side to their assistance fly
Their fellow soldiers, and with strong supply
Crowd to the battle, but no bloody stain
Tinctures their armour; sportive in the plain
Mars plays awhile, and in excursion slight
Harmless they sally forth, or wait the fight.
    But now the swarthy Foot, that first appear'd
To front the foe, his pond'rous jav'lin rear'd
Leftward aslant, and a pale warrior slays,
Spurns him aside, and boldly takes his place.
Unhappy youth, his danger not to spy!
Instant he fell, and triumph'd but to die.
At this the sable King with prudent care
Removed his station from the middle square,
And slowly retiring to the farthest ground,
There safely lurk'd, with troops entrench'd around.
Then from each quarter to the war advance
The furious Knights, and poise the trembling lance:
By turns they rush, by turns the victors yield,
Heaps of dead Foot choke up the crimson'd field:
They fall unable to retreat; around
The clang of arms and iron hoofs resound.
But while young Phoebus pleased himself to view
His furious Knight destroy the vulgar crew,
Sly Hermes long'd t' attempt with secret aim
Some noble act of more exalted fame,
For this, he inoffensive pass'd along
Through ranks of Foot, and midst the trembling throng
Sent his left Horse, that free without confine
Rov'd o'er the plain, upon some great design
Against the King himself. At length he stood,
And having fix'd his station as he would,
Threaten'd at once with instant fate the King
And th'Indian beast that guarded the right wing.
Apollo sigh'd, and hast'ning to relieve

admonitus: namque indefensum in morte elephantem
linquere se videt atque ambos non posse periclo
eripere, et fatis urgeri cernit iniquis.
cura prior sed enim est trepidum defendere regem,
quem rapit in dextrum latus: at niger emicat ense   50
stricto eques, et magnis elephantem intercipit ausis,
damnum ingens: neque enim est, saevae post virginis arma,
bellantum numero ex omni magis utilis alter.
'non tamen impune evades', ait acer Apollo;
et peditum cuneis, densaque indagine cingit.   55
ille igitur trepidare metu, certique pericli
frustra velle fugam: nam hinc fata minatur Amazon,
inde obstat conserta phalanx: tandem altius acto
virginis ense cadit, pulchrae solacia mortis.
aestuat alba cohors latere heu! minus utilis uno,   60
et magis atque magis furit acri accensa dolore.
sicut ubi dextrum taurus certamine cornu
amisit, dum se adverso fert pectore in hostem,
saevior in pugnam ruit, armos sanguine, et alte
colla animosa lavans: gemitu omnis silva remugit.   65
talis erat facies, caesi post fata elephantis,
candentis turmae: hinc furiis maioribus ardet
Phoebus, et ultrices hortatur in arma cohortes,
in ferrum, et caedes pronus cupidusque nocendi;
incautusque ambas perdit sine lege phalangas.   70
dumque hostes pariter cernat procumbere victos,
ipse suos morti indefensos obiicit ultro.

The straiten'd Monarch, griev'd that he must leave
His martial Elephant expos'd to fate,
And view'd with pitying eyes his dang'rous state.
First in his thoughts however was his care
To save his King, whom to the neighbouring square
On the right hand, he snatch'd with trembling flight;
At this with fury springs the sable Knight,
Drew his keen sword, and rising to the blow,
Sent the great Indian brute to shades below.
O fatal loss! for none except the Queen
Spreads such a terror through the bloody scene.
'Yet shall you ne'er unpunish'd boast your prize,'
The Delian god with stern resentment cries;
And wedg'd him round with Foot, and pour'd in fresh supplies.
Thus close besieg'd trembling he cast his eye
Around the plain; for here the Queen oppos'd,
The Foot in phalanx there the passage clos'd:
At length he fell; yet not unpleas'd with fate,
Since victim to a Queen's vindictive hate.
With grief and fury burns the whiten'd host,
One of their Tow'rs thus immaturely lost.
As when a bull has in contention stern
Lost his right horn, with double vengeance burn
His thoughts for war, with blood he's cover'd o'er,
And the woods echo to his dismal roar,
So look'd the flaxen host, when angry fate
O'erturn'd the Indian bulwark of their state.
Fired at this great success, with double rage
Apollo hurries on his troops t'engage,
For blood and havoc wild; and, while he leads
His troops thus careless, loses both his steeds:
For if some adverse warriors were o'erthrown,
He little thought what dangers threat his own.

LXV   MARCELLI PALINGENII

Zodiacus vitae

Si tibi suspecta est uxor dubiique pudoris,
non habeas pulchros famulos pulchrosve sodales
cum quibus illa domi versetur. decipieris
si quemquam fidum credes, est nemo fidelis
in Venere: illa dolis incautos fallere gaudet.   5
fraude paratur amor, Veneri gratissima fraus est.
sed tua praecipue non intret limina quisquam
frater, vel monachus, vel quavis lege sacerdos:
hos fuge. pestis enim nulla hac immanior. hi sunt
faex hominum, fons stultitiae, sentina malorum,   10
agnorum sub pelle lupi, mercede colentes
non pietate Deum, falsa sub imagine recti
decipiunt stolidos ac religionis in umbra
mille actus vetitos et mille piacula condunt:
raptores, moechi, puerorum corruptores,   15
luxuriae atque gulae famuli: caelestia vendunt.
heu quas non fugas, quae non miracula fingunt
ut vulgus fallant optataque praemia carpant?
inde superstitio et ludibria plurima manant
quae dii, si sapiunt, rident renuuntque videre.   20
non pretio, sed amore Deum vir iustus adorat.
deme autem lucrum, superos et sacra negabunt.
ergo sibi, non caelicolis haec turba ministrat.
utilitas facit esse deos: qua nempe remota
templa ruent, nec erunt arae nec Iuppiter ullus.   25
hos impostores igitur vulpesque dolosas,
pelle procul: quantumque licet, tua ianua vitet.

LXV   M. PALINGENIUS

The zodiac of life

If thou suspect thy wife of play, / then kepe no lusty men,
Nor fellowes fayre, with whom she may / be prating now and then.
Thou art deceaved, if thou dost thinke / that any kinde of man
Wyll faythfull be, in Venus case / no men are faithfull than.
For she rejoyseth to beguile. / by fraude is love possest
And unto Venus always fraude / a thing is counted best.
But as a chiefest thing take heede / there entre not thy dore
No fryer fatte, ne lusty Monke, / nor priest of any lore.
Eschewe the knaves, a greater plague / than these can none
    expresse,
These are the dregges of every sort / and springes of folishenesse
The common synke of mischiefes all, / and Wolves in felles of
    sheepe,
For pence and no devocion sure / to God these wretches creepe.
And with a colour false of truth / they symple soules beguile.
And underneath religions cloke / a thousande mischiefes vile.
A thousande haynous deedes they doe / deflouring mayde and
    wyfe,
Whore hunters vile, and Sodomites / the servaunts all their lyfe.
Of beastlinesse, and belly ioye, / the things divine they sell,
What wonders great invent they not? / What dreames doe they not
    tell?
The common people to deceive / and to procure againe.
Hereof doth superstition ryse / and thousande fansyes vaine,
Which if the gods be wyse they scorne, / and do refuse to vewe:
The Godly man doth worship God, / wyth earnest love and trewe.
And not for gold, away wyth gayne, / thou shalt see them denie:
All sacred service here on earth, / and God himself on hie.
Themselves therefore this flock doth serve, / and not the saincts
    above:
And profit causeth Gods to be, / which if thou once remove,
Both temples and their altare stones, / shall flat lie on the ground:
Nor any more amongst them al, / shall any God be found.
These juggling mates and foxes false, / expell from thee therfore:
And take good hede that none of them, / do enter at thy dore.

pelle procul, ne te probitas simulata, maritum
caprarum efficiat, nec si tibi compater ullus
contingit, nimium confidas: namque sub isto   30
nomine peccandi proclivior est via multis.
hoc etiam serva, ne saepius egrediatur
sola domum, neu tecta adeat vicina: frequenter
vicini latitare domo consuevit adulter.
illi da comites castas vitaeque probatae: 35
infames vetulas et lenas cautus avaras
secum stare veta, longeque arcebis ab illa.
nec tu aliam Venerem atque aliena cubilia quaeras,
nec te concubitus delectet pellicis: est nil
quo doleat magis ac vehementius excrucietur: 40
quod magis ulcisci cupiat, quam foedera lecti
instabili temerata fide, tunc ardet et odit,
fallere tunc vellet simili ratione maritum:
sique potest fallit. bilis tunc maxima fervet,
tunc furit, ut Thyas nimio stimulata Lyaeo.   45
crede mihi, rara est quae non sit adultera, quando
legitimo fraudata toro sua gaudia perdit:
saltem animo, si non concessum est corpore, peccat.
labitur in vitium vitio inritata voluntas.
si deprensa tamen fuerit, tunc legibus uti   50
ne pudeat, legum tibi sit reverentia semper
praecipua; est etenim nostrae lex regula vitae.
nec temere iratus maiorem crimine poenam
infligas, laedasque Deum vulgique sequaris
ingenium et mores: qui non ratione movetur   55
sed veluti pecudes furiis atque impete fertur.
nec ducta uxore idcirco non liber haberis,
quod tibi non licet esse malo, neque nocte vagari,
nec multis aliis rationibus insanire.
non haec libertas, sed prava licentia dici   60
debet, qui sic est liber, servire videtur.
talis libertas non est cupienda, frequenter
in mala praecipitem quam plurima mittit habentem.
est melius non posse malum committere, quam si
undique peccandi pateat via. quot perierunt   65
ob talem libertatem? quot saepe fuerunt

Least thou do cry the Cuckoes note, / through fayned vertue such:
Nor if thou any gossyps hast, / beleve them not to much.
For under colour of this name, / the Knaves do many play:
Take heede besyde that from thy house, / she often do not stray.
Nor let her haunt thy neyghbors house, / it hath bene sene ful oft:
That whoremasters have hid themselves, /amyd thy neighbours loft.
Appoynt her mates for company, / of chast and honest fame:
Let mother Bee, be put from thence, / and every bawdy dame.
And seeke thou not wyth other whores, / thy selfe for to relieve;
Nothing doth cause her more to frowne / nor nothing more her grieve
For nothing more revengement seekes, / than when she is begilde:
And sees that wyth unsteadfast love, / her bed is thus defilde.
Then all wyth ire she flames and hates, / then doth she eke begin
To work her husband like despite, / then choller boyles within.
Then rageth shee like Bacchus priest, / whom to much wine doth prick:
Beleve me well she is but rare, / that doth not use the trick,
That harlots use, when that she is / deceyvde of lawfull part:
At least if she can not in dede, / yet synnes she in hir heart.
For will with vice provoked thus / in vice will farther slide.
But if thou takst hir with the deede / let lawes on hir be tride.
Be not ashamed but let the lawes / be reverencde of thee,
For they are as a certaine rule / by which we guided bee.
Least thou shouldst give a greater paine / amind thy raging yre
(Offending God, in felowing men) / than doth the fault require.
For common people never use / the rule of reason sage,
But are seducde with furies fell / like beastes of brainles rage.
Ne hast thou lost thy liberty / by marrying of a wyfe
Because thou maist not walke ye stretes / and leade a ruffians lyfe.
This can be calde no liberty / but rather licence nought
Who so is free doth seeme to serve / such is not to be sought.
It brings the owner to much harme, / and not to can doe ill,
Is better farre than have such vice / adherent to thy will.
How many men have bene destroide / by to much liberty?
How many men in safety live / with bridles dost thou se?

incolumes, quoniam frenos habuere tenaces?
si vero nati morbo vexantur ab ullo,
quid facias? cur te crucies? succurre medelis.
quae si nil prosunt et mors tibi surripit illos,   70
aequo animo sufferre velis. non solus in isto
gurgite iactaris, comitum tibi maxima turba est.
quae mala cum multis patimur, leviora videntur.
nascimur hac omnes lege, ut moriamur: ab ortu
exitus ipse fluit. cunctis mensura dierum   75
certa datur, Stygias citius vel serius undas
quisque petit. quamquam mors ultima meta malorum est
nec forti metuenda viro. quid munere vitae
defunctos, tantis opus est deflere querelis?
estne adeo miserum, moriendo relinquere mundi   80
stultitiam et sese innumeris auferre periclis:
proque tot aerumnis, tranquillam acquirere pacem?
aut mors est aeterna quies, aut ianua vitae.

LXVI   SCAEVOLAE SAMMARTHANI

Paedotrophia

Hortus erat, rosei qua lucida pandit Eoi
se regio (Edenem dixerunt nomine patres)
dulcibus et pomis, et dulcibus utilis herbis,
lenis ubi zephyri molles tranquilla per umbras
aura susurrabat semper, caeloque sereno   5
perpetuum tepidi servabat Veris honorem.
hanc sedem, haec illis viridaria laeta benignus
indulsit genitor lectosque induxit in agros
primum hominem, verbis simul hunc adfatus amicis?
   'I, decus, atque operis merito summa ultima nostri,   10
quae tibi nunc habitare damus felicia rura
ingredere, et nostris actutum vescere donis,

And if thy children sicknesse vexe / why shouldst thou weepe or
    wale
So seeke in hast to make them whole / if that will not prevaile
And if that death will have them needes / then use a pacient minde
Thou art not in this case alone / but fellowes shalt thou finde.
The griefe that we with many beare / we better may sustaine.
We all are borne to this intent / to render lyfe againe.
For of our fyrst beginning doth / the fatall ende depende
And certaine is the time decreed / for all away to wende.
And either sone or latter doth / eche man his grave descende
To death which is of evils all / the last and finall ende.
Not of the valiaunt to be fearde, / what doth it ought availe:
The deathes of them with teares, ye here / have lost their lyfe to
    wayle.
Is it a thing so wretched here, / to leave this foolishe life:
To rid thereby our mortall corps / from all the unquiet strife,
And for the hurly burly here, / eternall lyfe to win:
Perpetuall reast by death we gaine, / or eke the comming in.

LXVI   GAUCHER DE SAINTE-MARTHE

Paedotrophia

In the bright regions of th'extended East
A garden rose, with bow'rs of roses grac'd,
With trees adorn'd, with fruits, with flow'rets crown'd,
In Eden plac'd, and o'er the world renown'd.
There gentle Zephyrs fann'd, with balmy wing,
The fragrant air, and brought perpetual spring:
The shades were cool, the leaves for ever green,
Each sun was bright, and ev'ry sky serene.
Our ancestor, to this delightful feat,
Alike from storms defended, and from heat,
The great Creator led; he bless'd the man,
And with all-cheering accents thus began:
Go, brightest work of this Almighty Hand,
Possess these flow'ry fields at our command;
Inhabit here, confess the power of Heav'n,

quae fecunda tibi, et male grati nescia cultus
terra feret, carae iucunda in munera vitae.
tantum (si qua tuae tangit te cura salutis)   15
huic uni memorem iubeo te parcere pomo'.
dixit, et ostendit pendentes arbore fetus,
quorum a vivifico rerum orta scientia succo
manabat primum, et studia inconcessa docebat.

Ille Dei monitis et amico numine plenus   20
ibat, et unanima cum compare laetus agebat.
una illis cura aetherium laudare parentem,
oblatisque bonis et libertate fruisci.
nondum turpe scelus, sceleris nec debita merces
prodierat labor, et queruli denso agmine morbi,   25
et curae vigiles et inevitabile fatum.
sed simplex animos candor, sed molle fovebat
corpus certa quies, et utrimque erat aequa voluptas.
felices ambo, nisi iam tum infesta maligni
daemonis ars nullum humanis durabile rebus   30
esse bonum, nullam pateretur vivere pacem.

Hos ille immemores violato ut foedere perdat,
adgreditur vafer atque dolos se vertit ad omnes,
ac velut adversis fetam legionibus arcem
captat ubi egregius tacito molimine ductor,   35
observat muros oculis et singula lustrat,
num qua parte minus firmo se moenia vallo
militibus praestent cupidis, aditusque patescat,
atque illuc toto inrumpens conamine tendit.
sic hominum insidians generi teterrimus hostis,   40

And freely feed on what to thee is giv'n;
The plants and trees will own thy nursing care,
And grateful nourishment for thee prepare,
But, as thou prizest life, at our decree
Forbear the tempting fruit of yonder tree;
'Tis knowledge call'd, will pain and woe produce,
And death is mingled with the fatal juice.
  So spake th'all-bounteous King, and shew'd around
The fruits, the flow'rs and all th'enamell'd ground,
Bestow'd on man; he nam'd them one by one,
And, of the whole, deny'd but this alone;
Whose unpermitted fruit sad knowledge gives,
And sheds the seeds of death on all that lives.
The fire obey'd, by Heaven itself inspir'd,
By Nature led, and by the mandate fir'd:
He found his fair associate, liv'd with her
In all the joys, that love and peace confer,
In pleasures pure, and, so complete their bliss,
Their wishes one, they but one soul confess;
Their only care to praise th'eternal King,
From whom life, joy and all their blessings spring.
No guilt they knew, nor pain, nor anxious fear;
Nor wasting care, nor gloomy death, was there.
There minds serene gave their pure bodies rest,
And equal pleasure reign'd in ev'ry breast;
Till the malignant fiend, possess'd with hate,
And baleful envy, saw their happy state,
By arts infernal made their joys to cease,
Destroy'd their bliss, and robb'd their souls of peace.
The daemon watch'd them in th'unguarded hour,
Seduc'd their minds and gain'd them to his pow'r.
As when a leader would, by fraud, obtain
A fort, attack'd by strength of arms in vain,
With eyes observing he begins to wind
Around the walls, the weakest place to find,
Surveys the works, and brings, with cautious art,
His soldiers to the most defenceless part.
So the fell daemon, our insidious foe,
Attempts the weakest of the two to know,

pectore quod mulier fragili magis esset, ab illa
ordiri, et primum placuit facere inde periclum.
   Nec mora, caerulei forma se callidus anguis
dissimulat: non ille ferus qui stridula vibret
sibila, tabificove minax livore tumescat: 45
sed blando sensim inrepens per gramina lapsu
arboris infaustae ramis fatalibus haesit
arduus implicito per mille volumina trunco.
tum molles aditus et tempora fraudibus apta
legit et humanis demum sic vocibus infit: 50
'nam quis te, mulier, tam vanus detinet error,
ut quos naturae dedit indulgentia fructus
ipsa tibi invideas demens, vescique recuses?
egregium vero imperium, memorandaque iura
ille parens, uni cui cuncta accepta refertis,   55
atque tibi atque tuo concesserit ante marito,
si vobis genus omne avium, genus omne ferarum,
atque adeo ingentem penitus subiecerit orbem:
vos autem rerum dominos subiecerit uni
arboris intactae pomo, nec mandere sit fas,   60
cuius partem imo tantum si admoveris ori,

Then with deceitful malice lain his plan,
And, in the woman, first attack'd the man.
   An earthly form he straight resolves to take,
And hides his cunning in a crested snake;
Not that ferocious kind, by lake or fen,
That feed on poisons in the hollow den,
Whose hissings, as their livid bodies swell,
Inform the traveller where dangers dwell;
But those more bright, who, twisting o'er the grass,
Then harmless lives in wanton gambols pass:
In such a serpent lurks the foe conceal'd,
And to the woman wondrous charms reveal'd.
Full in her sight he skims along the ground,
Draws her attention, as he plays around,
Displays, before the Sun, each op'ning fold,
And floats redundant, like a wave of gold.
Him, as she follows with transported eyes,
Still circling on, the fatal fruit he spies;
Then, from the ground, with spires unfolded sprung,
Mounts up the tree, and 'mid the branches hung,
The human voice, with artful cunning feigns,
And, with these tempting words, our mother gains.
   What cause, what error, foolish woman, draws
You from obedience to great Nature's laws?
Why should you shun this tree, you daily meet,
Or of its fragrant fruit forbear to eat?
Aspire you not to die, but more to live.
Say, could th'Almigthy Sire, by whom was giv'n
Whatever lies beneath th'expanse of Heav'n,
Each bird, each beast, each plant, and blooming flow'r
To thine alone, and to thy husband's pow'r,
Deny what grateful earth produc'd for thee,
Or give the garden, and refuse the tree?
Strange doctrine this! that you, tho' form'd divine,
Tho' lords of all, must your just rights confine,
Must be unblest, ev'n in this happy fate,
And to a tree subject your future fate!
This fruit, once tasted, shall enlarge your will,
Instruct you to distinguish good from ill,

protinus obscuram videas vanescere nubem
ex oculis, victaque iubar caligine oriri,
unde boni atque mali divina scientia vobis
prodeat, insignesque novo iam lumine spargat.   65
atque hinc (si nescis) iniusti numinis illa
invidia est, dum vos consortes laudis habere
abnuit et pomis ideo praestantibus arcet.
at tu pone metus et inania despice iussa,
(nam potes) erectoque iugum semel excute collo.   70
aspicis ut prona demissas ab arbore fetus
se virides inter tibi ramos offerat ultro
adridens, tangique tuo desideret ore?
carpe age et oblati ne respue muneris usum.'
sic ait occultoque implet muliebre veneno   75
pectus et inlicitum vescendi inspirat amorem.
illa levi iam tum ingenio male provida paret
ocius et vetito sese contaminat esu.
nec satis hoc: simili incautum capit arte maritum,
et vocat in partem culpae. exitialibus ambo   80
indulgent epulis miseri, numenque lacessunt,
atque hinc prima mali ventura in secula labes,
dum pater indignans haec lumine cernit iniquo
omnia et infandos ulcisci accingitur ausus.

Illume your minds with science all divine,
And make you like the pow'rs of Heav'n to shine.
Its wondrous virtue your Great Maker knows,
But this unjust restriction envy shews;
The Deity looks down, with jealous eye,
And fears lest you, with him, in knowlege vie.
Dismiss your terror, scorn the words he spoke,
And free your necks from this uneasy yoke.
Behold you not the loaded branches bend,
Each verdant bough in grateful clusters end?
The laughing apples, drest in flow'r of youth,
Spring of themselves, to your desiring mouth.
Refuse not then t'accept the fragrant load,
But pull, and eat, know, and be a God.
    He ceas'd. The woman heard the words he said,
Forgot her Maker, and the fiend obey'd:
She ate, she glutton'd on the food possest
With all the longings of a female breast,
And thus, betray'd by her impure desire,
Began what pregnant mothers yet require.
Nor ceas'd she thus; but, at that luckless time,
Made her fond husband partner of her crime:
She call'd: he came, partook with equal blame,
And bore an equal share of guilt and shame.
The miserable pair the fruit devour'd,
And drew the wrath of Heav'ns avenging Lord;
The Pow'r Omnipotent, who gave them breath,
Consign'd them o'er to woe, to sin, and death.

Court and ceremonial poetry

During the Renaissance, life at court assumes greater brilliance and importance. The example was set in certain Italian cities, notably in the Florence of the Medici; in France, it is during the reign of Francis I that court life makes notable strides, though Charles VIII and Louis XII had already realised the growing political importance of the court, which during the sixteenth century was to become rather more stable. England develops along similar lines under the Tudors and in Germany the various ducal courts improve their life-style. The sociological composition of the court was changing as it grew larger: for a start, the presence of woman assumes greater significance. As a French theoretician remarked towards the middle of the sixteenth century, one of the monarch's duties is to be seen by his people. Then one notes the increasing presence of noblemen at court, partly for political reasons as the central administrative structures acquire more power, partly because economic factors were loosening the ties that bound the nobleman to his region. Moreover, there were a considerable number of rulers whose cultural pursuits were more or less genuine, and the system of patronage encouraged artists and men of letters to cultivate the court. The need for parade and *paraître* entails the recruitment of the best artistic talent available, the (re)building of castles and palaces, the upsurge of the visual arts, often with a strongly classical character, the preparation of more sophisticated entries and the celebration of events at or beyond the court that were relevant to the prestige of the monarch and his entourage. The poet, for his part, views his role as an exalted one: quite apart from the neo-platonic theories in vogue, he might see himself a spokesman for his country's interests—especially in France where humanism often had a chauvinistic dimension; and he was keen to repeat the old topos that posthumous fame could be ensured by the pen, even more reliably than by the other arts. Thus the writer comes to play an increasingly substantial part in producing a literature that is ceremonial and, in moments of national crisis, outspokenly committed.

What is interesting of course is the extent to which Latin poetry flourishes as vigorously as the vernacular. In so far as culture adds grist to the national mill, classical humanism can acquire a serious status; moreover we have seen that, in the eyes of many contemporaries, there are themes of a certain elevation that can be adequately sung only in Latin; and it must be recognised that Latin verse, at critical moments, has a propaganda value beyond the frontiers of the country in question. It is notable that 'committed' texts will appear in Latin as well as in the vernacular, sometimes in bilingual presentation. And in France the appointments of poets laureate at court involved Latin and the vernacular: Faustus Andrelinus, Salmon Macrin (like Clément Marot a *cubicularius regius*), Jean Dorat, Ronsard's Latin counterpart. During the Wars of religion, French Neo-latin writers often became spokesmen for royal policies, and it is worth adding that the Calvinists, whom one might suspect *prima facie* of hostility to a language that was closed to the man in the street and the vehicle for pagan attitudes, swell the ranks of Latin versifiers to an uncommon degree.

Court poetry covers a wide range of activities. Festivities may include masques and ballets composed in Latin; then there are the usual—but often alembicated—celebrations of hatches, matches and dispatches; collective homages, often relating to the death of distinguished persons, become widespread. These *tumuli* not only reveal much literary virtuosity and exhibitionism, they often are an expression of solidarity with current political and religious attitudes with which the deceased had been associated. Particularly prominent are compositions celebrating military events. The forms in which these occurrences are sung tend predictably to be the more exalted genres: the genethliacon, the epinicion, the epicedion, the deploratio, all favouring the heroic metre; but the ode comes into its own as well and though it is generally thought that Ronsard's ventures into the Pindaric ode were a failure, the fact remains that in Northern Europe the Latin Pindaric ode enjoys a prolonged vogue that may also extend into the vernacular. As national states become more coherent and as Latin encomiastic verse is more and more affected by the standards of Ciceronian scholarship, this type of poetry tends to be more sophisticated, prolix, stilted and frankly dull. One has only to turn over the pages of the *Delitiae* of German poets to realise how ossified such verse could become; and in our time there is the additional disadvantage that the circumstances and persons sung in these compositions frequently remain outside the ken of the alert reader. This is the chief reason for so few poems being included in this section, though a further example will be found among the eclogues.

One ceremonial or celebratory genre which acquires a momentum of its own during the Renaissance is the epithalamium. There are wedding-songs that concern the private individual—of these the most memorable is probably that by Joannes Secundus, with its unusually frank eroticism and abundant linguistic vitality; but the main concentration is on the epithalamium that forms part of the rapidly expanding court poetry. It is a genre in the elevated style, but it also allows for a great variety of tone and theme. Apart from the inevitable references to personal happiness, innumerable offsprings to come, and reflections on love that makes the world go round, the poet may often take the opportunity to celebrate national pride, ambition and achievement. Where major royal persons are involved, the tradition of the *miroir des princes* may be introduced and room found for philosophical meditation of some range. As one would expect, the tendency for pastoral elements to invade court poetry will not leave the epithalamium unaffected. It may happen that poets will indulge in collective epithalamial tributes as was the case in England when Oxford and Cambridge humanists pooled their talents in 1613, 1625, 1662. In Germany the genre was very extensively exploited, though abundance was usually superior to quality. There were of course adequate classical models for poets to follow, and Scaliger stressed the importance of certain features being included as a matter of principle. Catullus, Statius and Claudian set the pattern; with the latter two a greater pastoral element is admitted and the mythological apparatus becomes very sophisticated as does the encomiastic dimension. Scaliger did however indicate a preference for Catullus as the model to be imitated, but modern poets were not insensitive to contemporary examples: Puttenham had kind things to say about Joannes Secundus' excursion into the genre and Ben Jonson admitted to following in the path of Daniel Heinsius when he composed his *Epithalamium* of 1608.

BIBLIOGRAPHY

Tufte, Virginia. *The Poetry of Marriage. The Epithalamium in Europe and its Development in England*, Los Angeles, 1970 (University of South California Studies in Comparative Literature, vol. II).

LXVII   IOANNIS SECUNDI

Epithalamium

Hora suavicula et voluptuosa,
hora blanditiis, lepore, risu,
hora deliciis, iocis, susurris,
hora suaviolis, parique magnis
cum dis et Iove transigenda sorte: 5
hora qua poterat beatiorem
nec Cnidi dea sancta polliceri,
nec qui cum pharetra pererrat orbem
curis gaudia delicata miscens,
penna splendidus aurea Cupido,   10
magni pronuba nec soror Tonantis,
nec qui floridulas Hymen puellas
raptas e gremio tenace matrum
involvit cupidis viri lacertis,
rupis incola floriger canorae,   15
advecta est serie rotante caeli.
o felix iuvenis, puella felix!

Felix sponse, cui cupita flamma
iam nunc in geminis quiescet ulnis,
puella aetheria beata forma.   20
qualem magna Venus velitque Iuno
et quae casside Martia refulget,

LXVII   JOANNES SECUNDUS

Epithalamium

The hour is come, with pleasure crowned
Borne in eternal order round!
Hour, of endearing looks and smiles,
Hour, of voluptuous sports and wiles,
Hour, fraught with fondly-murmuring sighs,
Hour, blest with softly dying eyes,
Hour, with commingling kisses sweet,
Hour, of transporting bliss replete,
Hour, worthy ev'n of gods above,
Hour, worthy all-commanding Jove!
For not a fairer-omened hour
Could promise the kind Cnidian power;
Nor tender Cupid could bestow,
The boy with silver-splendid bow,
And golden wing, delicious boy,
That sorrow still allays with joy:
Nor, wont at nuptials to preside
She that of Jove is sister bride;
Nor he, on tuneful summit born,
The god whom flowery wreaths adorn,
Who blooming beauty tears away,
Bears off by force the charming prey;
From the reluctant mothers tears,
To the rapacious lover bears.
Hour long desired! hour long delayed!
Thrice happy youth! thrice happy maid!

Thrice happy youth, supremely blest,
Of every wish in one possest!
To thee, the maid of form divine
Comes seeming loth, but inly thine:
Such form as Juno's self might choose,
Nor yet the martial maid refuse;
Though that th'aetherial sceptre sways,
And this the shining shield displays:

sancto vertice procreata Pallas,
si iunctae statuant adire valles
umbrosas iterum virentis Idae,   25
qua spectanda vel haec, vel haec, vel illa,
quovis iudicio superba malum
victrix aureolum reportet astris.
o felix iuvenis, puella felix!

Felix sponsa, cui cupitus ardor   30
adfusus modo lectulo in beato
stringet colla tenacibus lacertis,
insigni iuvenis venustus ore:
istis qui roseis tuis labellis,
istis qui niveis tuis papillis,   35
isto qui rutilante crine tactus,
isto lumine qui loquace victus,
iampridem tacito voratur igne
lentumque increpat usque et usque solem
tardamque invocat usque et usque lunam.   40
o felix iuvenis, puella felix!

Votis, fervide sponse, parce votis,
et suspiria mitte, mitte questus.
tempus accelerat suave; mitis
exaudit gemitus Venus suorum.   45
condit Cynthius ora, condit ora,
seque gurgite perluens Ibero
cedit noctivagae locum sorori.
et quo gratior haud relucet ignis
coniunctis animis amore dulci   50
producit caput emicatque caelo
ductor Hesperus aureae catervae.
o felix iuvenis, puella felix!

Nor yet the Cyprian queen disdain,
But, to re-seek the Phrygian swain
And cause of beauty re-decide
In shady vale of flowering Ide,
How sure to gain the golden prize,—
Though judged by less discerning eyes,—
She, in that matchless form arrayed;
Thrice happy youth! thrice happy maid!

Thrice happy maid, supremely blest,
Of every wish in one possest!
To thee on wings of love and truth,
Comes, all devote, the raptured youth,
Thy bending neck with eager hold,
Thy waist impatient to enfold;
While, for that hair of easy flow,
While, for that breast of virgin snow,
While, for that lip of rosy dye,
While, for that sweetly-speaking eye,
With silent passion he expires
And burns with still-consuming fires,
Now Phoebus, slow to quit the skies,
Now loitering Phoebus, slow to rise,
Persists alternate to upbraid!
Thrice happy youth! thrice happy maid!

Spare, youth, your vows, vain offerings spare:
Forbear your needless sighs, forbear;
Lo! Time, in ever-varying race,
Brings on at last the wished-for space.
Mild Venus, with propitious ears,
The sorrows of her votaries hears;
While Cynthius, down the western steeps,
Now plunges in Iberian deeps,
And quits the ample fields of air
To his night-wandering sister's care:
Than whom no light more grateful shines
To souls which mutual love conjoins;
Not he that leads the stars along,
Brightest of all the glittering throng,
Hesper, with golden torch displayed:
Thrice happy youth! Thrice happy maid!

iam virgo thalamum subibit, unde
ne virgo redeat, marite, cura.　　　　　　　　　　　55
iam virgo niveis locata fulcris
adventum cupiet tuum, tremetque,
perfusa ingenuo rubore malas.
forsan et lacrimis genae madebunt
et suspiria fundet et querelas.　　　　　　　　　　60
at tu nil remoratus et querelas
et suspiria lacrimasque tolles
abstergens oculos tuo ore, dulce
murmur pro querimoniis reponens.
o felix iuvenis, puella felix!　　　　　　　　　　　65

Ergo, membra ubi virginis decorae
felix candida lectulus fovebit,
membra languidulo parata somno,
et molli quoque te toro locatum
supra purpureos beata reges.　　　　　　　　　　　70
supra constituet Iovem Dione;
mox te blandidicis parare rixis,
mox te molliculae parare pugnae
motus occipies calore iusto
belli prospera signa non cruenti　　　　　　　　　　75
figens mille protervus hic et illic,
collo basia multa, multa malis,
labris basia plura, plura ocellis.
repugnabit et improbum vocabit
et dicet 'satis est' tremente voce　　　　　　　　　80
arcebitque manu proterva labra

See where the maid all panting lies,
Ah! Never more a maid to rise,
And longs, yet trembles at thy tread,
Her cheeks perfused with decent red,
Expressing half her inward flame,
Half-springing from ingenuous shame;
Tears from her eyes perhaps may steal,
Her joys the better to conceal;
Then sighs, with grief unreal fraught,
Then follow plaints of wrongs un-thought.
But cease not thou, with idle fears,
For all her plaints, or sighs, or tears:
Kissed be the tears from off her eyes;
With tender murmurs stopped, her sighs;
With soothing soft her plaints allayed;
Thrice happy youth! thrice happy maid!

The maid, in decent order placed,
With every bridal honour graced,
Through all her limbs began to spread
The glowings of the genial bed
And languid sleep dispose to take,
Did not the youth, more watchful, wake,
And the mild Queen of fierce desire
With warmth not disproportioned fire.
Taught hence, nor purpled kings to prize,
Nor sceptred Jove that rules the skies,
Soon for soft combats he prepares,
And gentle toils of amorous wars:
Declared, but with no loud alarms,
Begun, but with no dreaded arms:
Kisses, which, wanton as he strays,
He darts a thousand wanton ways
At mouth, or neck, eyes, or cheeks;
Him humbly she full oft bespeaks,
Entreats, an helpless maid to spare,
And begs with trembling voice, 'forbear';
Full oft his rudeness loudly blames;
His boundless insolence proclaims;

propelletque manu manum protervam.
o noctem ter et amplius beatam!

Pugnet strenua, pugnet illa; pasci
pugnando teneri volunt amores.   85
pugnando tibi duplicatus ardor
vires sufficiet novas in arma.
tunc per candida colla, tunc per illud
quod certat ebori nitore pectus,
tunc per crura tenella perque ventrem   90
et quae proxima sunt et huic et illis,
saltu volve agili manum salacem;
et tot milia iunge basiorum
quot caelum rutilos tenebit ignes.
o noctem quater et quater beatam!   95

Nec desint tibi blandulaeque voces
et quaecumque iuvant perita verba,
nec cum murmure sibili suaves,
quales dant zephyro sonante blandum
frondes, quale columba, quale cycnus   100
annosus moriente spirat ore;
donec victa potentibus sagittis
et caeco pueri volantis igne
paulatim minus et minus severa
ponet purpureum toro pudorem,   105
collum in bracchia nexuosa dedens,
collo bracchia nexuosa stringens.
o noctem quater, o quater beatam!

His lips with lips averse withstands;
With hands restrains his roving hands;
Resistance sweet, delicious fight:
O night! O doubly happy night!

Contention obstinate succeeds,
The tender Loves contention feeds.
By that, redoubled ardour burns;
By that, redoubled strength returns.
Now o'er her neck take nimble flight,
Her breast, as spotless ivory white,
Her waist of gradual rising charms,
Soft-moulded legs, smooth-polished arms;
Search all the tracts, in curious sport,
Conducive to the Cyprian court;
Through all the dark recesses go,
And all the shady coverts know:
To this, unnumbered kisses join,
Unnumbered as the stars that shine,
Commingling rays of blended light:
O night! O doubly happy night!

Then, spare no blandishments of love:
Sounds that with softening flattery move:
Sighs that with soothing murmur please
The injured virgin to appease:
Such, as when Zephyr fans the grove,
Or coos the amorous billing dove,
Or sings the swan with tuneful breath,
Conscious of near-approaching death:
Till, pierced by Cupid's powerful dart,
As by degrees relents her heart,
The virgin, less and less severe,
Quits by degrees her stubborn fear;
Now, on your arms her neck reclines,
Now, with your arms her neck entwines,
As love's resistless flames incite:
O night! O doubly happy night!

Tunc tunc oscula delicata sumes,
nullis contemerata quae rapinis 110
haerebunt vario morata nexu.
tunc lusus similes paresque virgo
reddet delicias, et os hiulcum
iampridem patulo licenter ori
committens animae libidinoso 115
fragrantis cupidum beabit haustu.
mox lusu quoque molliore ludens,
dicet blanditias suaviores.
emittet digitos licentiores,
finget nequitiam salaciorem. 120
o noctem nimis et nimis beatam!

Tunc arma expedienda, tunc ad arma
et Venus vocat et vocat Cupido.
tunc in vulnera grata proruendum.
huc illuc agilis feratur hasta, 125
quam crebro furibunda verset ictu
non Martis soror ast amica Martis
semper laeta novo cruore Cypris.
nec quies lateri laborioso
detur mobilibus nec ulla coxis; 130
donec deficiente voce anhela,
donec deficientibus medullis,
membris languidulis madens uterque
sudabit varii liquoris undas.
o noctem nimis, o nimis beatam! 135

Sudate, ut libet, et diesque longas
noctesque exigite impotente lusu.
et brevi date liberosque dulces
et longo ordine blandulos nepotes;

Sweet kisses shall reward your pains,
Kisses which no rude rapine stains,
From lips on swelling lips that swell,
From lips on dwelling lips that dwell,
That play return with equal play,
That bliss with equal bliss repay,
That vital stores from either heart
Imbibing, soul for soul impart,
Till now the maid, adventurous grown,
Attempts new frolics of her own,
Now suffers, strangers to the way,
Her far more daring hands to stray;
Now sports far more salacious seeks;
Now words far more licentious speaks,
Words that past suffering well requite:
O Night! O doubly happy night!

To arms! to arms! now Cupid sounds;
Now is the time for grateful wounds:
Here Venus waves the nimble spear,
Venus is warlike goddess here.
Here, not thy sister, Mars, presides;
Thy mistress in those conflicts prides
While close engage the struggling foes,
And restless, breast to breast oppose,
While eager this disputes the field,
And that alike disdain to yield,
Till Io! in breathless transports tost,
Till, in resistless raptures lost,
Their limbs with liquid dews distil,
Their hearts with pleasing horrors thrill,
And faint away in wild delight:
O night! O doubly happy night!

O may you oft these sports renew,
And through long days and nights pursue;
With many an early moon begun,
Prolonged to many a setting sun.
May a fair offspring crown your joys,
Of prattling girls and smiling boys;

quae vobis senii minuta turba   140
olim sollicitos levabit annos,
arcebit querulos toro dolores,
languentem tremulos fovebit artus,
componet tumulo pios parentes.
o felix iuvenis, puella felix!   145

LXVIII   GEORGII BUCHANANI

Francisci Valesii
et Mariae Stuartae Regum Franciae et Scotiae
Epithalamium

Unde repentino fremuerunt viscera motu?
cur Phoebum desueta pati praecordia anhelus
fervor agit, mutaeque diu Parnassidos umbrae
turba iterum arcanis renovat paeana sub antris?
nuper enim, memini, squallebat marcida laurus,   5
muta chelys, tristis Phoebus, citharaeque repertor
Arcas, et ad surdas fundebam vota sorores.
nunc Phoebi delubra patent, nunc Delphica rupes
panditur, et sacro cortina remugit ab antro.
nunc lauro meliore comas innexa sororum   10
turba venit, nunc Aeoniae non invida lymphae
inrigat aeternos Pimplei ruris honores,
laetaque Pieriae revirescit gloria silvae.
fallimur? an nitidae tibi se Francisce Camenae
exornant? tibi serta parant, tibi fronde recenti   15
templa novant? mutumque diu formidine Martis
gaudent insolitis celebrare Helicona choreis?
scilicet haud alius nemoris decerpere fructus
dignior Aonii, seu quem numerare triumphos
forte iuvat patrios, seu consecrata Camenis   20
otia. sic certe est. hinc laeto compita plausu

And yet another offspring rise,
Sweet objects to parental eyes,
The cares assiduous to assuage
That still solicit querulous age;
Careful your trembling limbs to stay,
That fail with unperceived decay;
Pious when summoned hence you go,
The last kind office to bestow,
Office, with unfeigned sorrow paid:
Thrice happy youth! thrice happy maid!

LXVIII   GEORGE BUCHANAN

*Epithalamium upon the Marriage of Mary Queen of Scots
to the Dauphin of France,
afterwards Francis the Second*

What sudden heat inspires my lab'ring Mind?
Why Phoebus, long a stranger, now so kind?
Parnassus Grove which had forbore to sing,
Does with revived Io Paeans ring.
Of late I mind the laurels with'red were,
My pray'rs to Muses vanisht in the Air;
Mercurius and Apollo, Gods of Wit,
Were stun'd, as with a melancholy fitt.
Now Phoebus Shrines are patent, and the sound
Of Mystic Oracles breaks from the ground.
The Muses with fresh Bayes adorn the Brow,
And ne're were seen more prodigal than now;
Their Fields are gay, their Waters flow a-main,
Their Woods with verdant beauty grace the plain.
If Fame erre not, great Sir, the splendid Show,
This mighty Change is wrought to honour you,
And who is worthier of the Muses care:
If we recount the Triumphs gain'd in War
By your Ancestors, or the Calm of Peace
Devoted unto Arts and Sciences
It's an undoubted Truth. Hence publick Joys

cuncta fremunt, legumque exuta licentia frenos
ludit. Hymen, Hymenaeus adest, lux illa pudicis
exoptata diu votis, lux aurea venit,
venit. habes tandem totiens quod mente petisti,   25
o decus Hectoridum iuvenis, iam pone querelas,
desine spes nimium lentas, iam desine longas
incusare moras, dum tardum signifer annum
torqueat, ignavos peragat dum Cynthia menses.
grande morae pretium fers: quod si prisca tulissent   30
saecula, non raptos flesset Menelaus amores,
et sine vi, sine caede Phrygum Cytherea probatae
solvere Priamidae potuisset praemia formae.
digna quidem facies, quam vel trans aequoris aestus
classe Paris rapiat, vel coniurata reposcat   35
Graecia, nec minus est animi tibi, nec minor ardor
quam Phrygio Graiove duci, si postulet arma
coniugii tutela tui. sed mitior in te
et Venus, et teneri fuit indulgentia nati,
qui quod ames tribuere domi: puerilibus annis   40
coeptus amor tecum crevit: quantumque iuventae
viribus accessit, tanto se flamma per artus
acrius insinuans tenerum pascebat amorem.
non tibi cura fuit, quae saepius anxia Regum
pectora sollicitat, longinquae obnoxia flammae,   45
nec metus is torsit, veri praenuntia fama
ne vero maiora ferat, dum saecula prisca
elevat, et primum formae tibi spondet honorem:
cera nec in varias docilis transire figuras
suspendit trepidam dubia formidine mentem,   50
nec tua commisti tacitis suspiria chartis,
rumorisque vagam timuisti pallidus umbram.
ipse tibi explorator eras formaeque probator,
et morum testis: nec conciliavit amorem
hunc tibi luxuries, legum indignata teneri   55
imperio, aut primis temerarius ardor ab annis.
sed sexu virtus, annis prudentia maior,
et decori pudor, et coniuncta modestia sceptris,

With loud Applause invade the Azure Skies,
Nothing is hear'd but Jollity and Love,
Which throw the universal Mass doth move.
Hymen's come, with him the happy day
So long expected chases Night away,
You've got, most noble Dauphin, your Desire,
What more cou'd Heav'n bestow, or Man require?
No longer blame your stars, nor dull delay,
Nor Sun, nor Moon for cutting slow their Way,
For all demurs you're largely recompens't,
Which had the Heav'ns to former times dispens't.
The Grecian had not mourn'd his ravisht wife,
No Trojan in the Quarrel lost his Life;
And without hundred part so much adoe,
Venus to Paris had been just and true;
She had to him the fairest woman giv'n
That ere was drawn by Art, or fram'd by Heav'n,
A Prize indeed fit for him to have ta'ne,
And for combyning Greece to seek again,
Nor is your zeal short of the Trojan Prince,
Or Grecian in your Spouses just Defence,
But kindly the indulgent Powers above
Gave you at home an object of your Love,
That Passion which with Infancy began,
Took firmer root still as you grew to Man,
You by no Proxie as most Monarchs woo'd,
Nor did you fear that Fame should you delude,
Which aggrandizes distand Qualities,
And barely shakes when they approach the eyes;
No sighs, nor am'rous Billets you did vent,
Nor fear'd divulging of the Message sent;
Your own dear self the God like Nymph survey'd
A constant Witness what she did or said;
Your flame did not from Luxury arise,
Which uncontroul'd, o'rleaps all legal Tyes,
From youthful Passion or unruly Heat,
But from a Virtue than her Sex more great,
From piercing Wit which in her early shin'd,
And bashful Modesty with Sceptres joyn'd,

atque haec cuncta ligans arcano Gratia nexu.
spes igitur dubiae lentaeque facessite curae,   60
ipse tuis oculis tua vota tuere probasque
speratosque leges sine sollicitudine fructus,
nullaque fallacis delusus imagine somni
inrita mendaci facies convicia nocti.
exspectatus Hymen iam iunget foedere dextras,   65
mox etiam amplecti, mox et geminare licebit
basia, mox etiam non tantum basia. sed tu
quamlibet adproperes, animo moderare, beatum
nobiscum partire diem, tu gaudia noctis
solus tota feres: quamquam neque gaudia noctis   70
solus tota feres: et nos communiter aequum est
laetitiam gaudere tuam: communia vota
fecimus, et sacras pariter placavimus aras,
miscuimusque preces, et spesque metusque tuosque
sensimus adfectus, aegre tecum hausimus una   75
taedia longa morae. superi nunc plena secundi
gaudia cum referant, sensus pervenit ad omnes
laetitiae, mentemque ciens renovata voluptas
crescit, et exsultant trepidis praecordia fibris.
qualis ubi Eois Phoebus caput extulit undis   80
purus, et auratum non turbidus extulit axem,
cuspide iucundae lucis percussa renident
arva, micat tremulo crispatus lumine pontus,
lenibus aspirat flabris innubilus aër,
blanda serenati ridet clementia caeli.   85
at si nubiferos effuderit Aeolus Austros,

From Divine Features, an unsampled Grace,
Which darted conqu'ring Beauty from her Face.
Avant uncertain and a ling'ring care,
Your utmost wishes to your sight appear,
The Mellow Fruits you coveted so long,
You may now gather unafrai'd of wrong,
No coy delusive Visions of the Night
Shall make you fret at your abused sight;
The Marriage God will now conjoin your hands
In the sure tyes of sacred Nuptial Bands,
E're long you may in soft embraces twine,
Snatch balmie smacks, and somewhat more Divine.
How violent so e're be your desire,
Let moderation quench the blazing fire,
Let others share with you the happy day,
You shall the lovely night alone enjoy.
Yet all its sweets you shan't monopolize
We in conjunction with you must rejoice;
We to the Gods with Vows and Prayers have fought,
And pious Off'rings to their Altars brought,
Whatever passion mov'd you, mov'd us too,
And thus we imitate whate're you do.
With great difficulty could we digest,
These loath'd retardments did your bliss molest,
Since now kind Heav'n doth solid mirth bestow,
A gen'ral gladness dimples every brow.
Such ponderous Joys Mens trembling heart-strings wear,
Too strong for weak Mortality to bear.
As the refulgent sun uprears his head
From eastern waves, and gilds the ocean's bed,
Without one cloud to intercept his beams,
His flaming axis with fresh glory streams;
Fields, struck with arrows of his joyous rays,
Shine forth, and sing their great Creator's praise;
And the vast main, curl'd with a trembling light,
With dazzling splendour quiver to the sight;
The fresh'ning calmness of a heaven serene,
Cheers every hill and glads the smiling plain;
But when stern Aeolus pours forth his store,

et pluviis gravidam caelo subtexuit umbram,
maesta horret rerum facies, deformia lugent
arva, tument fluctus, campis gravis incubat aër,
torpet et obductum picea caligine caelum.   90
sic ex te populus suspensus, gaudia, curas,
maeroresque trahit, rosea nec sola iuventa
florida, nec spatiis quae te propioribus aetas
insequitur, genio indulgent, vultuque soluto,
lusibus exhilarant aptos iuvenilibus annos.   95
hunc posita vultus gravitate severior aetas
laetatur celebrare diem, matresque verendae
non tacito hunc, tacitoque optat virguncula voto.
    Quid loquar humanas admittere gaudia mentes?
ipsa parens rerum totos renovata per artus   100
gestit, et in vestros penitus conspirat honores.
aspice iam primum radiati luminis orbem
semper inexhausta lustrantem lampade terras,
ut niteat, blanda ut flagrantes mitiget ignes
temperie, ut cupido spectacula vestra tueri   105
purpureo vultus maturior exserat ortu,
serius occiduas currus demittat in undas,
ut gelidos repetens flamma propiore triones
contrahat aestivas angusta luce tenebras.
ipsa etiam tellus virides renovatur amictus,   110
et modo pampineas meditatur collibus umbras,
et modo messe agros, modo pingit floribus hortos:

The cloudy south winds through the forest roar,
And overspread the sky, replete with rain,
Impel the river, and o'erflow the plain;
The loaded air presents a scene forlorn,
Looks terrible, while fields disfigur'd mourn,
And chills the heaven, with darkness cover'd o'er,
While raging billows lash the rocky shore.

So, 'tis from thee alone thy people share
Suspense or pleasure, misery or care;
Nor is it now the rosy youth alone
That makes thy bliss and ecstasies their own;
Even serious age a smile of gladness wears,
And quits the dullness of advancing years;
The matron loud, and oft repeats her prayer,
'Tis breath'd in silence by the blooming fair.

Shall I repeat, that human minds are prone
To make your joy, and even your griefs, their own?
Nature herself, who renovates, upholds,
And in her work God's wondrous power unfolds;
Throughout her bright and vast celestial fires,
Even to your joy, and dignity conspires.

Behold the gilded orb of radiant light
Who in his course divides the day from night,
The earth illumes with his exhaustless lamp,
Dispels the clouds, and clears away the damp;
His flaming heat to mitigate inclines,
And with his rays and gentle splendour shines;
Your nuptial day, the festive scene to view,
More early rises with his purple hue,
And later while the ocean Gallia laves,
Sends down his chariot in the Western waves,
With nearer blaze he glads the northern pole,
Cheers Nature bland, and animates the whole,
With genial brightness, ever radiant light,
Contracts the darkness of the summer night.
The Earth her verdant carpet fast assumes,
The hills and dales with floral shrubs perfumes;
Riches o'er every field with beauty showers,
The vineyards smile, the plains are deck'd with flowers;

horrida nec tenero cessant mansuescere fetu
tesqua, nec armati spina sua bracchia vepres,
nec curvare feros pomis aviaria ramos: 115
inque omnes frugum facies bona copia cornu
solvit, et omniferum beat indulgentior annum,
pignoris hoc spondens felices omine taedas.
   Fortunati ambo, et felici tempore nati,
et thalamis iuncti, vestram concordia mundi   120
spem fovet, aspirat votis, indulget honori:
atque utinam nullius umquam labefacta querelis
coniugium hoc canos concordia servet in annos.
et, mihi ni vano fallax praecordia Phoebus
impulit augurio, quem iungit sanguinis ortus,   125
et commune genus proavum, serieque perenni
foedus amicitiae solidum, quem more vetusto
sancta verendarum committunt foedera legum,
nulla dies umquam vestrum divellet amorem.
vos quoque felici lucent quibus omine taedae,   130
quo studium, populique favor, quo publica regni
vota precesque vocant, alacres accedite: tuque
tu prior, o reges non ementite parentes,
Hectoride iuvenis, tota complectere mente
quam dedit uxorem tibi lex, natura sororem,   135
parentem imperio sexus, dominamque voluntas,
quam sociam vitae tibi coniunxere parentes,
et genus, et virtus, et forma, et nubilus aetas,
et promissa fides, et qui tot vincula nectens
firmius arctat amor totidem per vincula nexus.   140
si tibi communi adsensu connubia Divae
adnuerent, Paris umbrosa quas vidit in Ida,
permittantque suo socias tibi iungere taedas

The tender fruits enrich the lonesome wild,
With varied colours, and with fragrance mild;
The blossoms of the bramble and the thorn
The woodlands paint, the rising bank adorn;
The spreading trees in each green vale are found,
Their boughs with apples bending to the ground;
Nature her horn abundant largely pours,—
Indulgent plenty through the nation's showers;
With omen kind, ten thousand boons appear
To crown the copious and productive year.
And by these blissful symbols deigns to prove
Your marriage fruitful in a pledge of love.
Thrice happy Pair, born in a lucky time,
And in a luckier, Marri'd in this Clime.
The Worlds united Harmony conspires
To feed your hopes and favour your desires:
And may you lead a long triumphant life,
Mar'd by no blemish of domestic strife:
If some Imposture genius do not move
My breast, there's nothing can disjoin your Love;
That Love join'd by the sacred Tyes of Blood,
Friendship, and Leagues and Laws, and all that's good,
Advance, then, to your Bliss, Illustrious Twain,
Let not the publick Vows and Pray's b' in vain.
You first, great Dauphin, whose Heroick veins
The Richest stock of Royal Blood contains:
Embrace with all the vigour of your mind,
The most accomplished Lady of her kind,
By Birth your Cousin, and your spouse by Law.
Made by her Sex of you to stand in awe,
Yet by your choice o're you, to carry sway,
Who through strong love her Beauty must obey,
By Parents will and helpful aid of Life,
Design'd by Birth and Vertue for your Wife.
And beauty plighted Faith, and Love which knites
Together all the rest and them unites.
If these bright Goddesses by Paris seen,
Of Old upon Mount Ida's shadie green,
Should with joint care you with a spouse provide,

arbitrio, quid iam, voti licet improbus, optes
amplius? eximiae delectat gratia formae? 145
aspice quantus honos frontis, quae gratia blandis
interfusa genis, quam mitis flamma decoris
fulguret ex oculis, quam conspirarit amico
foedere cum tenera gravitas matura iuventa,
lenis et augusta cum maiestate venustas. 150
pectora nec formae cedunt exercita curis
Palladiis, et Pierias exculta per artes
tranquillant placidos Sophia sub praeside mores.
si series generis longusque propaginis ordo
quaeritur: haec una centum de stirpe nepotes 155
sceptriferos numerare potest, haec regia sola est,
quae bis dena suis includat saecula fastis:
unica vicinis totiens pulsata procellis
externi immunis domini, quodcumque vetustum
gentibus in reliquis vel narrat fama, vel audet 160
fabula, longaevis vel credunt saecula fastis,
huc compone, novum est. ampla si dote moveris,
accipe dotales Mavortia pectora Scotos.
nec tibi frugiferae memorabo hic iugera glebae,
aut saltus pecore, aut fecundas piscibus undas, 165
aut aeris gravidos et plumbi pondere sulcos,
et nitidos auro montes, ferroque rigentes,
deque metalliferis manantia flumina venis:
quaeque beant alias communia commoda gentes.
haec vulgus miretur iners, quique omnia spernunt 170
praeter opes, quibus adsidue sitis acris habendi
tabifico oblimat praecordia crassa veneno.
illa pharetratis est propria gloria Scotis,
cingere venatu saltus, superare natando,

Cou'd your vast wishes crave a Nobler Bride?
If matchless Beauty your nice fancy move,
Behold an Object worthy of your Love!
How loftily her stately front doth rise,
What gentle lightening flashes from her eyes,
What awful Majesty her carriage bears,
Maturely grave ev'n in her tender years.
Thus outwardly adorn'd, her sacred mind
In purest qualities comes not behind;
Her Nature has the seeds of Vertue sow'n,
By Moral Precepts to perfection grown;
Her Wisdom doth all vicious weeds controul,
Such force has Right Instruction on the soul.
Are you Ambitious of an ancient Line,
Where Heraulds make the Pompous branches shine?
She can an hundred Monarchs reckon o're,
Who in a Race unbroke, the Royal Scepter bore.
What house of such Antiquity can boast,
Where full two thousand years in time are lost?
Tempestuous Storms have oft the hand assail'd,
Yet Foreign Conquest never here prevail'd.
What Storie tells, or what Romance dare feigne
Compar'd with this, is of a modern strain.
Are you affected with an ample dour?
Take all the Scots with all their Martial Pow'r.
I shall not here describe the fruitful soil,
Which copiously rewards the Lab'rers toil;
Their Mynes of Brass and Lead, Low hill and plain
Are fill'd with Beasts, as Waves with scaly train;
Nor shall I sing what Iron we command,
How golden ore lyes mixt with common sand,
How from Metallic Veins the streams do run;
These are admired by the Mob alone,
Or such who with vile avarice possest,
The more their wealth augments, for more they thirst.
These glories do the valiant Scots commend,
To which no Rival Nation must pretend,
In hunting bravely they surround the woods,
And swimming with address, divide the floods,

flumina, ferre famem, contemnere frigora et aestus;   175
nec fossa et muris patriam, sed Marte tueri
et spreta incolumem vita defendere famam,
polliciti servare fidem, sanctumque vereri
numen amicitiae, mores, non munus amare.
artibus his, totum fremerent cum bella per orbem,   180
nullaque non leges tellus mutaret avitas
externo subiecta iugo, gens una vetustis
sedibus antiqua sub libertate resedit.
substitit hic Gothi furor, hic gravis impetus haesit
Saxonis, hic Cimber superato Saxone, et acri   185
perdomito Neuster Cimbro. si volvere priscos
non piget annales, hic et victoria fixit
praecipitem Romana gradum, quem non gravis Auster
reppulit, incultis non squallens Parthia campis,
non aestu Meroë, non frigore Rhenus et Albis   190
tardavit, Latium remorata est Scotia cursum:
solaque gens mundi est cum qua non culmine montis,
non rapidi ripis amnis, non obiice silvae,
non vasti spatiis campi Romana potestas,
sed muris fossaque sui confinia regni   195
munivit, gentesque alias cum pelleret armis
sedibus, aut victas vilem servaret in usum
servitii, hic contenta suos defendere fines
Roma securigeris praetendit moenia Scotis:
hic spe progressus posita, Carronis ad undam   200
terminus Ausonii signat divortia regni.

Nor heat nor cold, nor hunger them appall,
Their Bodies are their Countrie's firmest wall.
Their love of fame is than of life more great,
What once they promised is of fixed fate:
None more the rights of friendship do regard,
And love the person, not his bright reward.
By such like arts when Blood War was hurl'd
With fatal Desolation throw the World,
And Nations did their ancient Laws forgo,
Because the Victors needs would have it so,
The Scots alone their pristine Right enforc'd,
And Liberty for which they Nobly dy'd,
Here stopt the Gothic fury, here was crost
The Saxon Brav'ries, and the Danish lust,
And all th'efforts which Normandy could boast.
If you the mouldy Annals will survey,
The Roman Conquest here was at Bay.
Their Eagles which to Southern Countrey flew,
And in revenge the rugged Parthians slew,
Whose flights th'Egyptian heats cou'd not confine
Nor all the chilling damps of frozen Rhine,
When they to Caledonia did resort
Their Pinions mouldered and their Arms fell short,
When Romans had with other Realms to do,
A ridge of mountains limited the foe,
Or some huge River interpos'd his Arms,
Or frontier Woods and Waste secured from harms,
These peaceful barrs by nature fram'd had been,
But art to keep off Scotland was call'd in,
A costly wall and French assistance lend,
Which did across from sea to sea extend,
Victorious Rome did other Nations drive
From their old seats, or forc't them meanly live,
With all the marks of servitude opprest,
Eternal drudgers, unacquaint with rest,
But here she rais'd (to keep her own content)
A Mound, the Scots incursions to prevent.
Dispairing of advance, the cause she yields
And to God Terminus a Temple builds,

neve putes duri studiis adsueta Gradivi
pectora mansuetas non emollescere ad artes,
haec quoque cum Latium quateret Mars barbarus orbem
sola prope expulsis fuit hospita terra Camenis.   205
hinc Sophiae Graiae, Sophiae decreta Latinae,
doctoresque rudis formatoresque iuventae
Carolus ad Celtas traduxit: Carolus idem
qui Francis Latios fasces, trabeamque Quirini
ferre dedit Francis, coniunxit foedere Scotos,   210
foedere, quod neque Mars ferro, nec turbida possit
solvere seditio, aut dominandi insana cupido,
nec series aevi, nec vis ulla altera, praeter
sanctius, et vinclis foedus proprioribus arctans.
tu licet ex illa numeres aetate triumphos,   215
et coniuratum cunctis e partibus orbem
nominis ad Franci exitium, sine milite Scoto
nulla umquam Francis fulsit victoria castris,
nulla umquam Hectoridas sine Scoto sanguine cladis
saevior oppressit: tulit haec communiter omnes   220
Fortunae gens una vices: Francisque minantes
saepe in se vertit gladios. scit belliger Anglus,
scit ferus hoc Batavus, testis Phaëthontias unda,
nec semel infaustis repetita Neapolis armis.
hanc tibi dat coniunx dotem, tot saecula fidam   225
coniunctamque tuis sociali foedere gentem,
auspicium felix thalamis concordibus, armis
indomitos populos per tot discrimina, felix
auspicium bellis, venturaeque omina palmae.
    At tu coniugio, Nymphe, dignata superbo,   230

Where Caron's waves glide through the fruitful Fields,
Think not these daring Sons of Mars inur'd
To arms, have all the liberal Arts abjur'd,
When Barbrous Foes the Roman bounds o'erspread.
Thither the Muses for Protection fled.
Hence Greek and Roman Learning in full store,
By Charle Main to France was wafted o're
And planted, throve as on their nat'ral shore.
That Charle Main, who liv'd and reign'd so well,
In goodness as in greatness did excell,
That willing Nations own'd him for their Lord,
And join'd to Gallick flowers th'imperial Bird.
This Emp'rour deem'd it no abusing thing
To strike a League with Caledonia's King
A League which neither dint of sword can break,
Nor wild Sedition from its Centre shake:
No mad desire of sway can give it date,
But only the resistless pow'r of Fate.
  Review your Triumphs since that famous Age,
And all Confed'rats which e're engage
To ruine France: France never won the day
Unless when Scottish Souldiers cutt the way:
France scarcely ever felt a dismal Blow,
But floods of Scottish gore the Fields o're flow;
This people shar'd their Fortune's ev'ry turn,
With France they're jovial, and with France they mourn,
Swords threatning France they on themselves have drawn,
A truth to Dutch and English fully known,
Witness the Po where Phaeton lay slain,
And Naples oft contended for in vain,
This Dour is brought to you by the Royal Maid,
The noblest Dourie ever Mortal paid,
A Nature trusty to the last Degree,
And leagu'd to yours in straitest Amity,
An happy omen of a cordial Bed,
A Nation never fully conquer'd,
Tho' tost with many perils; hence doth rise
A sure Presage of future Victories.
But you, fair Nymph, to whom propitious Heav'n

te licet et Iuno, et bellis metuenda virago,
et Venus, et Charitum larga indulgentia certet
muneribus decorare suis, licet ille secundus
spes votisque hominum Francae moderator habenae,
et solo genitore minor tibi Regia sceptra   235
submittat, blando et dominam et praedicet ore,
sexum agnosce tamen, dominaeque immunis habenae,
hactenus, imperio iam nunc adsuesce iugali.
disce iugum, sed cum dilecto coniuge, ferre,
disce pati imperium, victrix patiendo futura.   240
aspicis Oceanum saxa indignatus ut undis
verberet, et cautes tumida circumfremat ira:
rupibus incursat, demoliturque procellis
fundamenta terens, scopulisque adsultat adesis.
ast ubi se tellus molli substravit harena,   245
hospitioque Deum blande invitavit amoeno,
ipse domat vires, placidusque et se minor ire
in thalamos gaudet non torvo turbidus ore,
non spumis fremituque minax, sed fronte serena
litus inoffensum lambit, sensimque relabens   250
adrepit facilis cerni et, ceu mollia captet
oscula, ludentes in litore lubricat undas.
cernis ut infirmis hedera enitatur in altum
frondibus, et molli serpens in robora flexu
paulatim insinuet sese, et complexibus haerens   255
emicet, et mediis pariter caput inserat astris:
flectitur obsequio rigor, obsequioque paratur,
et retinetur amor. neu tu iactura relictae
sollicitet patriae, desideriumque parentis:
haec quoque terra tibi patria est, hic stirpe propinqui,   260
hic generis pars magna tui, multosque per annos
fortunatorum series longissima Regum,
unde genus ducis, rerum moderatur habenas.
quoquo oculos vertes, quoquo vestigia flectes,

A match most worthy of yourself has giv'n;
Tho' charming Wit and Beauty do conspire,
And all the Graces which the World admire,
Themselves with anxious consultation vex;
Tho' he whom Mankind wish to fill the Throne,
Inferior to his God-like Sire alone;
Tho' he to you the Royal Scepter vail,
And own you for the Empress of his Soul;
Yet know your Sex, and to the Marriage yoke
Inure yourself, which galls the more its chock,
Your sympathising Love will Love constrain,
And passive Valour will a Conquest gain.

Behold the foaming Ocean, how he roars,
And on with-standing Rocks his Billows pours,
With such vast Force his rageing Waves are born,
The Cliffs almost from their Foundations torn,
But when the Shoar in humble Sand is bow'd,
And makes a pleasant Lodging for the God,
He checks his full Carrier, and curbs his power,
Strives to be less that he may please the more;
No sullen Frown his angry Brows invest,
Nor froathing Menaces disturb his Breast,
But with a Visage calm, serene, and clear,
(Such at the Birth of Nature did appear),
He skims the bank, and glyding back apace,
Comes forward with a Lover's mild embrace.

See how the mantling Ivie doth infold
Her tender leafs, and on an Oak takes hold,
Till with the tall aspiring Tree she rise,
And both together reach the wond'ring skies:
Complying Arts will Sullenness enhance,
And Love is got and kept by complaisance.
Let not these fonder thoughts molest your mind,
Your Country and your Mother left behind:
This too's your native Soil, what shoals of Friends
And kindred on your Nuptial Pomp attends?
A long blest Race of Monarchs here have sway'd,
To whom in blood you nearly are ally'd.
Look round, all are akin, where e're you tread,

cognatis pars nulla vacat, locus exhibet omnis 265
aut generis socios, aut fastis incluta gentis
ostentat monumenta tuae. iam ut caetera mittam,
hic te, qui cunctis merito praeponderat unus
exspectat longe pulcherrimus Hectoridarum,
pene tibi stirpis communis origine frater. 270
mox etiam fratrem quod vincat amore futurus,
et matrem, et quicquid consanguinitate verendum
lex facit et legum quam iussa valentior ulla,
naturae arcanos pulsans reverentia sensus.
hic quoque, ni iustis obsistent numina votis, 275
falsaque credulitas frustra spem nutrit inanem,
filius ore patrem referens et filia matrem
sanguine communi vinclum communis amoris
firmabunt, brevibusque amplexi colla lacertis
discutient blando curarum nubila risu. 280
  Hunc vitae mihi fata modum concedite, donec
iuncta Caledoniae tot saeclis Gallia genti
officiis pactisque et legum compede, fratrum
subdita dehinc sceptris animo coalescat, et undis
quos mare, quos vastis caelum spatiisque solumque 285
dividit, hos populum Concordia nectat in unum,
aequaeva aeternis caeli Concordia flammis.

LXIX   IOANNIS AURATI

Paean sive Hymnus in triplicem
victoriam Caroli IX Galliarum regis.
Poeta et Gallia alternis canunt

P.   Incipe iam ter Io, ter mecum Gallia Paean,
       Carole, ter Paean, ter Io tibi, Carole victor.
       maxima qui tria bella tribus ter conficis annis.
G.   Carole Rex. ter Io, tibi ter Rex Carole Paean. 4
P.   Ad Druidas primos peperit tibi quercus honores:
       servans Parisios, fudit cum Guisius hostem,
       hostem Parisiis ausum succedere muris.
G.   Carole, etc. 8

The Mighty Living, and the Mightier Dead,
Whose Actions have Immortaliz'd their Name,
And struck their Merits in the Roll of Fame;
Besides, there's one behind doth you expect,
Compar'd to whom, all else you must neglect:
The fairest, bravest of the Royal Line,
By birth almost a Brother uterine;
But shortly he will to you above
A Brother's or a Mother's tender Love,
Or any thing that Laws do bid us prize,
Or Nature, stronger than all legal tyes.
   Now, if the Gods do not our vows deceive,
And we too fondly what we wish believe,
A numerous progenie from you shall spring,
Which may your Love to firm consistence bring,
Such pretty Boys and Daughters be your share,
One smile of whom may banish all your care,
Sons as the Father brave, Girls as the Mother fair.
   Grant me, ye Destinies, to live so long,
Till France and Scotland's Union be my Song;
An Union which may Time and Death defy,
And with the Stars have Co-eternity.

LXIX   JEAN DORAT

*Paean ou Chant Triumphal sur la victoire
de Charles Neuviesme Roy de France. France, et le Poëte
chantent par refrain*

P.   Chantons trois fois Io, Io d'esjouissance:
      Chantons trois fois Paean à Charles le vainqueur,
      Qui de trois camps domta en neuf ans la ranqueur.
G.   Trois Io, trois, Paean à Charles Roy de France.
P.   A Dreux un Chesne verd orna premier ta lance,
      Lors que Guise deffeit l'ennemy Francien,
      Qui osoit assaillir le mur Parisien.
G.   Trois Io, etc.

P. Ad Dionysiacum tuus hostis concidit alter,
    auspiciisque tuis Momoranci et fortibus armis
    mors cum pulchra Duci, victoria laeta superstes.

G.   Carole, etc.   12

P. Tertia praeteritis gravior ter pugna duabus
    auspice te, Duce fratre, ter uno fortiter anno
    est pugnata, Deis tua semper in arma secundis.

G.   Carole, etc.   16

P. Anni primus honor, Monpensius arma moventi
    contudit: alter honos stratus Condaeus in ulva:
    tertia palma ducis fuga Gasparis, agmine caeso.

G.   Carole, etc.   20

P. Proelia quis numeret Regis numerosa Ducisque
    cetera? tres validos incursus, hoste repulso
    sustinet Henricus, triplex velut aereus agger.

G.   Carole, etc.   24

P. At tu Germanis is, Carole, comminus ultro
    figis et Aurangi metas Metensibus oris:
    unde redux geminum Pontem excutis amne Vigennae.

G.   Carole, etc.   28

P. Scilicet omen erat felix in fratre paternum,
    sicut nomen inest Henrici: quo duce quondam
    signa domum totiens retulit victricia Gallus.

G.   Carole, etc.   32

P. Sed tamen accessit felicius omen ad omen
    te veniente tuum fraternis, Carole, signis:
    nam te fata vocant magnarum ad culmina rerum.

G.   Carole, etc.   36

P. Tu Marcellus eris, qui everso denique saeclo
    succurrasque sacris, meliore sed omine fati:
    illum ostenderunt terris, te fata tenebunt.

G.   Carole, etc.   40

P. Alter eris Fabius, qui Gallis restituas rem;
    ille tamen senior, tu vix iuvenilibus annis:
    ille diu cunctans, at tu ter victor in anno.

G.   Carole, etc.   44

P. Sed quid opus Fabiis, quid Marcellis opus ullis
    externis ducibus? tibi par tibi Carolus unus,
    cuius nomen habes, et cuius nominis omen.

P.   Du second ennemy sainct Denis veid l'offence,
       Qui par Mommorancy soubs ton heur fut batu:
       Quand laissant gloire aux siens, le Chef fut abbatu.

G.   Trois Io, etc.

P.   Plus grande que les deuz fut la troisieme outrance
       Que ton frere soubs toy gouverneur a vengé,
       Ayant trois fois dans l'an ton ennemy rengé.

G.   Trois Io, etc.

P.   Montpencier de Mouvant brida la violence:
       Le second heur Condé du cheval trebuchant:
       Le tiers Gaspart fuyant, son armée bronchant.

G.   Trois Io, etc.

P.   Qui d'autres faits nombreux nombreroit la vaillance?
       Trois grands assaults soustint Henry rompant l'effort
       (Comme un rampart d'airain) de l'ennemy si fort.

G.   Trois Io, etc.

P.   Et toy Charles tu mis la fiere outrecuidance
       Du Germain et d'Orange és mettes pres de Mets:
       De retour, les deus ponts loing de Vienne tu mets.

G.   Trois Io, etc.

P.   Certes de l'heur du pere Henry grande esperance
       (Qui a mis le François si souvent en renom)
       Estoit ja en ton Frere ayant un mesme nom;

G.   Trois Io, etc.

P.   Mais tu a redoublé le sort de sa naissance
       Par ton sort tresheureux à tous ses estendarts:
       Car le destin t'apelle à treshautains hazards.

G.   Trois Io, etc.

P.   Tu seras un Marcelle, ains qu'à la decadence
       Du siecle secourant, meilleur sort encourras:
       Il mourut avant terme, et long temps tu vivras.

G.   Trois Io, etc.

P.   Tu seras un Fabien, qui par ta grand prudence,
       L'affaire des François restaureras du tout:
       Ce qu'il feit seul, tu feras ieune, à coup.

G.   Trois Io, etc.

P.   Mais que sert de Marcelle ou Fabien la semblance?
       Seul à toy ressembla Charles du nom premier:
       Duquel tu es de nom et de sort heritier.

G.   Carole, etc.   48
P.   Non igitur temere primo praediximus anno,
     qui decies senos, quingentos milleque supra:
     nonus erat, felix tibi quod tuus hic foret annis.

G.   Carole, etc.   52
P.   Annus enim tuus est, tuus est hic, Carole, nonus:
     cuncta novem novat et tu Gallica regna novare
     in decus antiquum nono nunc incipis anno.

G.   Carole, etc.   56
P.   Triplex hic nonus (numerosum maximus unus)
     nominis, aetatis, Regni hoc tibi contigit anno
     namque Dei est decimus qui rex per saecula summus.

G.   Carole, etc.   60
P.   Fatalis numerus, fatalia nomina cum sint
     sorte tibi, fies tu Carole, Carolus alter:
     quo maior Gallis Regum non exstitit alter.

G.   Carole, etc.   64
P.   Haec ineunte tuus vates dum praecinit anno:
     accipio (dixit) Lotarenus Carolus omen:
     adsensuque ratum fecit suo ut alter Apollo.

G.   Carole, etc.   68
P.   Carolus ille fuit magnus, tu Maximus: idque
     non sine sorte tibi nomen puerilibus annis;
     quod tua iam pueri tot maxima facta probarunt.

G.   Carole, etc.   72
P.   Nam quod maius opus, quam quo non maximus ipse
     Iuppiter effecit maius? puer ille Gigantes
     Titanasque domat, domitas tener ipse Gigantes.

G.   Carole, etc.   76
P.   Iuppiter ut tu alter, sic est tua, Carole, mater
     altera nunc Cybele, genetrix fecunda deorum:
     cuius consiliis tot monstra rebellia vincis.

G.   Carole, etc.   80
P.   Et tibi frater adest, nunc pene tridentifer alter
     Neptunus, Gallis qui monstra Britannica terris
     reppulit Henricus, dum litora Picta tuetur.

G.   Carole, etc.   84
P.   Et tibi tertius est frater Dis parvulus alter
     Carole, Franciscus, te absente Palatia servat,

G. Trois Io, etc.

P. Or donc au mien sort n'eut aucune decevance,
    Que ie te dy en l'an cinq cens soixante neuf,
    Qu'en cest an tu rendrois l'heur de France tout neuf.

G. Trois Io, etc.

P. Ie dy en ce tien an(car tien est sans doutance
    Ce Neuf qui rend tout neuf) toy neuviesme en neuf ans
    L'heur de France banny remettras au dedans.

G. Trois Io, etc.

P. Ce nombre tres parfaict qui tous nombres balance,
    Est triple en toy, de nom, d'age, de regne. Mais
    Le dixiesme est à Dieu, qui regne pour iamais.

G. Trois Io, etc.

P. Puis que ce nombre et nom faict en toy concurrence,
    Un iour tu seras (dy-ie) un autre Charles Grand,
    A qui tous Rois François quittent le premier rang.

G. Trois Io, etc.

P. Cecy, ie te disoy, au iour que l'an commence,
    Quand le Charles Lorrain dist l'accepte ton sort:
    Et fit, comme un Phoebus, qu'à son effect il sort.

G. Trois Io, etc.

P. Charlemaigne fut grand, mais sans contredisance
    Tu seras le Tres-grand: car de ce fus sommé
    Quand, Maximilien, petit fut surnommé.

G. Trois Io, etc.

P. Tes grands faicts l'ont monstré dez ta premiere enfance.
    Que feit plus Iuppiter qui vainquit le Geant,
    Et Titan en ieunesse? et tu les vas tuant.

G. Trois Io, etc.

P. Si tu es Iuppiter, aussi par sa semence
    Ta mere est la Cybele enfantant les grands dieux,
    Qui te faict par conseil vaincre monstres hideux.

G. Trois Io, etc.

P. Tu as un frere aussi, qui par sa vigilance,
    Chassant du Poictevin l'Ourque Angloise, à bon droict
    Seroit dit un Neptun, si Henry dit n'estoit.

G. Trois Io, etc.

P. Ton tiers frere petit, qui garde la chevance
    Et palais, où du Roy tout le grand thresor gist:

       qui tua quique tuis thesauris incubat amplis.

G.   Carole, etc.   88

P.   Est tibi parva soror, ceu virgo parvula Iuno
       quam (nisi me fallunt numquam fallentia Vatem
       visa) sibi nuptam mox ducet Iuppiter alter.

G.   Carole, etc.   92

P.   Forsan et ultimus his iniens vel proximus annus
       (ni mea quae dixi multis, me somnia fallunt)
       non ter Io tantum, sed ter cantabit et Hymen.

P.   Desine iam ter Io, ter desine Gallia Paean.   96

G.   Desinimus ter Io, ter ut incipiamus et Hymen.

       Pourroist estre estimé un vray Ditis petit.

G.   Trois Io, etc.

P.   Ta ieune seur aussi a telle contenance
       Qu'une ieune Iunon: et (si le songe mien
       Ne me trompe) bien tost aura un Iuppin sien.

G.   Trois Io, etc.

P.   Que sçait on, si cest an par heureuse alliance,
       Ou l'an prochain fera (si mon songe ne fault)
       Que crirons pour Io trois Hymen clair et hault?

P.   Cesse trois fois Io, trois fois Paean ma France.

G.   Ie cesse trois Io, trois Paean resonner,
       Pour bien tost de rechef trois Hymen entonner.

The eclogue

The eclogue flourishes during the Renaissance, partly because of the status that Vergil in particular conferred upon the genre, but chiefly because of its exceptional flexibility, so that it ends up by becoming one of the most wide-ranging forms of poetry in the elevated style. The Idylls of Theocritus were well known, in part through the Latin verse rendering of Eobanus Hessus (1531), though Italian humanists were early acquainted with the Greek text; and the eclogues of Calpurnius Siculus and Nemesianus were no strangers to the Renaissance; but inevitably it was the example of Vergil that predominated. His highly stylised compositions set the pattern for many poets: the use of monologue or dialogue, the pastoral conventions, the use of mythology, stylistic symmetries and so forth, all these features will recur in Renaissance poetry, but the variety of theme and treatment is impressive. At one end of the spectrum, there will develop a sophisticated, formalised court allegory—first apparent in Italy—in which the pastoral decoration serves to conceal a political or topical reality; the allegorical interpretation of Vergil's eclogues goes back a long way, of course. The association of the eclogue with ceremonial court poetry helps to explain its development as commemorative verse of various kinds, for which the hexameter was in any case a traditional vehicle. Then in the religious climate of the age, it was put to devotional uses, and this development shows itself more especially at two different periods: the beginning of the sixteenth century and the early seventeenth century. The eclogue can also be the instrument of a more personal inspiration, and this type occurs sporadically, but persistently until the end of the seventeenth century. Finally, the eclogue becomes a vehicle for pedagogic satire and didactic purpose: the most successful were those by Mantuan. At the same time, attempts may be made to renew the formal aspects of the genre—though the thematic developments just mentioned will affect the proportions of the traditional conventions employed. Claude Roillet succeeded in drawing the eclogue more into the dramatic orbit, while Sannazaro's piscatory eclogues enjoyed extraordinary favour. The sixteenth century was fully aware of the theory underlying different genres, but in practice it often blurred the lines of demarcation; and some of the solid successes of Renaissance poetry occur when conventions of the individual genres have been flouted or blended with others.

BIBLIOGRAPHY

Grant, W. Leonard. *Neo-latin Literature and the Pastoral*, Chapel Hill, 1965.

Harrison, T. P. *The Pastoral Elegy*, Austin, 1939.

Hulubei, Alice. *L'Eglogue en France au XVIe siècle*, Paris, 1938.

LXX   F. PETRARCAE

Ecloga II: Argus

Ideus. Phitias. Silvius

Id. Aureus occasum iam sol spectabat, equosque
pronum iter urgebat facili transmittere cursu,
nec nemorum tantam per saecula multa quietem
viderat ulla dies; passim saturata iacebant
armenta et lenis pastores somnus habebat;   5
pars teretes baculos, pars nectere serta canendo
frondea, pars agiles calamos; tunc fusca nitentem
obduxit Phoebum nubes, praecepsque repente
ante exspectatum nox adfuit; horruit aether
grandine terribili; certatim ventus et imber   10
saevire et fractis descendere fulmina nimbis.
altior, aetherio penitus convulsa fragore,
corruit et colles concussit et arva cupressus,
solis amor quondam, solis pia cura sepulti;
nec tamen evaluit fatalem avertere luctum   15
solis amor, vicitque pium sors dura favorem.
praescius, heu! nimium vates tum, Phoebe, fuisti:
'dum sibi dumque aliis erit haec lacrimabilis arbor',
dixisti. ingentis strepitu tremefacta ruinae
pastorum mox turba fugit, quaecumque sub illa   20
per longum secura diem consederat umbra,
pars repetit montes, tuguri pars limina fidi,
pars specubus terraeque caput submittit hianti.
Silvius et Phitias scopulum fortassis eundem
praecipiti petiere gradu, geminisque cavernis   25
occuluere animas trepidi, nec pauca gementes.
post, ubi laxatis tempestas fracta parumper
nubibus et caeli siluerunt murmura fessi,
incipit inlacrimans Phitias: 'O Iuppiter alme,
si scelus hoc nostrum meruit, si rustica sordet   30
pastorum pietas, silvis ignosce, precamur,
innocui miserere gregis meliorque capellas
collige dispersas; teneris signata labellis
ubera te moveant, nisi forte oblivia lactis

LXX   F. PETRARCH

Eclogue II: Argus

Ideus. Phitias. Silvius

Id. Already the golden sun was looking westward and was urging on his horses to complete his downward journey with easy course; nor for many centuries past had any day known such deep quiet in the groves: here and there the well-fed flocks were lying and a gentle slumber held the shepherds in its grip: some were fashioning smooth staffs, some weaving leafy garlands as they sang, others shaping pliant reeds for their song. Then a black cloud darkened radiant Phoebus and night was on them with a sudden rush before the expected time; the air became stiff with a terrible hailstorm; wind and rain raged in rivalry, while lightning descended from the rent clouds. A lofty cypress torn from its roots by the tumult of the heavens crashed down and shook both hills and fields, once the beloved of the sun, the cherished care of the now buried sun; nor yet did the sun's love avail to turn away the grievous catastrophe, and harsh fate overcame the object of his cherishing devotion. Alas, Phoebus, too true a prophet were you then: 'Some day to itself, some day to others this tree will be an object of grief', you said. Terrified by the crash of its mighty downfall the crowd of shepherds soon fled, all who had sat safely in its shade throughout the long days. Some made their way to the hills, some to the threshold of their trusted cottage, some hid their heads in caverns and the gaping earth. Silvius and Pythias by chance sought with hurried step the same rock and terrified found shelter in twin caves, groaning not a little. Later when the clouds scattered and the force of the wind was broken for a time, and when the noises of the wearied skies fell silent, Pythias, in tears, began: 'O bountiful Jupiter, if our crime has deserved this, if the rustic piety of the shepherds has lost your favour, spare our woodlands, we beseech you. Take pity on the innocent flock and, more benevolently inclined, bring together the scattered goats; may their udders once marked by your tender lips sway your feelings, unless perhaps the

illius astrigerae nectar tibi suggerit aulae: 35
de grege nempe fuit nutrix tua!' talia questus,
subticuit, pectusque manu percussit et ora.
Silvius, audita rupis de parte querela
(nam neque se coram cernebant, obice parvo
praetentae silicis ramoque comante dirempti)   40
concussa sic mente refert, gemitumque coercens:
'o Phitia, Phitia, fateor, sic astra minari
iampridem adverti, postquam flammantia Martis
lumina, et imbrifera Saturnum in parte morantem
obsessumque Iovem, et Venerem transversa tuentem, 45
sibila ventorum postquam peregrina notavi.
nonne procul nebulas, limo exhalante palustri,
surgere et in nostrum delatas vidimus axem?
nonne grues profugas, turpesque ad litora mergos?
num corvos, fulicasque vagas, num sidera maesta   50
vidimus et nimbo velatam abscedere Phoeben,
tum quae multa olim nascentis signa procellae
silvicolae cecinere senes? sed ferre necesse est.
haec est vita hominum, Phitia; sic laeta dolendis
alternat fortuna ferox. eat ordine mundus   55
antiquo; nobis rerum experientia prosit;
quo grex cumque miser ruerit, consistere pulchrum est.'
'care mihi in primis et semper maxime Silvi',
respondit Phitias, 'oculos, te consule, tergam;
tu modo, si quod habes damni solamen acerbi,   60
tempestiva graves relevent oblivia casus'.
'imo', ait ille, 'tuum est quae condita carmina servas
mecum partiri: Daphnis pastoribus olim,
et tibi nunc ingens merito cantabitur Argus.
quid tibi, non nobis, Phitias? num tu quoque carmen 65
Argeum vocitare libet? nimis omnia celas.
incipe; forte sequar, nisi vox tua terreat', inquit
Silvius. ille alta fregit suspiria voce:
Phit. Arge, decus rerum! silvae dolor, Arge, relictae!
hoc licuit rapidae sacro de corpore morti?   70
hoc ausa est tellus? te, qui stellantis Olympi
iam solus spectator eras, humus obruit atra?
quo favor, et nostri rediit quo gloria saecli?

nectar of the starry court has made you forget their milk. To be sure, your nurse was of the flock!' After such laments he held his peace and with his hand he beat his breast and face. When Silvius heard him complain from his side of the cliff (for they could not make each out clearly, separated as they were by the small outcrop and by a leafy branch), greatly disturbed he thus replied, holding back a groan: 'Pythias, Pythias, I confess that for a long time I remarked that the stars were threatening such disasters, after I noticed the flaming eyes of Mars, Saturn lingering in the rainy region, and Jupiter under siege and Venus watching obliquely, and after I noticed the whistlings of strange winds. Did we not see from a great distance the clouds rising from the marshy, stinking mire and borne towards our skies? Did we not see the cranes in flight, the foul gulls by the shores? or perhaps the ravens and the wandering coot? Did we not see the dejected stars and Phoebe vanish behind the cloud? then the numerous signs of a growing storm which the old men of the wood foretold at one time? Yet we must endure it. Such is the life of man, Pythias; thus does cruel fortune make joy and sorrow alternate. Let the world go on according to its ancient code; let us learn by our experience of life. Wherever the wretched flock takes its course, there is our honourable station. 'Silvius, dear to me above everything and ever most cherished,' replied Pythias, 'on your advice, I shall wipe my eyes dry. If only you have some solace to bring to bitter loss, let timely oblivion lighten our harsh misfortunes.' 'Rather', he said, 'it is your task to share with me these songs that you have kept hidden. Daphnis was once sung by the shepherds and now great Argus will rightly be the object of your song. Why sung by you and not by both of us, Pythias? Are you not in a mood to sing in honour of Argus? You are too willing to keep everything to yourself. Begin; perhaps I shall join in, unless your voice should put me off', said Silvius. With a loud voice Pythias interrupted his sighs. *P.* Argus, glory of the world! Argus, sorrow of the abandoned wood! Was fierce, consuming death allowed to act thus with your sacred body? Did earth dare to do this? Has the black earth buried you, who were already the only observer of starry Olympus? Whither has returned the ornament, whither the

quis tempestates praenoscet ab aethere longe?
quis mihi voce feras quercusque et saxa movebit, 75
aut longam dulci traducet carmine noctem?
quis terrebit apros? quis tendet retia dammis?
quis visco captabit aves? quis, flumine mergens,
ah! miseras curabit oves? quis sacra Cybeles,
atque humilem, Admeti famulantem in gramine, Phoebum 80
rite canet? quem nocturnus trepidabat abactor?
quem noscent dociles alta sub rupe capellae?
quem vigiles fidique canes? quem dulcis amica?
quis mihi sollemnes statuet per litora ludos,
insuetam patrio renovans ex more palaestram? 85
a quo consilium dubii, divinaque late
silvestres responsa ferent? quis tempore in arto
supplicibus praestabit opem? pulcherrime quondam
Arge, amor ac luctus Dryadum, quid silva, quid antrum,
quid sine te colles? et post te vivere quisquam 90
aut volet, aut poterit? pastores, credite, mors est
vivere post Argum. iam nunc arescere circum
stagna, lacus, fontes, ipsumque videbitis aequor;
spiritus alter erit ventis, color alter in herbis,
floribus alter odor; solitos nec poma sapores 95
servabunt, nec prata comas, nec flumina lymphas,
vellera nec pecudes, nec opimas campus aristas,
omnia namque oculis unus (nec fallimur) ille
laetificare suis et fecundare solebat.
illo silva fuit semper sub principe tuta, 100
pax inerat fronti, purgabat nubila verbo.
ille abiit; fortuna suos mutata fatigat.
Sil. Extorques lacrimas; nec iam mihi vivere dulce est
post Argum. sed vivaci parebimus astro.
Phit. Effugis! agnosco. nusquam sine carmine, Silvi. 105
si libet ire, cane; post i, tua damna recense.
Sil. Pastorum rex Argus erat, cui lumina centum
lyncea, cui centum vigiles cum sensibus aures,
centum artus, centumque manus, centumque lacerti,
lingua sed una fuit, cum qua rupesque ferasque 110
flecteret et fixas terrae divelleret ornos.
ille diu clarus silvis, perque omnia notus

glory of our times? Who will forecast far ahead the storms from the skies? Who will charm wild beasts and oaks and rocks with his voice? or who will beguile the long night with his sweet song? Who will scare away the wild boars? who will lay traps for the deer? who will snare the birds with lime? Ah, who will look after our unhappy sheep, bathing them in the river? Who will, according to religious observance, sing the rites of Cybele and humbled Phoebus toiling as a servant in the pastures of Admetus? Whom will the cattle thief in the night fear? Whom will the obedient she-goats recognise as their master under the lofty crag, or the faithful watchdogs, or his sweet mistress? Who, then, will organise the sacred games on the shores, renewing the old-established contest, now fallen out of use? From whom will those in doubt take advice and the woodlanders far and wide receive divine oracles? Who in time of need will bring help to those that ask for it? Argus, once most handsome, the love and sorrow of the Dryads, what will the wood, what will the cave, what will the hills become without you? And after your passing, will anyone wish or manage to live? Believe me, shepherds, it is death to live without Argus. Now soon you will see drying up everywhere the pools, the lakes, the springs, the sea even. Different will be the breath of the wind, different the colour of the grass, different the fragrance of the flowers. Nor will fruits retain their accustomed taste, nor meadows their greenery, nor rivers their waters, nor sheep their fleece, nor the field its rich ears of corn. For he alone with his gaze (nor am I mistaken) was wont to bring joy to all things and make them fruitful. Under his guidance the woodland was always safe; peace was on his brow; with a word he dismissed the clouds. Now he has departed; changed fortune troubles his people. *S.* You bring me to tears, no longer is life sweet to me without Argus. But we shall obey the star of our lives. *P.* So you are leaving us! I see that; but not without a song, Silvius. If you wish to go, sing first and then depart, tell us your own sorrows. *S.* Argus, king of the shepherds, possessed a hundred Lyncean eyes, a hundred keen ears with their senses, a hundred limbs, a hundred hands, and a hundred arms, yet he had only one tongue and with it he could move rocks and animals and uproot the firm ash trees from the ground. He was long renowned in the woods, known throughout the pastures, sung everywhere by

pascua, formosis cantatus ubique puellis,
mille greges niveos pascens per mille recessus.
postquam pertaesum est nemorum longique laboris,   115
inrediturus abit, volucrique per avia saltu
evolat in montes. illinc de vertice summo
despicit et nostras curas nostrosque tumultus,
regnataeque videt quanta est angustia silvae;
adloquiturque Iovem et viduum commendat ovile.   120
Arge, vale! nos te cuncti, mora parva, sequemur.
Id. His dictis, abeunt; patrii Sulmonis ad arva
contendit Phitias, silvas petit alter Etruscas;
solus ego adflicto maerens in litore mansi.

LXXI   BAPTISTAE MANTUANI

Ecloga VII: Pollux

De conversione iuvenum ad religionem,
cum iam auctor ad religionem aspiraret

Alphus.   Galbula

A. Galbula, quid sentis? Pollux doctissimus olim
fistulicen subito quodam quasi numine tactus
destituit calamos, tunicas, armenta, sodales;
bardocucullatus caput ut campestris alauda
quattuor ante dies in religiosa recessit   5
claustra. ferunt illum, pecudes dum solus in agris
pasceret, effigiem quandam vidisse deorum.
cetera non memini, sed tu quid, Galbula, sentis?
G. Vt dixere patres, iaciens primordia rerum
(magna canam nobis quae quondam tradidit Vmber)   10
instituit Deus agricolas pecorisque magistros.
primus agri cultor rudis, immansuetus et asper
qualis humus segnis, lapidosa, rebellis aratro.
ast ovium primus pastor, mitissima proles,
instar ovis quae bile caret, quae lacte redundat,   15
mitis erat, nullis umquam pastoribus asper.
de grege saepe suo sacrum ponebat ad aras;

fair maidens, driving to pasture a thousand snowy flocks in a thousand hidden places. Having grown weary of the groves and the long labour he has departed never to return; like a bird he flies swiftly through remote regions into the mountains. Thence from the top of the peak he looks down and observes our cares and commotion and sees how great are the difficulties of the wood that he ruled formerly. Now he speaks with Jupiter and entrusts to him the orphaned fold. Argus, farewell! Before long, we shall all be following you. *Id.* With these words they take their leave; Pythias wends his way to the fields of his native Sulmo; the other one seeks his Etruscan woods. I remained alone with my sorrow on the desolate shore.

LXXI   MANTUAN

Eclogue VII: Pollux

Here Galbula extols The Shephierds to the Skie:
And tels how Pollux did convers that saw the Sainct with eie

The Speakers' names.   Alphus.   Galbula.

A. What thinkst thou, Galbula? / Sir Pollux passing fine
In piping earst (I wotte not howe) / inspirde with powre devine
Forwent his Pipe, his Weede, / his charge of Beasts, his Mates,
And hooded (as the Lapwings are / with crists upon their pates)
Foure dayes agoe himselfe / to holie house did yelde.
Some think that whilst his flock he led / alone in open fielde,
He saw some godlie shape / from Heaven to appeare,
(The rest I have forgot) but what /thinkst thou? I long to heare.
G. As sages sayde, when God / eche creature gan to make,
(No trifles I will tell, but such / of yore as Umber spake)
Both Clownish country wights / and Shephierdes he ordainde:
The Tylman tough, unmilde, in ci-/vill nurture never trainde,
Much like the lumpish clay / that Culter doth controll:
The Shephierd of a softer kinde / a siely hurtlesse soule.
As simple as the Sheepe, / devoide of wrathfull gall,
The Sheepe that yelds the milk, and likes / his keeper aye withall.
From flocke to Altare he / would bring when so he came

nunc ove, nunc pingui vitulo faciebat, et agno
saepius, et magno divos ambibat honore.
sic profecit apud superos, sic numina flexit,   20
ut fuerit primo mundi nascentis ab ortu
tempus ad hoc caelo pecoris gratissima cura.
Assyrios quosdam (sed nescio nomina; curae
diminuunt animum) Deus ex pastoribus olim
constituit reges qui postea murice et auro   25
conspicui gentes bello domuere superbas.
cum Paris Iliaca tria numina vidit in Ida
(aut Paris aut alius puerum qui obtruncat ad aram)
pastor erat. quando caelesti exterritus igne
venit ad ostentum pedibus per pascua nudis,   30
pastor erat Moses. Moses a flumine tractus
exsul apud Graios Amphrysia pastor Apollo
rura peragravit posito deitatis honore.
caelestes animi Christo ad praesepia nato
in caulis cecinere Deum pastoribus ortum.   35
et nova divini partus miracula docti
pastores primi natum videre Tonantem
et sua pastores infans Regnator Olympi
ante magos regesque dedit cunabula scire.
se quoque pastorem Deus appellavit, ovesque   40
mitibus ingeniis homines et mentibus aequis.
et, ne vana putes haec somnia, nuper ab urbe
rus veniens picto perlegi haec omnia templo.
sunt pecudes pictae, parvi sub matribus agni
in tellure cubant, ingens equitatus ab alto   45
monte venit, radiant auro diademata divum
et suspensa tenent vaga lumina praetereuntum.
non igitur mirum noster si numina Pollux
vidit; amant villas et oves et ovilia divi.
simplicibus praesens Deus est, offenditur astu.   50

Sometime a Sheepe, a fatted Calfe, / sometime a sucking Lambe.
To Gods their honour due / he gave with good intent:
His service so prevailde with them, / he so their Godheads bent,
As since the time the worlde /created was and made,
Unto this houre most gratefull was / to Gods the Shephierdes trade.
And more than this, he callde, / Assyrians a sort
(Their names through care I have forgot) / to Mace and kingly port,
That Shephierds were afore / who garnisht brave in Golde
And purple roabes, proude countries oft / in battaile have controlde,
That Paris that behelde / three Goddesses in Ide,
With Paris eke the syre that would / have forc'd his sonne to have dide,
A Shephierd was. When Moy-/ses searde with heavenly fyre
Came barefoote through the fieldes to see / the signe with great desyre
A shepherd then he was / and lately come from floud.
Apollo (as a banisht man) / in Greece did think it good
His Godhead layde aside / a Shephierds charge to take
And so th' Amphisian fields to walke / and Bowe and shafts forsake.
Those sacred Angels eke / when Christ in Oxen stall
Was born, forspake for Shephierds sake / that would be a thrall.
And Shephierds being taught / the miracles divine
Of heavenly birth, did first beholde / the thundring Impe with eyen.
The mightie Infant gave / the Shephierds libertie
Before the wise and royale kings / in Cradle him to see.
A Shephierd he himselfe / disdained not to call,
Those men he termed Sheepe that sim-/ple were and meeke withall.
And least you thinke I lie, / from Citie home againe
To Countrie as I came, In Church / I redde them painted plaine
There portrayde are the Beasts / and little Lambes that lie
On soile beside their dames. A hu-/gie troupe from mountains hie
Of Gods on horseback commes, / their Diademes do blaze
With glittering Golde this sight doth make / the passers by to gaze.
No marvell then if gods / appearde to Pollux sight:
In Villages, in Sheepe and home-/lie Sheepecots they delight:
GOD is a guest to simple men, / the haughtie he doth spite.

A. Vera refers. pecori sic sint innoxia nostro
pascua, vidi asinum, vidi praesepe bovemque.
iam memini turbae venientis, et ora videre
Indica iam videor regum sua dona ferentum.
unum oro, quaenam Polluci occurrit imago?   55
Galbula, si nosti. ne sit labor omnia fari.
G. Et novi et memorare libet; res digna relatu,
res digna auditu, pia, sancta, imitabile factum.
durus et immitis pater atque superba noverca
Pollucem graviore iugo pressere iuventae   60
tempore cum dulces animos nova suggerit aetas;
et eum iam invalidae longo sub pondere vires
deficerent nullaque odium mansuesceret arte,
constituit temptare fugam. res una volentem
ire diu tenuit: nimis impatienter amabat;   65
error enim communis amor iuvenilibus annis.
res est fortis amor, violentia fortior; ivit.
et tales abiens (mihi namque solebat amores
enarrare suos) maesto dedit ore querelas:
'O Virgo lacrimaene tuis solventur ocellis   70
cum te tam caro cernes ab amante relictam?
ullane discessu duces suspiria nostro?
tune mei crudelis eris forte immemor umquam?
usque adeone tuum poterit frigescere pectus,
pectus quod totiens, quod lumina fletibus implet?   75
tune trahes crebros gemitus et pallida fies?
cerno oculos, cerno lacrimas, cerno anxia corda
virginis. huc tantum qua dissimulare dolorem
fas erit arte? dolor duplex mea pectora torquet,
illius atque meus. sed fas mihi, flere, quod illi   80
non licet; occultus longe magis aestuat ignis.
incolumem mihi vos, divi, servabitis illam,
ut, quando exsilio repetam mea rura peracto,
fiat amor, felix saltem semel ante senectam.'
talia pergebat memorans, voluitque reverti   85
(tantus amor iuvenem, vis tanta furoris agebat),

A. Thou telst the truth, I wish / the fieldes as hurtlesse bee
Unto your Beasts. The Asse, the rack, / and Bullocke I did see.
A call to minde the route / that thither flockt apace,
Me thinkes I see the Kings of Inde / that brought their gifts in
    place.
One thing I crave, what kinde / of shape did Pollux see?
And if thou knowst it (Galbula) / do daine to tell it mee.
G. I know it well, and will / rehearse the storie true,
A worthie fact to tell or heare / for all men to ensue.
The froward Father, and / the Stepdame full of pride,
Had pressed Pollux necke with yoake / uneasie to abide,
In tender yeares when youth / sweet pleasures doth persuade:
But when he fealt his force to faile / through such a weary trade,
And sawe no arte prevailde / their rigor to relent,
He thought it best to runne away: / and thus to flight ybent
His onely let was this, / he lov'd impatiently.
For doting love (a common fault) / doth Youth accompany.
Love of it selfe is strong, / the violence doth passe.
He went: At parture (these complaints / to me he wonted was
His dolours to declare) / with mournful voice he spake:
Wilt thou (O Virgin) shead thy teares / for such a traytors sake?
And when thou seest thy selfe /by Lover so betrayde,
Wilt thou bewaile the want of him / that such a pranke hath
    playde?
Wilt thou thy cruell Friend / remember in distresse?
Or shall that lovyng breast of thine / a chillie colde possesse?
That breath that hath provokte /so many weeping eyes,
Wilt thou wax wan for grief? Wilt thou / sende sighings to the
    Skies?
I see the Virgins eyes, / his eares, his panting hart.
Alas may any cunning now / conceale my secrete smart?
A double dolour doth / distraine my troubled minde,
Hir griefe and my distresse: my wo / to waile is me assignde,
But not to hir: my fire / more covertly doth burne.
You Gods (I trust) will hir preserve / in health till my returne,
That after my exile / when I shall backe retire,
Our love may have a good successe / ere youthfull yeares expire.
Thus talking he did passe, / and would have turned againe:
Such love had bleard the boy. such frensie / he broylde in youthfull

sed iam iacta fuga cunctis erat alea nota.
fronde sub Herculea fessus maerore sedebat;
ecce puellari virgo stipata corona
ora, manus, oculos habitumque simillima Nymphae.   90
et tali adfata est puerum sermone dolentem:
'Care puer, quo tendis iter? vestigia verte.
nescis, heu nescis quo te via ducat et audes
ignotis errare locis nihil insidiarum
per campos ratus herbosos, nihil esse pericli.   95
omnia tuta putas et quod placet utile credis
more iuventutis stolidae. collectus in orbem
saepe latet molli coluber sub graminis umbra;
est facile incautos offendere. parvulus infans
innocuos rutilum digitos extendit in ignem: 100
nec nisi iam laesus vires intellegit ignis.
haec regio intrantes aditu consuevit amoeno
fallere, delicias offert et gaudia; verum
ingressis, cum triste nihil superesse putatur,
mille parat laqueos et mille pericula profert.   105
trames hic, ut collem gressu superaveris illum,
ducit in umbrosam silvam, crudele ferarum
hospitium, loca taetra situ et caligine opaca.
quisquis eo deceptus abit remeare vetatur,
et piceis primum velatur lumina vittis,   110
deinde per omne nemus, dumeta per aspera tractus
transit in effigiem monstri. dum volvere linguam
atque loqui temptat, mugit; dum attollere sese
credit, humi graditur quadrupes neque suspicit astra.
ima tenebrosae vallis lacus aequore nigro   115
occupat et nigris mons plurimus imminet undis.
huc tracti in Stygios latices altumque barathrum
praecipites dantur rapidaque voragine mersi
in Styga et aeternas Erebi rapiuntur in umbras.
heu quot pastores istis ambagibus acti   120

braine.

But now the Die were cast, / decreed was the flight,
He underneath a Popple tree / sate downe a wofull wight.
Beholde a Virgin crownde / with Garlande he did see,
Hir face, hir eyes, and habite were / Nymphlike in eche degree.
She did approche, and thus / the sorie boy bespake.
(Sweet Lad) where wilte thou wander now? / thy purposde pathes forsake.
Alas thou wottst not where / this way woulde bring thee streight,
Yet darst thou goe to places straunge: / and thinking no deceipt
To lurke in grassie fielde, / eche perill thou neglectst,
All safe thou deemst, that which likes / thee best, thou most respectst
Like unadvised youth. / The adder knit in knot
And lurking in the grasse doth bite / the man that saw him not.
Th'unware is soone begilde. / The Infant dares assay
Withouten dreade in burning Coates / with tender hands to play,
And thinkes it but a sport / untill he feele the fire.
This Countrie traines the Passengers / at first with sweete desire,
And proffers pleasures rife / with joyes exceding all:
But entred once, foreseeing not / the hurte that may befall,
It lets a thousand shares / and planteth perills more.
This path as soone as you have past, / that hill you see before
Leades to a shadie wood / where cruelle beasts do dwell,
To dungeons deepe and loathsome vauts, / as blacke as any Hell.
And who is so intrapt / shal thence retire no more:
For first he hath a fillet swarth / and vaile his eyes before.
Then drawne about the wood / through sharpe and shrubby thornes,
To Monster he transformed is: / and whilst his tongue he turnes
And thinks to speake, he howles, / and coveting upright
To go, he groveling creepes on foure, / the heavens are barrd his sight.
Beneath a Valley darke, / a Pit with waters blake
Doth stand, and then a mountayne huge / doth overlooke the Lake.
Thus drawne to stinkyng Styx, / is headlong downe prast
Into the filthy foorde, the Sinke / down swallowe him in hast:
Thus damnde to Styx in shade / for aye he must abyde.
Alas, how many Shephierds through / these dotyng fitts have dyde:

cum gregibus periere suis! ego sedula semper
monstro iter; hic ad opem vigilo indefessa ferendam.
tolle moras igitur, mortis fuge blanda propinquae
atria; secreti tutam pete litoris oram
qua contra Idalios fluctus mihi tollit in altum   125
aëra Carmelus viridi caput arbore cinctum.
primus hic antiquis patribus spelaea domosque
praebuit arboreas intra nemus ilice densum.
ex hoc in vestros deducta cacumine montes
religio venit, sicut de fonte perenni   130
flumina, et ex uno multi genitore nepotes.
illius in silvis abies ubi plurima surgit,
pinguis ubi piceae sudat liber et terebinthi.
innocuum postquam feliciter egeris aevum,
mox tua mutatis aetas renovabitur annis.   135
in loca te tollam meliora virentia semper;
immortalis eris divum comes, ire per astra
inter Hamadryades et Oreadas atque Napaeas
flore coronatas caput et redolentibus herbis
fas erit ac super et subter cognoscere caelos.'   140
    Sic effata leves virgo discessit in auras.
tum sua iuravit Pollux mutata repente
pectora et extemplo victum exspirasse furorem
non aliter quam flumina cadet, si ardentibus agris
effluat et totas praeceps Padus evomat undas.   145
sic abiit crudelis Amor qui saepe pharetram
in iuvenem, dum principiis obstaret amandi,
dum tepet ac timide insanit, consumpserat omnem.
sic igitur Pollux in claustra silentia venit.
A. Sunt quibus aspirent etiam nolentibus ultro,   150
sunt quibus infensi sine causa et crimine di sint.
G. Quod nos in pecudes, in nos id iuris habent di;
hoc rus scire sat est, sapiant sublimius urbes.

And perisht with theyr flocks? / but I am busie still
As one untirde, to shewe the way / and wrest thee from the yll.
Wherefore do way delayes / and flie the flattering dore
That traines to death, go seeke the coast / that leades to secrete shore,
Against th'Idalian floods / where Carmelus is seene.
To lift his head aloft the Skies / bedeckt with Garlande greene,
To aun, cient fathers first / this Hill gave dwellings good,
As caves and houses made of trees / within a bushy wood.
From thence Religion first / deriv'd his offspring tooke
And came amongst your hills as from / his head, the running brooke,
And from one Grandsire as / do many Nephews sproute.
In those same woods, where Beechy boughes / are growing all about,
Where fattie Pix doth sweate / and Terebynth doth shed
His glewlike gum, and clammie juyce. / There after thou hast led
A happie hurtlesse life / devoide of vile offence:
Then into places ever greene / and flourishing from thence
I will advance thee streight, / a better lodge to dwell:
Immortall shalt thou waxen then, / and (marke what tale I tell)
Thou shalt as fellowes made /unto the heavenly States,
Get up above the starres, and have / the Nimphs unto thy mates
Both Hamadriads and / the hillie Orcads bright,
And Napes, Ladies that in sweetes / and Garlands doe delight:
With lawfull leave to have ye skies / both up and downe in sight.
Thus having tolde hir tale / to Skie the Virgin flewe.
Then Pollux sware his mind was turnd, / and heart ychangde anew
Forwent his furies fitte. / Even as the firie flash
Is quencht, when Padus with his streame / the frying fields doth wash,
So parted cruell Love, / that earst his Arrowes shot
At him (good youth) that striving would / those colde hote fitts forgot:
And so good Pollux he / to silent cloister came.
A. Yea mary. Gods some men inspire, / that looke not for the same,
But they with other wroth / and causelesse angry bee.
G. Such powre have Gods on us as on / our sielly sheepe have wee.
This knowledge will suffice / us simple Countrie clownes:

sic docuit rediens aliquando ex urbe sacerdos
Iannus et in magno dixit sibi codice lectum.   155
A. Sol cadit et Baldi vix summa cacumina tangit,
nos quoque iam sero cum sole recedere tempus.
Galbula, sarcinulas ne sit tibi ferre molestum,
pera levis, levis est et cantharus; omnia parvus
ferre labor sero, grave mane sed utile pondus.   160
ipse pecus ducam, mihi pars erit ista laboris.

LXXII   B. CASTILIONIS

Ecloga: Alcon

Ereptum fatis primo sub flore iuventae
Alconem nemorum decus, et solacia amantum,
quem totiens Fauni et Dryades sensere canentem,
quem totiens Pan est, totiens miratus Apollo,
flebant pastores; ante omnes carus Iolas,   5
tristia perfundens lacrimis manantibus ora,
crudeles superos, crudeliaque astra vocabat.
ut gemit amissos fetus Philomela sub umbris,
aut qualis socia viduatus compare turtur,
quam procul incautam quercu speculatus ab alta   10
immitis calamo pastor deiecit acuto;
non viridi sedit ramo, non gramine laeto,
non vitrei dulcem libavit fluminis undam,
sed gemitu amissos tantum testatus amores,
languidulus maestis complet nemora alta querelis.   15
nulla dies miserum lacrimis sine vidit Iolam,
nec cum Sol oritur, nec cum se condit in undas:
non illi pecudes, non pingues pascere tauros
cura erat, aut pastos ad flumina ducere potum,
haedorumve gregem aut vitulos includere septis: 20
tantum inter silvas, aut solo in litore secum
perditus, et serae oblitus decedere nocti,
rupibus haec frustra et surdis iactabat harenis:
'Alcon deliciae Musarum et Apollinis, Alcon

Let them contende for greater witte / that weare the scarlet gownes
And in the Citie woonne. / Thus person Ianus tolde
Returnde from towne, and sayd he sawe / it writte in storie olde.
A. Nowe goes the sunne to glade / he toucheth top of hills,
Wherefore that wee with him depart / his wonted parting wills.
O Galbula get up / those trinkets on thy backe
The Scrippe is light, the bottle light, / no payne to beare the packe,
For though the burthen way / yet is it good to beare,
Do that, and I will fetch our flockes, / for nowe the day doth weare.

LXXII   BALDASSARO CASTIGLIONE

Eclogue: Alcon

Alcon, snatched away by the Fates in the first flower of his youth,
the ornament of the groves and the solace of lovers, whom so often
the Fauns and Dryads heard sing, whom so often Pan, so often
Apollo admired, Alcon was mourned by the shepherds. Iolas, dear
above all, with tears running down his sad face, invoked the cruel
gods above and the cruel stars. Like Philomela, who in the shadow
of the trees bewails her lost offspring, or like the turtle dove bereft
of his mate and companion whom a harsh shepherd has spied
unsuspecting from a distance and has felled to the ground from a
tall oak with a sharp arrow; he did not rest on the green bough or
on the lush grass, he did not taste the sweet water of the crystal
stream, but with his laments invoking his lost love, he faintly filled
the high groves with mournful complaints. Not a day saw sad Iolas
without tears, either when the sun rose or when it sank into the
waves; he cared not to feed the flocks or the well-conditioned bulls,
or to drive them after their feed to the rivers to drink; nor did he
heed to enclose in their pens the flock of kids or the bullocks; only
in the woods or on the lonely shore, left to himself in his despair
and forgetting to avoid the gloom of night, in vain he uttered these
words to the rocks and sands that heard him not: 'Alcon, the
darling of the Muses and of Apollo, Alcon, the half of my life,

pars animae, cordis pars Alcon maxima nostri,   25
et dolor, his lacrimas oculis habiture perennes,
quis deus, aut quis te casus miser abstulit? ergo
optima quaeque rapit duri inclementia fati?
ergo bonis tantum est aliquod male numen amicum?
non metit ante diem lactentes messor aristas,   30
immatura rudis non carpit poma colonus:
at fera te ante diem mors nigro immersit Averno.
iniecitque manus rapidas crescentibus annis.
heu miserande puer! tecum solacia ruris,
tecum Amor et Charites periere, et gaudia nostra.   35
arboribus cecidere comae, spoliataque honore est
silva suo, solitasque negat pastoribus umbras.
prata suum amisere decus, morientibus herbis
arida; sunt sicci fontes, et flumina sicca.
infecunda carent promissis frugibus arva,   40
et mala crescentes rubigo exedit aristas.
squalor tristis habet pecudes, pecudumque magistros:
impastus stabulis saevit lupus. ubere raptos
dilaniatque ferus miseris cum matribus agnos:
perque canes praedam impavidus pastoribus aufert.   45
nil nisi triste sonant et silvae, et pascua, et amnes,
et liquidi fontes tua tristia funera flerunt,
et liquidi fontes, et silvae, et pascua, et amnes;
heu miserande puer! tangunt tua funera divos.
per nemora agricolae flentes videre Napaeas,   50
Panaque, Silvanumque, et capripedes Satyriscos.
sed neque iam lacrimis aut questu fata moventur
impia, nec nostras audit Mors surda querelas.
'vomeribus succisa suis moriuntur in arvis
gramina, deinde iterum viridi de cespite surgunt;   55
rupta semel non deinde adnectunt stamina Parcae.
aspice, decedens iam sol declivis Olympo
occidit, et moriens accendit sidera caelo;
sed tamen occiduo cum laverit aequore currus,
idem iterum terras orienti luce reviset.   60
ast ubi nigra semel durae nos flumina mortis
lavere, et clausa est immitis ianua regni,
nulla umquam ad superos ducit via, lumina somnus

Alcon, the chief part of my heart and object of my grief, who wilt keep these my eyes for ever wet with tears, what god or what wretched chance snatched thee from me? Does then the severity of cruel fate carry off all that is best? Is there then some deity hostile only to the good? The reaper does not gather in the green corn before the appointed time; the rough farmer does not pick the unripe fruit; but savage death has plunged thee into black Avernus before thy time, and has laid impetuous hands upon thy growing years. Alas, luckless youth! with thee has perished the solace of the countryside, with thee have perished Love and the Graces and our joys. The trees have shed their tresses, the wood is deprived of its splendour and denies the shepherds their wonted shade. The meadows have lost their beauty with their grasses dying and their surfaces parched; the springs have run dry and the rivers are dry. The barren fields are without their promised crops and wicked blight has devoured the growing wheat. Bleak squalour possesses the herds and the masters of the herds; the hungry wolf rages in the enclosures and savagely tears to pieces the lambs and their unfortunate mother from whom he has seized them, and making his way through the dogs he fearlessly carries off his prey from the shepherds. Nothing but mournful sounds are heard in the woods, the pastures and the rivers; and the running springs mourned thy sad funeral rites, the running springs, the woods, the pastures and the rivers. Alas, luckless youth! Thy death affects the gods. Through the groves the farmers saw the wood-nymphs weeping, and Pan and Silvanus and the little goat-footed Satyrs. Yet no longer are the cursed Fates moved by tears or laments, nor does inexorable Death listen to my cries. 'Mown down by the plough, the grasses die in their fields, then once again rise up from the green turf; the Fates do not then bind together again the threads once they are broken. Behold, the dying sun now sinking in the heavens is setting, and as it dies kindles the stars in the sky; yet when it has laved its chariot in the western sea, it will again revisit the lands with eastern light. But when once we have bathed in the black waters of harsh death and the door of that inexorable kingdom has been closed, no way ever leads to the gods above, everlasting sleep

urget perpetuus, tenebrisque involvit amaris:
tunc lacrimae incassum, tunc inrita vota, precesque   65
funduntur. fert vota Notus, lacrimasque, precesque.
heu miserande puer, fatis subrepte malignis!
non ego te posthac pastorum astante corona
victorem aspiciam volucri certare sagitta,
aut iaculo, aut dura socios superare palaestra.   70
non tecum posthac molli resupinus in umbra
effugiam longos aestivo tempore soles;
non tua vicinos mulcebit fistula montes,
docta nec umbrosae resonabunt carmina valles:
non tua corticibus totiens inscripta Lycoris,   75
atque ignis Galatea meus, non iam simul ambos
audierint ambae nostros cantare furores.
nos etenim a teneris simul usque huc viximus annis,
frigora pertulimusque aestus, noctesque, diesque,
communique simul sunt pasta armenta labore.   80
rura mea haec tecum communia: viximus una;
te moriente igitur cur nam mihi vita relicta est?'
'heu male me ira deum patriis abduxit ab oris!
ne manibus premerem morientia lumina amici,
aut abeuntis adhuc supremum animae halitum in auras   85
exciperem ore meo, gelidis atque oscula labris.
invideo, Leucippe, tibi; suprema dolenti
deficiens mandata bonus tibi praebuit Alcon,
spectavitque tuos morienti lumine vultus:
frigida tu maesto imposuisti membra feretro,   90
sparsisti et lacrimis bustum, ingratumque sepulcrum:
inde ubi defletum satis est, et iusta peracta,
Alconem ad manes felix comes usque secutus,
amisso vitam socio non passus inertem es;
et nunc Elysia laetus spatiaris in umbra,   95
Alcone et frueris dulci, aeternumque frueris.
atque aliquis forsan pastor pius ossa sepulcro
uno eodemque simul florentis margine ripae,
amborum sacro manes veneratus honore,
composuit, lacrimasque ambobus fudit easdem.   100
ast ego nec tristes lacrimas in funere fudi,
debita nec misero persolvi iusta sodali.

lies heavy on our eyes and enfolds us in bitter darkness. Then vainly tears, then useless vows and prayers are uttered, and the wind bears away vows, tears and prayers. Alas, luckless youth! snatched away by spiteful Fates, no more shall I see thee in a circle of shepherds victoriously contending with winged arrow or with javelin, or outstripping thy comrades in hard-fought wrestling. No more shall I, lying on my back in the gentle shade with thee, avoid the hot sunny days of a long summer; nor will thy pipe again soothe the nearby hills, nor the shadowy valleys echo with thy expert songs. Thy Lycoris, with her name so often scratched on the bark, and my flame Galatea, no more will they both hear us singing together of our passionate love. For we have lived together from our tender youth on until now, together we have endured cold and heat, nights and days, and our herds were fed together with common effort. These my fields I shared with you as well; we lived together. Then why since thy death has life been left to me?' 'Alas, wrongfully did the wrath of the gods take me away from my native shores, lest with my hands I might close the eyes of my dying friend or with my mouth catch the last breath of his spirit, while it departed into the air, and the kisses from his ice-cold lips! Leucippus, I envy thee; good Alcon, as life ebbed, handed over his last charges to thee in thy sorrow and he looked with dying eye on thy countenance. Thou laid'st his cold limbs out on the mournful bier, thou sheddest tears over his grave and ungrateful tomb, whence, after the mourning and the funeral rites had been properly observed, thou, happy companion, didst follow Alcon as far as the world of shades, and after the loss of thy friend, wouldst not suffer a pointless life. And now thou walkest happily in the shades of Elysium, and enjoyest the society of dear Alcon and shalt enjoy it for ever. And maybe some good shepherd has laid to rest thy bones in the very same grave with him on the edge of a flowering bank, worshipping the shades of both with religious respect, and has wept the same tears on both. But I neither shed sad tears at his death nor did I pay due homage to my luckless comrade. But rather, unaware

quin etiam, sortis durae ignarusque malorum,
vana mihi incassum fingebam somnia demens:
'haec ego rura colam celeberrima; tum meus Alcon   105
huc veniet linquens colles, et inhospita saxa,
infectasque undas, et pabula dira veneno.
molliaque inviset prata haec, fluviosque salubres.
occurram longe, et venientem primus amicum
agnoscam; primus caris complexibus ora   110
impediam; excutient hilares nova gaudia fletus.
sic tandem optato laeti sermone fruemur,
aerumnasque graves, olim et transacta vicissim
damna referre simul, rursusque audire iuvabit;
tum veteres sensim fando repetemus amores,   115
deliciasque inter pastorum, et dulcia ruris
otia, securae peragemus tempora vitae.
haec amat arva Ceres, iuga Bacchus, pascua Apollo;
ipsa Pales herbas pecori, lac sufficit agnis.
montibus his passim tenerae adsuevere Napaeae   120
saepe feras agitare, et saepe agitare choreas.
his redolens sacros primaeve gentis honores
perluit antiquas Tiberis decora alta ruinas.
hic umbrae nemorum, hic fontes, hic frigida Tempe,
formosum hic pastor Corydon cantavit Alexin.   125
ergo ades, o dilecte puer: te pascua et amnes
exspectant, tibi iam contexunt florea serta,
adventuque tuo testantur gaudia Nymphae,
summittitque novos tellus tibi daedala flores.'

  'Haec ego fingebam miser ab spe ductus inani,   130
nescius omne nefas morti fatisque licere.
at postquam frustrata leves abiere per auras
vota mea, et vivos Alconis cernere vultus
non licuit, vivasque audire et reddere voces,
huc saltem, o saltem umbra levi per inania lapsu.   135
advolet, et nostros tandem miserata dolores
accipiat lacrimas, imo et suspiria corde
eruta, quasque cava haec responsant antra querelas.
ipse meis manibus ripa hac Aniensis inanem
constituam tumulum, nostri solacia luctus,   140
atque addam pia tura focis, manesque ciebo.

of his cruel fate and misfortunes did I, vainly in my delirium, imagine futile dreams: 'I shall dwell in these famous fields; then my Alcon will come hither, forsaking the hills and the unwelcoming rocks, the tainted waters and poisonous nourishment, and he will visit these fair meadows and healthful streams. I shall run to meet him from a long way off and shall be the first to recognise my friend as he approaches; I shall be the first to clasp him in affectionate embraces; our new joys will cause tears of happiness to flow. Thus at last we shall happily enjoy our long wished for conversation, and we shall take pleasure in recounting in turn our great tribulations and harm formerly endured and in listening to them again. Then gradually, as we speak, we shall renew our old loves and amongst pastoral pleasures and the sweet leisure of the countryside while away the time in carefree peace. Ceres loves these fields, Bacchus these ridges, Apollo these pastures, Pales herself provides grass for the flock, milk for the lambs. In these mountains, here and there, the gentle wood-nymphs were accustomed to pursue wild animals, and to pursue their dances. Here the Tiber, rich with the sacred glories of our ancient people, washes the time-honoured ruins, lofty ornaments. Here are woodland shades, here springs, here cool valleys, here the shepherd Corydon sang of his beautiful Alexis. Therefore come, beloved youth: the pastures and rivers await thee, for thee the Nymphs are now weaving garlands of flowers, and declare their delight at thy coming, and the wonder-making earth puts forth fresh flowers for thee!' In my misery, I imagined such fictions, spurred on by a vain hope, unaware that every crime is allowed to the Fates and Death. But after my disappointed prayers had vanished on the light winds and I was not allowed to behold the living features of Alcon, to hear and exchange living words with him, hither at all events, yea, at all events may his shade fly through the air with gentle flight and, taking pity at last on my sorrows, receive my tears and sighs brought forth from the bottom of my heart, and the lamentations echoed by these hollow caves. With my own hands I shall build an empty tomb on this bank of the Anio, as a solace for my grief, and I shall place loyal incense on the altars, and I shall invoke his

vos mecum o pueri beneolentes spargite flores,
narcissum, atque rosas, et suave rubentem hyacinthum,
atque umbras hedera lauroque inducite opacas.
nec desint casiae, permixtaque cinnama amomo,   145
excitet ut dulces aspirans ventus odores.
nos Alcon dilexit multum, et dignus amari
ipse fuit nobis, et tali dignus honore.
interea violas intertexent amaranthis,
et tumulo spargent flores et serta Napaeae,   150
et tumulo maestae inscribent miserabile carmen:
'Alconem postquam rapuerunt impia fata,
conlacrimant duri montes, et consitus atra est
nocte dies; sunt candida nigra, et dulcia amara.'

LXXIII   I. SANNAZARII

Ecloga piscatoria II: Galatea

Forte Lycon vacuo fessus consederat antro
piscator qua se scopuli de vertice lato
ostentat pelago pulcherrima Mergelline.
dumque alii notosque sinus piscosaque circum
aequora conlustrant flammis aut linea longe   5
retia captivosque trahunt ad litora pisces,
ipse per obscuram meditatur carmina noctem:
immitis Galatea, nihil te munera tandem,
nil nostrae movere preces? verba inrita ventis
fudimus et vanas scopulis impegimus undas.   10
aspice, cuncta silent, orcas et maxima cete
somnus habet, tacitae recubant per litora phocae.
non Zephyri strepit aura, sopor suus umida mulcet
aequora, sopito conivent sidera caelo;
solus ego (ei misero) dum tristi pectore questus   15

shade. You boys, come with me and scatter fragrant flowers, narcissus and roses, and the sweetly blushing hyacinth, and create dense shade with ivy and laurel. Nor let there be lacking cassia and cinnamon mingled with amomum, so that the wind, as it breathes on them, may stimulate their sweet perfume. Alcon loved me greatly and himself was worthy of my love and worthy of such an honour. Meanwhile, the wood-nymphs will weave violets together with amaranth and will scatter flowers and wreaths on the tomb, and they in their grief will inscribe these mournful lines on the tomb: 'Since the cursed Fates snatched Alcon away, the unfeeling mountains weep greatly and day has been overcast with black night; white is now black and sweet is now bitter.'

LXXIII   J. SANNAZARO

Piscatory Eclogue II: Galatea

Lycon, to ease the Weariness of Day,
Within his loanly Cave extended lay;
Where on a stately Rock, to seaward, stands
Fair Mergillen', and far the Sea commands:
While other Fishermen, with Blazer try
Each hidden Creek, and tempt the scaly Fry;
Or spread their Nets, or drag to Shore their Prey,
All Night, he meditates this mournful Lay:
Ah! cruel Galatea, why so long!
Deaf to my suit, and heedless of my Song!
Pour I, to Rock and Winds, my Vows in vain!
Sink all my Wishes in the rueful Main!
Now all is hush, now, peaceful Hours prevail,
Soft Slumbers seize the Dolphin, and the Whale;
The drowsy Sea-Calves, in their Cells, are lost,
Scarce breathes a Zephyr o'er the winding Coast;
Smooth is the surface of the mighty Deep,
And the declining Stars retire to Sleep;
I, I alone, in gloomy Shades complain
Of inward Racks, and of tormenting Pain:

nocte itero, somnum tota de mente fugavi,
nec tamen ulla meae tangit te cura salutis.
at non Praxinoe me quondam, non Polybotae
filia despexit, non divitis uxor Amyntae,
quamvis culta sinu, quamvis foret alba papillis.   20
quin etiam Aenaria (si quicquam credis) ab alta
saepe vocor; solet ipsa meas laudare Camenas
in primis formosa Hyale cui sanguis Iberis
clarus avis, cui tot terrae, tot litora parent
quaeque vel in mediis Neptunum torreat undis.   25
sed mihi quid prosunt haec omnia, si tibi tantum
(quis credat, Galatea?) tibi si denique tantum
displiceo? si tu nostram crudelis avenam
sola fugis, sola et nostros contemnis amores?
ostrea Miseni pendentibus eruta saxis   30
mille tibi misi, totidem sub gurgite vasto
Pausilypus, totidem vitreis Euploea sub undis
servat adhuc; plures Nesis mihi servat echinos
quos nec vere novo foliis lentiscus amaris
inficit aut vacuae tenuant dispendia Lunae.   35
praeterea mihi sub pelago manus apta legendis
muricibus; dedici Tyrios cognoscere sucos
quoque modo plena durent conchylia testa.
quid refugis? tingenda tibi iam lana paratur
qua niteas superesque alias, Galatea, puellas,   40
lana maris spumis quae mollior. hanc mihi pastor
ipse olim dedit, hanc pastor Melisaeus, ab alta
cum me forte senex audisset rupe canentem,
et dixit, 'puer, ista tuae sint praemia Musae,
quandoquidem nostra cecinisti primus in acta.'   45

And whilst these Moans, by Night disturb my Breast,
They drive away the very Thoughts of Rest.
Yet, You, the cruel Cause of all my Grief!
Still urge my Passion, yet deny Relief.
Not so in former Times, Praxinoe strove
To cross my Hopes, or check my proffer'd Love;
Not so, Polybota my suit return'd,
Not so, the Wife of Rich Amyntas scorn'd,
Whose snowy Breasts, and Swan like Neck might vie
With downy Jove descending from the Sky.
   Oft am I call'd from Ischia's rocky Brow,
If ought I say, may be believ'd by you;
My melting Lays fair Hyale commends,
Who from Iberia's ample Realm descends,
Whom distant Lands, and different Isles obey,
Westward from Gades, and the mighty Sea.
But what avail a thousand Loves like these,
If I, my Galatea still displease?
If you, relentless, from my Musick fly,
Sport when I weep, and triumph when I sigh?
To you, a thousand Oysters I present,
Deep from Mysenus' rocky Caverns, rent;
A thousand too, fair Pausilipe sends,
Euploea's Shore another share commends.
I've store of Cray-Fish, Nesis' chief Renown,
Untoucht by Mastick, or the waning Moon.
Well can these Hands the deepest Seas explore,
And gather Shell-fish from the rocky Store;
I know the Fish that gives the Tyrian Juice,
And know to save the Dye, for future Use.
Why flies my Fair? for thee my Fingers cull,
And stain, with purest Dye, the richest Wooll,
Softer than Foam just rising from the Sea,
This Melissaeus gave, long since, to me;
When, from a pointed Rock, he heard me play,
The hoary Shepherd was observed to say,
Take this, the Prize of thy victorious Lay;
Since Thou, the first of all our youths, hast strove
To touch the Pipe, and tune thy Notes of Love;

ex illo in calathis servavi, ut mittere possem.
sed tu (ne qua mihi superet spes, ne qua futuri
condicio, Galatea) manum mihi dura negasti.
hoc est, hoc, miserum, quod perdidit. ite Camenae,
ite procul, sprevit nostras Galatea querelas.   50
scilicet (exiguae videor quod navita cymbae,
quodque leves hamos nodosaque retia tracto)
despicis. an patrio non hoc quoque litore Glaucus
fecerat, aequoreae Glaucus scrutator harenae?
et nunc ille quidem tumidarum numen aquarum.   55
sed nec (quae nimium vel me sic falsa fatigat)
fabula te moveat Lydae, licet illa puellis
iactet nescio quas mihi se misisse corollas;
non me Lyda tamen, non impulit aequora testor
Nereidasque omnes. si fallo, naufragus illas   60
experiar salsosque bibam sub gurgite fluctus.
heu quid agam? externas trans pontum quaerere terras
iam pridem est animus. quo numquam navita, numquam
piscator veniat; fors illic nostra licebit
fata queri. boreae extremo damnata sub axe   65
stagna petam et rigidis numquam non cana pruinis
an Libyae rapidas austrique tepentis harenas,
et videam nigros populos solemque propinquum?
quid loquor infelix? an non per saxa, per ignes,
quo me cumque pedes ducent, mens aegra sequetur?   70
vitantur venti, pluviae vitantur et aestus,
non vitatur amor; mecum tumuletur oportet
iam saxo meme ex illo demittere in undas
praecipitem iubet ipse furor. vos o mihi Nymphae,
vos maris undisoni Nymphae, praestate cadenti   75

The Prize, in Basketts stor'd, I now prepare
To send, a grateful offering, to my Fair.
But you, lest such a Favour should impart
Some secret Hope to my desponding Heart,
Refuse my Gift: Hence, hence! all earthly Joys!
This, this alone a wretched Youth destroys!
Away my Pipe! my rural Strains, away!
Fair Galatea scorns my mournful Lay.
Shun you my Suit, because my Boat's so mean?
Or Nets and Hooks, in these harsh Hands, are seen?
Once a poor Fisherman, in quest of Gain,
But now, the mighty Ruler of the Main.

   Be not with Lyda's idle Tales possest,
Tales! which, however false, disturb'd my Rest:
Still let her boast (if you from Fears are free)
Corals, and God knows what, convey'd to me;
Yet ne'er could Lyda my Affections move,
Witness, yee Waves, if I inclin'd to Love!
Witness, ye Nymphs, if I the Truth deny,
Shipwreck'd, your watry Vengeance let my try,
And in some Eddy, feast the scaly Fry.

   Oh! whither shall I fly? I've long design'd,
Beyond the Seas some foreign Shore to find,
Where never Fisherman, nor Sailor came,
And there, in briny Tears, bewail my Flame?
Say, shall I steer to Zembla's distant Coast,
Doom'd to thick Darkness, and eternal Frost?
Or Southern Shores, and Lybia's burning Sand,
And view black Nations, and a barren Land?
Wretch that I am! Condemn'd to lasting Love,
Thro' seas, thro' Fires, o'er rising Hills of Snow,
Where'er my weary Feet a Passage find,
I'm still pursu'd by a distemper'd Mind;
Winds may be shun'd, and Rains, and scorching Heat,
From Love alone, no Mortal can retreat.

   Now from this Rock, my Frenzy bids me leap,
And drown my Sorrows in the raging Deep,
But oh! each azure Goddess of the Main!
Ye Nymphs and Nereids! all, attend your Swain;

non duros obitus saevasque exstinguite flammas.
scilicet haec olim, veniens seu litore curvo
Caietae, seu Cumarum navalibus altis,
dum loca transibit, raucus de puppe magister
hortatus socios 'dextrum deflectite' dicet   80
'in latus, o socii, dextras deflectite in undas;
vitemus scopulos infames morte Lyconis!'
talia nequiquam surdas iactabat ad auras
infelix piscator et inrita vota fovebat,
cum tandem extremo veniens effulsit ab ortu   85
Lucifer et roseo perfudit lumine pontum.

LXXIV   GEORGII BUCHANANI

Silva II: Desiderium Ptolemaei Luxii Tastaei

Usque adeo patrii sordet tibi ripa Garumnae,
Pictones ut scopulos, atque horrida tesqua frutetis
durus ames? nec te socium pecorisque larisque
cura tenet, nec quam sociis pecorique larique
praetuleras; cui saepe rosas, cui saepe solebas   5
pallida cum niveis vaccinia ferre ligustris:
quam tu sideribus, quam tu componere soli
ausus eras: cuius nitidis radiantia gemmis
sola tibi purum fundebant lumina lumen.
nunc tamen (heu numquam constans in amore voluptas!)   10
tu procul hinc steriles rupes colis immemor Agrii
Vasconicique gregis, Nymphaeque oblitus amatae:

Let not poor Lycon unregarded die,
Nor may my Flames in long Oblivion lie.
  So, down to latest Times, as Ships explore
Cuma's high cliffs, or Baia's winding shore,
When they too nigh these fatal Shallows fall,
Then the hoarse Master, from the Deck, shall call:
Haste, Sailors! haste! your Course to Sea-ward bend;
Sheer off, ye Winds, our swelling Sails befriend,
To shun the Rocks, defam'd by Lycon's End.
Thus, did the Wretch pour forth his Moans in vain,
To senseless Winds, and sooth'd his raging Pain:
Till Morn, at length, the happy Land survey'd,
And, o'er the Waves, her purple Wings display'd.

LXXIV   GEORGE BUCHANAN

Silva II: Agrius

Still do Garumna's shores offend thine Eye?
Still must thy native Climes neglected lie?
Still do Pictonian Prospects please thy Taste?
Her rocky Mountains, and her barren Waste?
Nor can the Fields, nor can thy downy Rest,
Nor Flocks, nor Folds, nor Swains, engage thy Breast?
Nor ev'n the Nymph, whose charmes, alone, controul'd
The Flocks, the Shepherds, and the fleecy Fold;
To grace whose beauteous Bosom, you have chose
The snowy Privet, and the purple Rose?
  Her Eyes, in Raptures, you would oft compare
To Sol's bright Rays, or to the Morning Star,
Whose radiant Beams, with generous Love inspir'd
Struck thro' the Soul, and all the Senses fir'd.
But now alas! (for so the Fates ordain,
Lest long the Pleasures of our Lives should reign)
You, far from hence, thro' sandy Desarts stray,
When rugged Rocks their hoary Heads display,
Heedless of Flocks, on fair Vasconia's Plain,
Leave the sad Nymph, and the lamenting Strain;

forsitan et stupidas bona carmina perdis ad aures.
interea nostris pastoria fistula silvis
muta silet, mutae pecudes, mutaeque volucres,   15
nec strepit adsueto Zephyri levis aura susurro.
noctua successit philomelae, et acanthidi bubo,
strixque nocens pueris, et tristis ad omina cornix,
raucaque flumineae recinunt convicia ranae.
sicubi fausta sedet volucris, non gutture laeto   20
mulcet agros, non in tractus lasciva volatu
emicat aërios, tristi sed murmure maestum
et lugubre sonans sedet in dumis desertis
abdita, turbatis deformis et horrida pennis.
ipse ego cum calamos maesti solacia luctus   25
sumere tentarem, crudumque levare dolorem
carmine, vix primis admoram labra cicutis,
sive fuit casus, seu (quo magis auguror) omen,
et mala quae mentem numquam praesagia fallunt,
flebile raucisonae responsavere cicutae.   30
ipsae etiam in tumidis Nymphae Oceanitides undis,
ipsae etiam in placidis Nymphae Dordonides antris,
ipsi etiam montes, ipsae etiam convalles
auditae longas per noctem iterare querelas.
sed neque te tantum, quamquam te flumina lugent,   35
nec tantum Nymphae, silvae, volucresque feraeque,
quantum te in solis solus gemit Agrius antris.
illum ego congressusque hominum et consortia tecta

And now your sweetest Notes, perhaps, are lost
In empty Air, on some forsaken Coast.
Mean while, our Woods no rural Strains salute,
The Flocks, the Shepherds, and the Birds are mute;
The lagging Zephyrs scarcely seem to breathe,
Nor, to these Shores, their spicy Gales bequeath;
The frightful Bird of Night alarms the Throng,
Where Philomela tun'd her midnight Song;
The Bittern mourns in ev'ry marshy Pool,
In Woods the Raven, and the screaming Owl;
From muddy Lakes the Frogs extend their Throats,
Deaf'ning the Shepherds with their hoarser Notes.
If, in the Groves, some tuneful Bird remain,
No more he warbles forth his wonted Strain;
No more the Race, which in the Woods reside,
The liquid Air with wanton Wings divide;
But each, in loud Complaints and bitter Moans,
Thro' solitary Scenes, relentless groans;
Or, screen'd from Sight, where gloomy Thickets rise,
From Bough to Bough, with lazy Pinions flies.
    Even I, myself, when first I strove to play,
And touch'd the Reed to chase dull cares away,
When, with my Strains, I sought to ease my Grief,
The only Hope I had known of Relief,
Scarcely the Sound could reach my list'ning Ear,
But, on Mischance, or, what I rather fear,
Some dreadful Omen was by Fates design'd,
And dire Events foreboding Omens find.
For in like Sounds the Grasshoppers complain'd,
And their hoarse Throats to mournful accents strain'd;
The Sister Nereids in the swelling Waves,
And the fair Dryads in Dodona's Caves,
The very Mountains, and the Valleys groan'd,
And oft, by Night, my bitter Fates bemoan'd;
But though the Rivers, and the Groves lament,
Tho' Nymphs, and Birds, and Flocks their Passions vent,
Not all their Tears such melting Anguish show,
As weeping Agrius in his Grott below.
Him, from the Towns and buisy Crowds withdrawn,

vitantem, tacitae per muta silentia silvae
dum sequor, et voces capto, et vestigia servo,   40
haec memini maesta convicia fundere lingua.
   Pictones o scopuli, et nudis impervia saxis
culmina, et exiguae male pinguis culta Crotellae,
quaeque paris raras tantum silva horrida glandes,
ah! quibus infames magicis in collibus herbas   45
gignitis? Aeaei quae vis occulta veneni
hinc procul in vestris Ptolemaeum detinet oris?
certe ibi purpureis non lotos aquatica baccis,
quae tenuit socios tarde redeuntis Ulyssei,
non Cereri lustratus ager, non commoda bubus   50
pascua, non virides generoso palmite colles,
qualia Vasconicae felicia iugera glebae.
ceteraque ut constent, non quae dedit ubera primum
hic genetrix, non quod tua primum infantia caelum
hausit, et infirmis pulsus vagitibus aër,   55
reptatumque solum puero: non falce notata
silva sub hirsuto servat tua carmina libro,
carmina nequicquam memorem spondentia mentem.
quid tamen hoc prodest, patrii quod ripa Garumnae
et viridis frondes, et amoenam in frondibus umbram   60
praebeat, et primas meditanti carmina cannas
prima tibi dederit, si tu non tangeris istis?
at te si capiunt inamoeno robore colles,
quodque per incultas arescit gramen harenas,
raraque quae canis languet vindemia saxis,   65
ipse suas vites, sua pinguia culta Garumna
oderit, et nulla redimitus harundine frontem
in mare per steriles lente prorepet harenas.
quid precer, o silvae, vobis, quid saxa, quid undae?

And to the silent Woods retir'd alone,
Whilst I, with Sighs and inward Sorrows, view'd,
Caught at his Words, and with swift Steps pursu'd,
Those deep Reflections I remember well,
From his pale Lips, in broken Accents fell.
   O Rocks! O Cliffs! O dire Pictonian Rills!
Ye hoary Valleys! Ye exalted Hills!
Ye blasted Woods! To you a Shepherd calls!
Ye barren Fields, around Crotella's Walls!
Alas! what Magick Herbs your Meads produce!
What secret Poysons! What infernal Juice!
What Force, what Art, what everlasting Chain,
In these dire Coasts my Ptolomy detain?
There with its purple Fruit, no Lotos grows,
Which lull'd Ulysses' Mates to long repose;
No Fields rejoice with Loads of waving Corn,
No Flocks, like ours, these barren Plains adorn;
Nor are thy Mates, nor is thy Parent there,
Who fed and nurs'd thee with a tender Care:
Thy blooming Years more wholsome Breezes drew,
A richer Soil thy native Country knew:
Still, in a verdant Grove, the Verses stand,
Grav'd in the Bark by the auspicious Hand,
Lines, which their Author's early worth explain,
Yet promise an Eternity in vain.
   But what avail thy far Garumna's Shores,
Her greenwood Shades, and her delicious Bowers:
If Thee, Pictonia's rugged Wilds command
To live a stranger, in a foreign Land?
But if those Hills, with blasted Oaks, invite,
Yet bleak Heaths, and barren Sands delight,
If still the slender Vintage suits thy Eyes,
Where craggy Cliffs, and rocky Prospects rise,
No more will Agrius then his Vines admire,
But from Garumna's fruitful Fields retire,
Tear the fresh Garland from his youthful Brows,
Nor scorching Sands, nor swelling Seas refuse.
But why should I of Sylvan Shades complain,
Of Rocks of Mountains, or the raging Main?

quid campis precer, et pecori, pecorisque magistris,   70
quos mihi, quos patriae Ptolemaeus praetulit orae?
silva neget glandes, et Bacchi munera colles,
torreat arva sitis, scabies pecus, atra magistros
pestis et insani perimant contagia morbi,
sospite Tastaeo patriaeque mihique sibique,   75
immemor ut visat memores invitus amicos.
Ei mihi! quid silvae et campi, quid saxa, quid undae?
quid pecus, et pecoris quid commeruere magistri?
haec ego devoveam, patriis quae praetulit arvis
pascua Tastaeus? piget, et mea vota retracto: 80
rursus et iratae linguae maledicta recanto.
   glande nemus, fetu pecus, uva vitis abundet,
puraque perspicuis manet de fontibus unda,
pabula dent campi, silvae pastoribus umbras,
sub quibus arguta carmen modulentur avena.   85
quae te cumque tenet tellus, quaecumque tenebit;
sive per aestiferas Libyae sitientis harenas
pastor ages pecudes, Boreae seu iuncta nivali
rura coles, Libycum Boreas riget imbribus axem,
et rigor Arctous tepido mitescat ab Austro;   90
et quacumque feres gressus, tibi balsama sudet
quercus, mella rubis, tribulisque legatur amomum;
dum neque terra ferax mellis, neque dives amomo
esse tibi patrio videatur amicior arvo.
me miserum! quid vana queror? procul ille remotis   95
saltibus externos forsan suspirat amores.
at vos o venti, tuque o pulsata querelis

Why Flocks, or Fields, or rural Scenes implore
Again my roving Shepherd to restore?
Which he prefers in wandring Wishes lost,
To me, his Phyllis, and his native Coast.
   Let Oaks their Fruits, and Hills their Wines withhold,
Droughts parch the Fields, and Murrains seize the Fold,
Each trembling Swain a dire Infection dread,
And sweeping Plagues around their Poysons spread,
If my Tastaeus, from the Dangers free,
Tho' heedless of his Country, or of Me,
Again to these inviting Realms return,
Which grieve his Loss, and his long Absence mourn.
   Why should my Rage to Fields and Woods extend?
How could the Shepherds, and their Flocks offend?
Why should I choose to curse the Climes unknown,
Which, heedless, he prefers before his own?
Ev'n now I'm sorry and retract my Vows,
And curb the Railings of a headstrong Muse:
May Woods their Fruits, the Vines their Grapes bestow,
And limpid Streams from Crystal Fountains flow.
Fields lend their Grass, the Groves their wonted Shade,
And rural Strains resound from every Glade.
   Where-e'er Thou art, or shalt for ever stray,
If, as a Swain, thy wandring Steps survey
The burning Sands of Lybia's thirsty Plain,
Or Icy Realms beneath the rigid Wain,
Thro' Lybian Climes may Northern Showers be sent,
And Icy Realms by southern Gales relent;
What Paths so'er thy weary Feet shall fill,,
From their rough Oaks may sov'reign Balm distil,
From humble Shrubs the choicest Honey flow,
And barren Heaths the Myrtle Wreath bestow;
Since Realms devoid of Honey, Balm, or Oyl,
Seem still more pleasing than my Native Soil.
   Wretch that I am! Why should I still renew
My moving Moans, and still my Swain pursue?
He, far from hence, perhaps, in foreign Groves,
Breathes forth in Sorrows his successless Loves.
But, O ye Winds! ye Zephyrs! send Relief,

aura meis totiens, et amari conscia luctus
partem aliquam duras Ptolemaei perfer ad aures.
ille licet scopulis (quod non puto) durior ipsis   100
fiat, et antiqui (quod nolim) oblitus amici,
cum tamen audierit gemitus, moturaque rupes
verba mei luctus, nostro ingemet ille dolori,
dicet et, hic nostrae fuit admirator avenae.
   plura locuturo vultum sub nube recondens   105
tristior occiduas Phoebus descendit in undas.

Mov'd by my Sighs, and conscious of my Grief,
Some Part, at least, of these Petitions bear
To my Tastaeus' unattending Ear.
　He, tho' forgetful of his rural Swain,
Tho' deaf as Rocks, remorseless as the Main,
Yet, when my Moans his rugged Heights ascend,
My piteous Moans which Rocks themselves might rend,
He, at the melting Sound, will sigh and say,
This was a Lover of my mournful Lay.
More he'd have sung, but Phoebus seem'd to shroud
His setting beams behind a Western Cloud.

Notes

Two sources of English translations are referred to here by abbreviations: Kendall and *Sales Epigrammatum*. See above, Select List of Neo-latin Anthologies, p. 15, for the full description under 1577 and 1663 respectively. For the *Delitiae delitiarum* which reprints some of the Jesuit poems quoted here, see the same list under 1637.

I   Poliziano, Angelo (1454–94). His family name was Ambrogini; he studied under Ficino and Landini in Florence, where Lorenzo dei Medici soon took him under his wing. He attained great distinction as a classical scholar; but his poetical output in Latin——he also wrote in Greek and the vernacular——is confined to a few elegies, silvae, odes and considerable number of epigrams, many written to his patron. These helped to set an example for later epigrammatists.

See: I. del Lungo, *Florentia, uomini e cose del quattrocento*, Florence, 1897; Ida Maïer, *Ange Politien, la formation d'un poète humaniste, 1469–1480*, Geneva, 1966.

Source: *Opera*, Lyon, S. Gryphius, tome II, 1528, 574. Modern edition: I. del Lungo (ed.), *Prose volgari inedite e poesie latine e greche edite ed inedite di A. Ambrogini Poliziano*, Florence, 1867.

The practice of extempore verse is very common among humanists of all countries. It is often popular in poetic circles and may form a substantial part of collective volumes.

II   Strozzi, Tito (*c.* 1425–1505). Of Florentine origin, he was born in Ferrara where he rose to high office under Ercole I. A humanist of wide range, he is now remembered for his six books of elegies and four books of miscellaneous verse which also mirror his political involvement. His son Ercole (1475–1508) showed great promise as a Latin poet, but was murdered, for political reasons, shortly after his marriage.

See: A. della Guardia, *Tito Vespasiano Strozzi. Poesie latine tratte dall'Aldina e confrontate con i codici*, Modena, 1916; Walter Ludwig, *Die Borsias des Tito Strozzi, ein lateinisches Epos der Renaissance*, Munich, 1977 (this epic is published here for the first time).

Source: *Strozzii Poetae pater et filius*, [Venice], Aldus, (1533), second part, separately foliated, fol. 146*r*. Transl.: Kendall, fol. 48*v*.

6 Fabricius, Roman commander famed for his sober style of life.

III   Pontano, Giovanni Giovano (1426–1503). Born in Cerruto, he soon entered the service of King Alfonso and then of Ferdinand I of Naples, to whose son he became tutor. He enjoyed a prominent political and diplomatic reputation; he also became the leading member of the Academy. When the French invaded Naples, he changed sides so that, with the return of the house of Aragon to power, he retired into political obscurity. His Latin verse, of considerable distinction, ranges from love poetry—to Fannia first, later to his wife—to scientific verse; and his humanist interests were equally wide-ranging. His poetry sets models that were to be followed by later writers throughout Europe; here there is not space to show his talents in all the genres in which he excelled.

See: A. Altamura, *L'umanesimo nel mezzogiorno d'Italia*, Florence, 1941; F. Arnaldi, 'Rileggendo i carmi di Pontano', *Atti dell' Accademia Pontaniana*, n.s. I (1948), 55 ff.; E. Percopo, *Vita di Giovanni Pontano*, Naples, 1938.

Source: *Opera poetica*, Venice, Aldus, vol. I, 1518, fol. 88*r-v*. There are modern editions of the Latin poems by B. Soldati, Florence, 1902 and J. Oeschger, Bari, 1948. Note the dialogue form. For convenience, the speakers are clearly shown here.

IV   Source: *ibid.*, I, fol. 85*r*. Many humanists will compose mock-epitaphs of this nature in which word-play is a key device.

V   Source: *ibid.*, II (1533), fol. 234*v*.

VI   Castiglione, Baldassare (1478–1529). Of Spanish origin, but born in Mantua, he had a distinguished career as a diplomat, serving the duke of Urbino and later the Pope. In 1506 he visited England. He became a naturalised Italian and was appointed bishop of Avila. His fame rests chiefly on *The Courtier*, but he was also an accomplished Latin poet read with profit by Milton among others.

See: Walther Schrinner, *Castiglione und die englische Renaissance*. Berlin, 1939.

Source: *Carminum quinque illustrium poetarum*, Venice, 1558, fol. 42*r*. Transl.: T. Heywood, *Pleasant Dialogues . . .*, 279.

VII Flaminio, Marcantonio (1498–1550). The son of a Latin poet, Joannes Attonius, he soon came under the influence of Castiglione; in due course he saw service under various prelates and especially Leo X. He accompanied Cardinal Reginald Pole to the Council of Trent. His travels brought him into contact with the leading Latin poets of Verona, Rome and Naples; and he distinguished himself in the field of nature poetry (with strong mythological harmonics) and of the pastoral, but his fame extends to his religious verse, including psalm paraphrases, and in which some have detected evangelical leanings. His poetry found favour with the circle of Marguerite de France; his paraphrases were frequently reprinted with those of Buchanan.

See: Carol Maddison, *Marcantonio Flaminio: poet, humanist and reformer*, London, 1965.

Source: *Carminum libri IIII . . .*, Florence, 1552, 237.

VIII Vitalis, Ianus (1485–*c.* 1560). Of Sicilian origin, Vitalis first emerged as an encomiastic poet; much of his writing reveals a strong patriotic vein. A fairly prolific author, he is remembered almost exclusively for the following poem on Rome, first published in 1552 and imitated or translated by poets including Du Bellay in his *Antiquitez*. It contributed to the current of verse concerned with the ruins of the past, a current that has medieval ancestry.

See: G. Tumminello, 'Giano Vitale, umanista del secolo XVI', *Archivo storico siciliano*, n.s. VIII (1883), fasc. 1–2; Roland Mortier, *La poétique des ruines en France*, Geneva, 1974, 46–59. Edmund Spenser translated Du Bellay's version (1569).

Source: *Theodori Bezae Vezelii poematum editio secunda*, [Geneva], 1569, second part (separately paginated), 191–2. Transl.: Thomas Heywood, *The Hierarchie of the Blessed Angells*, London, 1637, 459. See Malcolm Smith, 'Looking for Rome in Rome: Janus Vitalis and his disciples', *Revue*

> *de Littérature Comparée* LI (1977), 510–27. Early printings
> show a number of variants (e.g. l. 9).

IX   Sannazaro, Jacopo (Actius Syncerus) (1458–1530). Was
closely associated with the rulers of Naples, notably Alfonso
duke of Calabria and Frederic II; after the fall of the house of
Aragon, he went into exile (1501–4) in France. He was a firm
friend of Pontano and after the latter's death became the leader
of the Accademia Pontaniana. His fame rests chiefly on the
Arcadia, but his verse and especially his piscatory eclogues
were famous throughout Western Europe, as was the pastoral
poem *Salices*. His religious poetry (e.g. the *De partu virginis*)
enjoyed respect during the Counter-reformation.

    See: A. Altamura, *Giacopo Sannazaro*, Naples, 1934.

    Source: *Opera omnia*, Venice, Aldus, 1535, fol. 38*v*. Transl.:
Thomas Heywood, *Pleasant Dialogues and Dramma's*,
London, 1637, 274–5. See also Roland Mortier, *op. cit.*,
39–41.

    3 The phrase *Tarpeias Iuppiter arces* occurs in Ovid, *Metam.*,
xv, 866. The reference is to the Capitoline Hill in Rome.

X   Navagero, Andrea (Naugerius) (1483–1529). Born in Venice,
Navagero enjoyed a distinguished career as scholar, diplomat
and poet. He studied in Padua and, under Sabellicus, in
Venice. He learned Greek from Marcus Musurus; among his
friends he counted Fracastor, Bembo, Castiglione and the
painter Raphael. In Venice he was closely associated with
Aldus Manutius' scholarly printings, became librarian of St
Mark's (1516) and spent much of the last ten years of his life
on ambassadorial missions, particularly in Spain. He died
suddenly in Blois whither he had been sent on official business.
His *Lusus*, collected posthumously by admiring friends, have
their niche in European literature. They were first published in
1530 (Venice) and soon found their way into Neo-latin
anthologies. The 1718 edition, by G. A. Volpi, with ancillary
material, is still worth consulting.

    See: *Andrea Navagero: Lusus*. Text and translation, ed. with
an introduction and a critical commentary by Alice E.
Wilson, Nieuwkoop, 1973.

    Source: *Doctissimorum nostra aetate Italorum Epigrammata*,
Paris [?1546], fol. 40*v*–41*r*. Navagero's *Lusus* did much to
popularise the *votum*, which Du Bellay adapted to the
French vernacular.

XI   Source: *ibid.*, fol. 44*r*. A very popular poem, translated into
various languages. In England Thomas Lodge provided a
version. See J. G. Fucilla, 'Navagero's De Cupidine et

Hyella', *Philological Quarterly* XVII (1938), fasc. 3, 288–96.

XII   Alciat, Andrea (1492–1550). Born near Milan, Alciat studied in that town and later at Pavia and Bologna, taking his doctorate of laws in 1514. He taught law at Avignon (1518–21) and after troubled years in Italy went to Bourges where he taught 1529–33. He returned home to a chair at Pavia, but before his death taught at Bologna and Ferrara. In 1531 he brought out his *Emblemata*, which went through many editions (with added material and commentaries) and exercised an European influence, both developing emblematic literature and boosting gnomic and iconic verse.

See: Henry Green, *Andrea Alciati and his book of emblems*, London, 1872; P. E. Viard, *André Alciat 1492–1550*, Bordeaux, 1926; Mario Praz, *Studies in seventeenth-century imagery*, 2 vols. London, 1939–47.

Source: *Emblemata*, Lyon, G. Rouillé, 1551, p. 224. Transl.: *Sales Epigrammatum*, 62.

XIII   Cordus Euricius (1486–1535). Born in the Hesse, he studied at Erfurt, where he taught for a time before going on to Kassel. He then moved on to Italy where he studied medicine at Ferrara, and on returning home, taught the subject at Bremen. A friend of Eobanus Hessus and Camerarius, he acquired a high reputation as a scholar and doctor; he also left a name for himself as a Latin poet (eclogues and epigrams); his Muse was strongly in the service of his fervent Lutheranism. His Epigrams first appeared at Erfurt in 1517.

See: K. Krause, *Euricius Cordus. Eine biographische Skizze aus der Reformationszeit*, Hanau, 1863.

Source: *Opera poetica omnia*, n.p., n.d., fol. 122*v*. The epigrams were edited by K. Krause in 1892, Berlin. Cordus tilts at various targets of the Reformers, who complained not only of the interval between priestly rule and practice but also of the whole concept of celibacy. Here Cordus uses terms from Ecclesiastical Latin.

XIV   Source: *ibid.*, fol. 201*r*.

XV   Bourbon, Nicolas (1503–after 1551). Born at Vandoeuvre, he was a precocious versifier, writing a poem on his father's forge by the age of fourteen. In the 1520s he was studying under Toussaint and others in Paris, where he learned Greek and was exposed to evangelical currents. He taught in various towns, especially Troyes, and later became tutor to Jeanne d'Albret. His poetry shows the influence of the Greek Anthology, of

Italian humanism and Petrarchism. His *Nugae*, first published in 1533, brought him into trouble with the Sorbonne and he was put in prison until he recanted under rather humiliating circumstances. He went off to England for a spell and was tutor to the sons of some noblemen at the court of Anne Boleyn. In the mid–1530s he was closely associated with the Lyon *sodalitium* and in 1538 published the second, augmented edition of the *Nugae*, which tell us a good deal about his time in England and are more prudent in religious matters. Bourbon published a number of pedagogic works, but faded out during the 1540s, though he composed some verse to celebrate the new reign of Henri II. Marguerite de Navarre procured for him a benefice at Candé; the last we hear of him is contributing a poem to her second *tombeau* (1551). He can write well in the field of amatory, satirical and religious verse.

See: G. Carré, *De Vita et scriptis Nicolai Borbonii Vandoperani*, Paris, 1888.

Source: *Nugarum libri octo*, Lyons, 1538, 80–1.

XVI   Source: *ibid*., 338. Holbein drew Bourbon's portrait during his sojourn at the English court; it is preserved in Windsor Castle and reproduced in L. Febvre, *Le Problème de l'incroyance au XVIe siècle—la religion de Rabelais*, Paris, 1942, facing p. 25.

4 It was a humanist commonplace to compare contemporary artists to Apelles, a famous Greek painter who lived in the fourth century B.C.

XVII   Bèze, Théodore de (1519–1605). Born at Vézelay, he was brought up by his uncle who knew Melchior Wolmar, the German reformer; hence his study at Bourges before proceeding to Orléans to take his law degree. In 1539 he moved to Paris, where he mingled in humanist circles and published his *Poemata* (1548) shortly before he departed for Lausanne. His *Abraham sacrifiant* was published in 1550 and three years later his French psalm paraphrases. In 1559 he became a minister of the city of Geneva, attended the Colloque de Poissy in 1561 and after Calvin's death was head of the Protestant Church 1564–80. Thereafter he led a more retired life and died in 1605. He was a man of immense scholarship—in 1549 he had been appointed professor of Greek at Lausanne—and he continued to compose Latin verse throughout his life. His *juvenilia* achieved widespread fame in the sixteenth century, though later editions of his poems seek to reduce or destroy verse that was contrary to Protestant principles. His youthful poetry is reprinted in the eighteenth century.

See: P. F. Geisendorf, *Théodore de Bèze*, Geneva, 1949; Ann Lake Prescott, 'English Writers and Beza's Latin Epigrams: the uses and abuses of Poetry', *Studies in the Renaissance* XXI (1974), 83–117.

Source: *Poematum editio secunda*, Geneva, 1569, pp. 160–1. This is an acknowledged imitation of one of his friend George Buchanan's *Fratres* (publ. 1566), *Pistoris et Pictoris dialogismus*. The contrast-model goes back to the *Greek Anthology*, XI, 233 (Lucilius). Transl.: Kendall, 74r–v.

XVIII Source: *Poemata*, 1548, 68. The poem is slightly modified in 1569 (editio secunda), 173 to become *Religio*. The general pattern, apart from the subject obviously, follows Buchanan's *Amor* (see below, XLIII). Transl.: L. R. Merrill, *The Life and Poems of Nicholas Grimald*, New Haven-London, 1925, p. 389.

XIX Du Bellay, Joachim (1522–60). Studied law at Poitiers, came to know Peletier du Mans in 1546 and Ronsard at the Collège de Coqueret in 1547. He wrote the *Deffence et illustration* in 1549 and was a leading member of the Brigade (later the Pléiade). He was in Rome 1553–7 where he wrote his *Regrets* and *Antiquitez* (in great part), and also his *Poemata* (1558). It is interesting to compare his treatment of certain themes in Latin and the vernacular; a friend of Buchanan's, he translated some of the Scotsman's verse, and there are thematic parallels in their writings.

See: H. Chamard, *Joachim du Bellay 1522–1560*, Lille, 1900; V. L. Saulnier, *Joachim du Bellay, l'homme et l'oeuvre*, Paris, 1951; G. Dickinson, *Du Bellay in Rome*, Leiden, 1962. There is an unpublished thesis on Du Bellay's Latin poetry by Dr George Sutherland (Paris, 1954).

Source: *Poematum libri quattuor*, Paris, 1558, fol. 148r (see also E. Courbet's uncritical ed. of the *Poésies françaises et latines*, 2 vols., Paris, 1918). Transl.: *Sales Epigrammatum*, 57.

XX Dorat, Jean (*c.* 1508–88). Born in the Limousin, he went to Paris, it is thought, *c.* 1540; later he taught J.-A. Baïf and became principal of Coqueret, where he influenced the future members of the Pléiade; only recently have notes on his lectures on Pindar been discovered (by Dr Peter Sharratt of Edinburgh). In 1553 he was appointed tutor to the duc d'Angoulême. In 1556 he became a royal reader (in Greek), a post which he was to relinquish in 1567 in favour of his son-in-law Nicolas Goulu. He was made *poeta regius* in the mid-1560s—the Latin counterpart of Ronsard. He married Marguerite de Laval in 1548, and after her death, Mlle Chippart, the poetic licence of an elderly scholar. His contributions to classical studies are only now coming to be understood; he was also a prolific poet in French, Latin and sometimes Greek. His work is rather uninspiring, but he is important as an accomplished court poet. Many of his poems were published in volume form shortly before his death, but the edition is a careless one.

See: P. de Nolhac, *Ronsard et l'humanisme*, Paris, 1921; J. Robiquet, *De Ioannis Aurati poetae regii vita et latine scriptis poematibus*, Paris, 1887. This carious work will shortly be superseded by Mme Geneviève Demerson's state thesis on the humanist's Latin poetry,

Source: *Poematia*, Paris, 1586, part II (separately paginated), 42. Transl.: *Sales Epigrammatum*, 54–5.

XXI   Bauhusius, Bernardus (van Bauhuysen) (1575–1619). Born at Antwerp, he entered the Jesuit order at the age of sixteen and in the course of time became a noted preacher. He later taught at the Jesuit college in Burgos. His *Epigrammatum libri V* (Antwerp, 1616) were reprinted on a number of occasions.

Source: Erycius Puteanus, *Pietatis thaumata ...*, Antwerp, 1617. This monostich, it appears, is capable of being rearranged 1022 times, without impairing the sense or the rhythm. The total number of stars was estimated by Ptolemy to be 1022: see A. D. S. Fowler, *Spenser and the Numbers of Time* (London, 1964), pp. 237–8.

XXII   Benedicti, George (1563–88). Was born in Harlem; he spent some time in England and was at Cambridge at one period. He died too early to fulfil his promise. His poems may be read in the *Delitiae Poetarum Belgicorum*; he is one of a number of Dutch humanists who write encomiastic verse on Elizabeth and prominent figures at her court. A paper on this humanist was given at the Third Congress (Tours) of the International Association for Neo-latin studies in 1976 by Marc de Schepper. On the relations between various Leiden poets and the English court *c.* 1585, see J. A. Van Dorsten, *Poets, Patrons and Professors. Sir Philip Sidney, Daniel Rogers and the Leiden humanists*, Leiden-London, 1962, (for Benedicti, see 80–81 and 162–63). Not all these poets can be represented here.

Source: *Delitiae Poetarum Belgicorum*, I, 534. This is one of a series of eighteen poems composed by Benedicti on Sidney's death.

XXIII Catsius, Jacobus (Kats) (1577–1660). Studied at Leiden; he became involved in political issues rather late in life, and among other duties was entrusted with a mission to Charles I, which resulted in his being knighted. He wrote poetry in Latin and the vernacular; his racy, rough, though prosaic writing was exceedingly popular with the Calvinists. His contribution lies in the gnomic and emblematic tradition more particularly.
See: G. Kalff, *Jakob Kats*, 1901.
Source: T. Heywood, *The Hierarchie of the Blessed Angells*, London, 1637, 555 (with translation). Heywood includes several poems by Kats in his two anthologies.

XXIV Posthius, Joannes (1537–97). Studied in Heidelberg, Italy and France and then practised as a doctor in Antwerp. In 1568 he was appointed physician to the bishop of Würzburg and later to the Elector Frederick IV at Mainz. His *Parerga poetica* first appeared at Würzburg in 1580 and were reprinted later.
Source: *Delitiae Poetarum Germanorum*, V, 193. Tobacco is a subject treated by various poets, the most extended composition being by J. Thorius.

XXV On Politian see poem I.
Source: *Opera*, Lyon, 1528, 598. Transl.: Kendall, fol. 38*v*–39*r*.
With its development of contraries, dependent in part on the Petrarchan tradition, this type of love poem becomes widespread.
4 Tantalus was punished by Jupiter for divulging divine secrets and sent to the nether regions where he stood in water with a fruit-tree above his head; both receded when he tried to eat or drink.

XXVI On Strozzi, see poem II.
Source: *Strozzi pater et filius*, Aldus, 1513, part II, fol. 17*r*.
12 *Dictynne*: another name for Diana.

XXVII On Pontano, see poem III.
Source: *Opera poetica*, Venice, vol. II, 1533, fol. 199*r*.
1–2 I have followed modern editions; 1533 has: *Dum furtim mihi connives ocello / Flectis mox aciem, simulque rides.*
15 *speculam*: the original edition has *speculam*, which we have followed. Laurens and Balavoine in their anthology *Musae reduces* suggest that *speculum* (mirror) might be a more satisfactory reading.

XXVIII Source: *ibid.*, vol. I, 1518, fol. 6*r*–7*r*; Oeschger, 394–5. Metre: iambic trimeter followed by iambic bimeter.

    3   The Ethiopian king Memnon was the son of Tithonus and Aurora.

    22   *fascia*: the bands that covered the breasts.

    36   One suspects a error on Pontano's part: Hesperus is of course the evening star, but the context shows clearly that Pontano is referring to the morning star.

XXIX   Source: *ibid.*, vol. I, 1518, fol. 110*v*–111*r*.
       Transl.: Kendall, fol. 72*r*–73*r*.

    10   Kendall's translation refers to the Fates.

XXX   Marullus, Michael Tarchaniota (? –1500). Born in Constantinople, of partly Greek origin, he came early to Italy. For a time he resided in Naples and became friendly with Pontano, then moved to Florence where he was involved in a celebrated dispute with Politian, and married the poetess Alessandra Scala. He was drowned when trying to cross the river Cecica in midwinter. His collection of poems include successful love compositions, elegies of some distinction, polished epigrams and a series of hymns on cosmic themes. His influence in Germany, France and the Low Countries was considerable.

    See: B. Croce, *Michele Marullo Tarcaniota*, Bari, 1938; A. Sainati, *La lirica italiana del Rinascimento*, Pisa, 1919, vol. I, 69–161.

    Source: *Hymni et epigrammata Marulli*, Florence, 1597, fol. a vii*r*–*v*; modern ed.: *Carmina* ed. A. Perosa, Zurich, 1951, 13.

XXXI   Source: *ibid.*, fol. b viii*v*-c*r*; Perosa, 4.
       Transl.: Kendall, fol. 54*r*-*v*.

XXXII   Angeriano, Girolamo (? – ?). Little is known of his life except that he was of Neapolitan origin; he probably frequented Neo-latin circles in Rome, and in 1520 brought out his *Erotopaignion*. His verse, exclusively amatory, has anacreontic harmonics and remained popular right through to the eighteenth century.

    Source: *Erotopaignion*, fol. b viii*v*. Transl.: Kendall, fol. 57*v*.

XXXIII   On Navagero, see poem X.

    Source: *Doctissimorum nostra aetate Italorum Epigrammata*, Paris, ? 1546, fol. 44*r*.

    9   Cf. Catullus, lxiv, 259, *pars obscura cavis celebrabant*

orgia cistis.

10   refers to Ceres. Eleusis was famous for its mysteries in honour of Ceres.

14   Cf. the Ovidian nutrix.

XXXIV   Secundus, Ioannes (Jan Everaerts) (1511–36). Born in The Hague, was one of the children of a distinguished lawyer who became President of the Council in Mechlin. He came to study law under Alciat at Bourges, but on the death of his father in 1532 was appointed secretary to the Archbishop of Toledo, where his reputation grew rapidly. Illness obliged him to return home and he obtained a similar post with the Archbishop of Utrecht. A recurrence of his illness overtook him in Tournai where he died in October 1536. His travel diaries are still worth reading; he left prose letters and a considerable variety of Latin verse which is of some distinction, but it is the *Epithalamium* (see below, poem LXX) and the *Basia* which are remembered. The latter set a fashion which spread rapidly in the sixteenth century.

Source: *Opera* (1541), fol. k*r–v*. Transl.: *Anacreon, Bion, Moschus, kisses by Secundus. Cupid crucified by Ausonius. Venus Vigils Incerto Authore*, 1651 (by Thomas Stanley), 56–57. There is a modern edition of the *Basia* by K. Ellinger, Berlin, 1899, which gives extensive information on the fortunes of the poems, as well as some biographical information. Giles Fletcher and William Drummond certainly owe something to Secundus. See also D. Crane, *Johannes Secundus, his Life, Work and Influence on English Literature*, Leipzig–London, 1931.

1   Ascanius was the son of Aeneas and later the founder of Alba Longa.

5   Adonis was beloved of Venus; when he was killed, some say because of Mars' jealousy, he was changed into a flower by Venus.

11   Dione was mother of Venus.

17   Triptolemus, the king of Eleusis and Metanira, who invented agriculture.

XXXV   Source: *ibid.*, fol. L3*r–v*. Transl.: Stanley, 60–1.

XXXVI   Source: *ibid.*, fol. L6*v–7r*. Transl.: Stanley, 62–3.

6 Charon, the ferryman who transported the dead across the river Styx.

XXXVII   On Bourbon, see poem XV.

Source: *Nugarum libri octo*, Lyon, 1538, 114–15. Cf. above the poem by Angeriano; the themes of the last lines recall

Ronsard's poem to Hélène, *Quand vous serez bien vieille, au soir, à la chandelle.*

XXXVIII Muret, Marc-Antoine de (1526–85). Born in the Limousin, he showed great precocity in his studies. He taught in Auch, Poitiers and Bordeaux before going to Paris where he was closely associated with the Pléiade. Accused of sodomy, he left for Toulouse and then Italy where he first led a peripatetic, but brilliant career. He was later appointed professor of philosophy in Rome; in 1576 he took holy orders and died a canon of the Vatican. He left a considerable name as an orator and towards the end of his career composed a number of Christian hymns; he was also a classical scholar of distinction (Catullus, Venice 1554); but for our purpose it is the *Juvenilia*, 1552, that are important. They contain a play *Julius Caesar*, elegies, epigrams and occasional verse. Muret was known in England to some extent.

See: Charles Dejob, *Marc-Antoine Muret; un professeur français en Italie dans la seconde moitié du seizième siècle*, Paris, 1881 (there is no up-to-date biography); P. de Nolhac, *Ronsard et l'humanisme*, Paris, 1921.

Source: *Juvenilia*, Paris, 1552, 71. Transl.: Kendall, fol. 49*r*.

XXXIX On Du Bellay, see poem XIX.

Source: *Poematum libri quattuor*, Paris, 1558, fol. 37*r–v*.

The older view that the Faustina poems reflected an attachment in Rome is now discredited; it is possible that Du Bellay chose the name Faustina because there were some statues of a Roman lady of this name in the garden of his uncle, Cardinal Jean du Bellay.

XL Buchanan, George (1506–82). Born near Killearn, Buchanan spends much of his life before 1561 on the continent, mainly in France (1520–2, 1525–35 approximately, 1539–47 and 1552–61) with visits to Portugal and Italy. After he returns home, he is appointed tutor to Mary Queen of Scots and later her son James VI, takes an active part in the political, religious and educational life of his country, and finishes the major works: poems, psalm paraphrases, *De Jure Regni apud Scotos*, *Rerum Scoticarum Historia*. In his youth he was exposed to the religious winds of change in Paris, though his general attitude was pretty flexible until the return home; in his middle years he was a close friend of humanists and poets associated with the Pléiade. His reputation for a long time rested on his poetic compositions circulating mostly in manuscript, and on his scholarship; he seems to have been a useful textual critic in both Latin and Greek, though no work has survived. He was acclaimed as *poeta sui saeculi facile princeps* by Henri Estienne and others, and his poems are among the finest in sixteenth-century Europe. They were regularly reprinted until the nineteenth century.

See: I. D. McFarlane, *George Buchanan 1506–82*, London, 1979.

Source: *Opera omnia*, ed. Ruddiman-Burmann, Leiden, 1725, vol. II, 391–2. This extremely popular poem has a number of Renaissance analogues (Alciat, Marullus, Muret, Pamfilo Sasso) which probably all go back in some measure to Ausonius' *In simulachrum Occasionis et Poenitentiae* and the *Greek Anthology*, XVI, 275. Bèze's poem on *Descriptio Virtutis* (see above, poem XVIII) is influenced by Buchanan and possibly Muret. This poem has been translated several times since the eighteenth century; it seems to leave traces in a poem by the Earl of Oxford (Breton's *Bower of Delights*, 1591: 'Of the birth and bringing up of desire') and in a sonnet by Griffin (*Fidessa*, s. xliii).

XLI Melissus, Paulus (Schede) (1539–1602). Born in Franconia, he studied in Erfurt, Zwickau, Jena and Vienna. For his poetic activities in Vienna he was raised to noble status. He travelled widely, in Hungary, France (1567), Geneva, Italy, and England, where his verse impressed Queen Elizabeth. In the final stage of his career he became Librarian at Heidelberg. Though he translated some psalms into German (1572), he wrote mostly in Latin. The *Schediasmata* appeared first in 1574, the *Poemata* at Paris in 1586. A number of poems are addressed to English worthies.

Source: *Schediasmata poetica*, 1586, part III, 164–5.

This is a translation of a poem from Ronsard's *Continuation des Amours* (ed. Laumonier, *Oeuvres complètes*, VII, 129). In the last decades of the sixteenth century in France, poetic translation enjoys a renewed and vigorous popularity; and there were contemporaries in whose eyes Ronsard's fame would be best ensured for posterity by translation into Latin. Melissus adapts the French model to suit his own series of poems to Rosina, and maintains the same number of lines as the original.

XLII Bonefons, Jean (1554–1614). Born at Clermont d'Auvergne, Bonefons followed his father's profession and studied law at Bourges, where he became a close friend of Cujas' son. He went on to Paris where he led a rather gay life, but also took care to obtain the favour of various legal notabilities. His *Pancharis*, apparently in honour of a lady whose identity has not been established, was written then but did not appear until 1587, by which time he was lieutenant-général at Bar-sur-Seine. Though he continued to write a lot of encomiastic and sometimes rather formal pieces to colleagues, he is remembered for the *Pancharis* which develops neo-catullan and secundan themes in the direction of a very sophisticated preciosity; these poems were immensely successful in France and England.

See: Jean Bonefons, *La Pancharis*, publiée et traduite d'après le texte de 1587 par André Berry et Edgar Valès. Paris, J. Hammont, 1944. After Bonefons' death there appeared the *Poematum libri II ad manuscriptum authoris* collati et recogniti a Nicolao Blancardo, Leiden, 1654 (which shows a certain number of variants). In early editions the numbering of the *Pancharis* poems is affected by the fact that two liminary poems are introduced as part of the series.

Source: 1587 as reproduced by Berry and Valès (checked against R. Gherus, *Delitiae Poetarum Gallorum*, 1606, vol. I); See also 1654 edition, 27–8. Transl.: *Pancharis, Queen of Love or the Art of Kissing: in all its varieties*. Made English from the Basia of Bonefonius by several Hands. The second edition, London, 1722, 24–7.

16   line missing 1654.

23   Tibullus was a Roman elegist contemporary with Horace and Ovid; in the Renaissance his works were often published together with those of Catullus and Propertius.

XLIII   Source: *ibid.*, 54; 1654, 40. Transl.: *Pancharis*, 4–5.

XLIV   Source: *ibid.*, 70; 1654, 44. Transl.: *Pancharis*, 15.

XLV   On Pontano see poem III.
Source: *Opera poetica*, Venice, Aldus, vol. I, 1518, fol. 28*r*.
1   *Casis*, the Casi (Umbria).
3   *Lycaei*, Arcadian mountain sacred to Pan.
5   *Maenalioque*, Arcadian.
17   *Pelignosque*, inhabitants of what today is the Abruzzi.

XLVI   On Sannazaro see poem IX.
Source: *Opera*, Venice, Aldus, fol. 22*v*–23*r*.
On this poem, see Roland Mortier, *La poétique des ruines en France*, Geneva, 1974, 39–41. Cumae was a town on the coast of Campania, renowned for its Sibyl.
5   Daedalus escaped to Cumae from Crete where Minos had opposed his departure.
27   the seven hills of Rome.

28   Venice.

29   Naples.

XLVII   On Bourbon, see poem XV.

Source: *Recueil de vers latins et vulgares de plusieurs Poëtes françoys composés sur le trespas de feu Monsieur le Daulphin*, Lyon, F. Juste, 1536, fol. a 6*v*, reprinted in *Nugarum libri octo*, Lyon, 1538, 283–4. This elegy, which could have been included in the section of ceremonial verse, appeared first in a collective *tumulus* to the memory of François the Dauphin who was believed at the time to have been poisoned, but probably died of miliary tuberculosis. The enterprise was organised by Etienne Dolet, and constitutes an early French example of a *tumulus* by various hands, a genre that developed greatly in the second half of the sixteenth century. The volume was also intended to boost the claims of Neo-latin poetry. The year 1536 was noted for its drought; portents and supernatural phenomena will occupy a greater place in Neo-latin poetry in France during the last third of the century. See V.-L. Saulnier, 'La Mort du Dauphin François et son Tombeau poétique 1536', *BHR* 6 (1945), 50–97.

5   *Matrona*, the Marne. *Alba*, the Aube, a tributary of the Seine.

26–8 Renaissance topos of the immortality conferred by poetry.

XLVIII   Lotichius, Petrus Secundus (1528–60). Studied at Franfurt under Micyllus, and then at Marburg and Wittenberg. His scholarly interests were wide-ranging and he was an ardent Protestant, particularly devoted to Melanchthon under whom he had studied. As a tutor he was able to travel in France (where the first edition of his *Elegiae* was published in 1551) and in Italy. He died at Heidelberg where he held a chair of medicine and botany.

See: Walther Ludwig, 'Petrus Lotichius Secundus and the Roman elegists: prolegomena to a study of Neo-latin elegy', in *Classical Influences on European culture A.D. 1500–1700*, ed. R. R. Bolgar, Cambridge, 1976, 171–90.

Source: *Poemata*, Leiden, 1733, pp. 6–10. The elegy first appeared in 1551, but was much altered when it was next published in 1563. The poem is coloured by the fact that Lotichius had himself seen military service; the elegy is of course an excellent development too of the Renaissance interest in the contrast of arms and letters.

2   *Zobelle*, Melchior Zobel acquired military fame before

being appointed to the bishopric of Herbipolis (Graz); he was assassinated by a ;nefaria ... turba'. Burmann, the eighteenth-century editor of his poems, thinks that the elegy was written after the peace of Erfurt.

53   *Caesar*, Charles V: the general reference is to the war in the Balkans against the Turks.

XLIX   On Pontano, see poem III.

Source: *Opera poetica*, Venice, Aldus, vol. I, 1518, fol. 92*v*–93*r*.

2   *Patulci*, Pontano has personified his villa at the foot of the Vomero, near Naples.

3   *Pausilypi*, mountain between Naples and Puteoli.

4   *Antiniana*, another villa owned, and here personified by the poet, at Antigniano on the Vomero hill.

10   *Melisaeus*, Pontano.

12   *Menalcas*, probably Sannazar who also sang Mergellina where he had his residence (see below, poem LXXVI).

20   original reading *arripisse*, corrected in modern editions on metrical grounds.

21   *Palaemon*, a sea-god formerly called Melicerta, the son of Athamas and Ino; mentioned by Ovid and Vergil, he was the protector of harbours.

24   *Triton*, son of Neptune and Salacia.

29   refers to Patulcis and Antiniana.

L   On Navagero, see poem X.

Source: *Doctissimorum nostra aetate Italorum Epigrammata*, Paris, ? 1546, fol. 54*r*–*v*.

In classical legend, Aurora (the Dawn) was the wife of the aged Tithonus.

34   *Daulias*, Daulis, a city of Phocis, was the scene of the drama between Tereus, Philomela and Progne (see Ovid, *Metam.*, vi, 440 ff.). Progne was changed into a swallow.

LI   On Marcantonio Flaminio see poem VII.

Source: *Carminum libri IIII*, Florence, 1552, 105–6.

LII   Macrin, Jean Salmon (1490–1557). Born at Loudun, Macrin studied in Paris where he later taught for a while. He acquired a modest reputation as a scholar, was among the early French humanists interested in Greek literature, and was encouraged in various ways by Guillaume Budé. As a poet he emerges during Louis XII's reign in the field of aulic and religious verse; twelve years later he published in 1528 his *Carminum libellus* which marks a new departure in the French Neo-latin field, with its development of love poetry influenced by

Catullus and the elegists, perhaps also by Italian models. The volumes of the years 1528–31 show him to be a lyric poet much attracted by Horace, but also conversant with Marullus, Pontano and others. Like Pontano he sings his wife who remains one of his main sources of inspiration. Appointed *cubicularius regius c.* 1533, he follows the court in its peregrinations. Much of his later work is encomiastic, religious or domestic; there is no clear evidence that he was a Huguenot, though most of his children seem to have been converted. He helps to acclimatise Horatian themes and metres in France, develops religious poetry and contributes to the development of the collective *tumulus* by his *Naeniae* published in 1550 in memory of his wife. His poetry often prefigures features associated with members of the Pléiade.

See: I. D. McFarlane, 'Jean Salmon Macrin 1490–1557', *Bibliothèque d'Humanisme et Renaissance*, 1959 and 1960.

Source: *Carminum libellus*, Paris, Colines, 1528, fol. a iiiv–iv. An edition of a substantial number of the poems published between 1528 and 1531 has been prepared by Georges Soubeille (Toulouse) and will soon be on the market.

2   On the west side of Loudun there is the stream called Brisseau, whose source is in a secluded wood. Like the Pléiade (and Horace) Macrin links his inspiration to his *pays* and peoples it with mythical figures.

21   *platani*, a Horatian echo: plane trees were introduced into France slightly later, by Pierre Belon.

25   the *gigantomachia* is a well-known theme in sixteenth-century French poetry, and recurs in the work of one of Macrin's good friends, Joachim du Bellay.

33   *Flaminius*, Pierre Boursault, Macrin's brother-in-law, a young man of considerable promise who died young.

51   Macrin styled himself Iuliodunensis. The earlier name of Loudun was Lugdunum, and the association with Julius Caesar is a poetic attempt to confer distinction on the town and no doubt the poet.

LIII   On Flaminio, see poem VII.
Source: *Carmina de rebus devinis*, 1551, fol. Avv–vir.

LIV   Source: *In Librum psalmorum brevis explanatio* ..., Paris, Dupuy, 1551, fol. 383r–v.
Some of Flaminio's paraphrases found their way into H. Estienne's *Davidis Psalmi aliquot* ..., Paris, 1556; this volume also contains Macrin's verse of Psalm 128. Both may be compared with Buchanan's rendering.

LV   Billy, Jacques de (1535–81). Studied early in Paris, then at the age of eighteen he went to read law at Orléans which he disliked. He went on to Lyon and Avignon; there he appears to have studied Hebrew. Some time after 1559 he took up residence at St Michel en l'Herm (Vendée) where he had inherited a benefice from his brother. The troubles of the religious wars drove him to Paris and Laon. He died in Paris. He was a good Greek scholar, editing texts by Church Fathers, and wrote his *Sonnets spirituels* (1573, 1577) under the influence of the Counter-reformation. He was a friend of Jean Dorat.

Source: *Anthologia sacra*, Paris, N. Chesneau, 1575, fol. 43*v*; Transl. (or rather version): *Sonnets spirituels*, Paris, 1573, fol. 35*v*. Curiously Billy published his religious poems in Latin and in French at separate times. Dates of publication suggest strongly that the Latin versions were written after the original French. The *Sonnets spirituels* are accompanied by lengthy commentaries which include the patristic and biblical sources on which they are based. Billy was known in England; Heywood refers to him on more than one occasion, and the Bodley copy of the *Anthologia sacra*, 1575, was once owned by one of the Christ Church Latin poets active at the beginning of the seventeenth century.

LVI   Bettinus, Marius (1578–1657). Born in Bologna, he entered the Jesuit order and taught mathematics and philosophy for many years in Parma. He died in his native town. He published a number of volumes of verse (e.g. *Florilegium*, which went through as many as seven editions by 1632, Bologna).

Source: *Delitiae delitiarum*, 76.

LVII   On van Bauhuysen, see poem XXI.

Source: *Bernhardi Bauhusii et Balduini Cabillavi … Epigrammata. Caroli Malaperti … Poemata*, Antwerp, 1634 (the volume also has poems by F. Remond).

LVIII   Bidermann, Jacob (1578–1639). Born in Swabia, he entered the Jesuit order and spent an industrious, uneventful existence. He wrote a life of Ignatius Loyola and published various volumes of verse: *Delitiae sacrae*, Rome, 1636; *Heroum epistolae, Epigrammata et Herodias*, Antwerp, 1634, and others.

Source: *Delitiae delitiarum*, 140.

LIX   Source: *ibid.*, 138–9.

LX   Hugo, Hermannus (1588–1629). Entered the Jesuit order in

1607. He was a linguist of considerable ability, and became confessor to several German counts. He died of the plague. His *Pia desideria*, published in Antwerp in 1624, went through many editions down to the eighteenth century; they were translated into English by Edmund Arwaker, a version that was also very successful (1686, 1690, 1702, 1727?). But before the English version, they had been read by Catholic poets and left their mark on Francis Quarles' *Emblesmes*.

Source: *Pia desideria Emblematis illustrata*, Antwerp, 1624, 297–8. Transl.: *Pia desideria ... Englished by Edm. Arwaker*, London, 1686, 94–7.

LXI Remond, François (1558–1631). Born in Dijon, he entered the Jesuit order. He was a prolific versifier, and published his epigrams and elegies at Antwerp in 1606. He died of the plague in Mantua.

Source: *Francisci Remondi S. J. Elegiae. Alexis. in Bernhardi Bauhusii et Balduini Cabillavi ... Epigrammata. Caroli Malaperti ... Poemata*, Antwerp, *634, 247–9*. Transl.: Richard Crashaw, *Sacred Poems, the Third Elegie, The Poems English, Latin and Greek*, ed. L. C. Martin, Oxford, 1957, 336–7.

LXII On Pontano, see poem III.

Source: *Opera*, vol. II, 1533, Aldus, Venice, fol. 6*v*–7*r*.

The extract comes from Book I of the *Urania*; each book is sub-divided into sections with separate titles. The definitive version of the poem seems to have been written not earlier than 1490, though the first draft probably belongs to the 1470s. See Benedetto Soldati, *La poesia astrologica nel Quattrocento*, Florence, 1906, especially ch. V, 254–314. English scientific poetry rarely comes into the purview of students on their first-degree course, but Pontano is such an important figure in the development of Latin and vernacular poetry of this kind that a short sample of his writing in this vein is desirable. Pontano, like other scientific poets of the Renaissance, owes a good deal to Manilius, Lucretius and Vergil.

26 *Tethys*: wife of Oceanus and mother of sea-nymphs.

LXIII Vida, Marcus Hieronymus (1490–1566). Born in Cremona, he entered the religious life, eventually reaching the rank of Prior and then of Bishop of Alba (1532). His existence was uneventful. His contribution to Neo-latin poetry lies not in his rather cramped lyric compositions, but in his epic poem *Christias*, his *Ars poetica* (1527), and the *Game of Chess* which combines the technical poem with elements of the mock-epic.

See: Mario di Cesare, *Vida's Christiad and Vergilian Epic*, New York, 1964; and by the same author *Bibliotheca Vidiana*, Florence, 1974.

Source: *De arte poetica* ..., Rome 1527, fol. v*r–v*, and vi*r–*vii*v*. See *Text, English translation and commentary* by Ralph Williams, Dissertation, University of Michigan, 1968; Bernard Weinberg, *A History of Literary Criticism in the Italian Renaissance*, 2 vols., Chicago, 1961; Baxter Hathaway, *The Age of Criticism: the late Renaissance in Italy*, Ithaca, 1962. The translation used here is: *Vida's Art of Poetry* translated into English verse by the Reverend Mr Christopher Pitt, London, 1725, 10–14.

LXIV   Source: *De arte poetica* ..., Rome, 1527, fol. K vi*r–*vii*v* Transl.: Oliver Goldsmith, *Works*, ed. P. Cunningham, London, 1854, vol. IV, 377–94.

See: *The Game of Chess: Marco Girolamo Vida's Scacchia Ludus*, with English verse translation and the texts of the three earlier versions, ed. Mario di Cesare, Nieuwkoop, 1975.

10   *atque] iamque   iam* omitted 1527.

It should be added that not all critics accept the attribution of the translation to Goldsmith; it is, for instance, not included in the latest edition of the Complete Works by Freedman, 1966. On this matter, see M. di Cesare, *Bibliotheca Vidiana*, 159–60.

LXV   Palingenius, Marcellus (?1500–43). His real name was Pier Angelo Manzoli; he appears to have frequented the court of duke Ercole d'Este, whose wife Renée of France protected many Reformers and where he may have absorbed the elements of his own religious attitude. His *Zodiacus Vitae* was written after 1520 and came out in Venice in 1534. He died in 1543 and six years later his book was placed on the Index. It became very popular in Protestant countries, but ranges more widely than committed literature; it includes moral reflections, astronomic indeed cosmic themes and satirical passages (e.g. against Church abuses). There is no doubt a stoic infrastructure—praise of reason, and of true knowledge, an ascetic code of behaviour—but God is placed firmly at the centre of his universe.

See: G. Borgiani, *Marcello Palingenius Stellato e il suo poema lo Zodiacus Vitae*, Città di Castello, 1913; F. W. Watson, *The Zodiacus Vitae of Marcellus Palingenius Stellatus: an* old *school-book*, London, 1908; Luzius Keller, *Palingène, Ronsard, Du Bartas. Trois études sur la poésie cosmologique de la Renaissance*, Berne, 1974.

Source: *Zodiacus Vitae*, Basel, 1563, 102–5 (from Book V, Leo). Transl.: *The Zodiack of Life* ... newly translated by Barnabae Googe, London, 1565, fol. O *v*–Oiv*v*. (Scholars' Facsimiles and Reprints edition with introduction by Rosamond Tuve, 1947 reprinted New York, 1976.)

LXVI   Sainte-Marthe, Scévole (Gaucher) de (1536–1623). A member of a distinguished Poitou family, he studied under Muret, La Ramée and Turnèbe towards the time the Pléiade was emerging; later he studied law at Poitiers, before entering public life in various towns. He defended Henri III against the Ligue. He made his name as a poet in Latin and in French, translated various Neo-latin poems into vernacular verse and also wrote *Elogia* of his contemporaries. His Latin poems appeared first in 1575, and were reprinted with additional material on several occasions. The *Paedotrophia* is of interest because of its advocacy of breast-feeding, one of the reasons why it was restored to popularity in the eighteenth century; it also includes a poetic description of the Fall, which is reproduced here.

See: J. Plattard, *La Vie et l'oeuvre de Scévole de Sainte-Marthe*, *Bulletin de la Société de l'Ouest*, 1941.

Source: *Opera*, Paris, 1616, 16–19. Transl.: *Paedotrophia*, translated from the Latin of Scévole de Sainte-Marthe ... by H. W. Tytler, Esq., London, 1797, 42–8.

LXVII   On Secundus see poem XXXIV.

Source: *Opera* (1541), fol. R*r*–R4*r*. Transl.: George Ogee, trn. of *Epithalamium* published in 1731.

LXVIII   On Buchanan, see poem XL.

Source: *Opera omnia*, ed. Ruddiman–Burmann, Leiden, 1725, vol. II, 332–9; Transl.: *Epithalamium on the Marriage of Francis and Mary, Queen of Scots*. Translated from the original by George Buchanan. Edinburgh, 1845 (from a ms text dated Edinburgh 1711 Feb.). Lines 80–118 are not rendered in this version, and are here taken from George Provand, *The Franciscan Friar ... and the Marriage Ode of Francis of Valois and Mary Sovereigns of France and Scotland ...*, Glasgow, 1809, 109–11.

Mary and Francis were betrothed on 19 April, 1558; the wedding ceremony took place on Sunday 24 April. The whole affair was of course dictated by the political circumstances of France in their Epithalamia.

See: Antonia Fraser, *Mary Queen of Scots*, London, 1970; J. E. Phillips, *Images of a Queen—Mary Stewart in Sixteenth-century Literature*, Los Angeles, 1964.

Buchanan's poem was however not published immediately.

16–17 refers to the period before the Treaty of Cateau-Cambrésis.

26 Reference to the Trojan myth of the origins of the French monarchy.

166 Contemporary Scottish historians mention that, even before Jesus Christ, the Scots had been famed for their wealth in metals rather than in agriculture.

173 Reference to the Scottish archers famous in Europe then; they formed part of the French king's bodyguard.

176 John Major mentions in his History that the Scots refused to fortify their castles and forts lest these might become a place of refuge for their enemies. The wall in question is either Hadrian's or the Antonine wall that stretched from Clyde to Forth; the latter suits the context better.

184 *Gothi*, perhaps refers to the Picts annihilated by Kenneth.

186 The Saxons were defeated near Edinburgh during the reign of Eugenius V. Danish incursions were apparently frequent until the beginning of the eleventh century.

190 *Meroe*, a large island of the Nile, in Ethiopia.

200 *Carronis*, the river Carron near Falkirk. In Buchanan's time there stood a round tower nearby which he assumed to be a temple to the God Terminus. The Dunipace mounds erected by the Romans were a symbol of peace.

205ff. According to ancient myth, the Celts were considered to have cultural priority over the French. Charlemagne was believed to have invited two Scotsmen, Joannes and Clemens, to preside over the academic establishments he had recently founded. The Auld Alliance was founded by Charlemagne and Achaius in 809. Bishop Leslie and Buchanan perpetuate this legend in their histories.

223 refers to the Po, and therefore to the military campaigns being conducted in Italy by the maréchal de Brissac-Cossé, to whose son Buchanan was still tutor.

235 *genitore*, Henri II.

259 Mary was the daughter of Marie of Lorraine (Guise), the second wife of James V of Scotland.

LXIX   On Dorat, see poem XX.

Source: *Paean sive Hymnus in triplicem victoriam Caroli IX* ... (with author's own French translation), Paris, 1570, fol. Aiir–Br.

5   *Druidas*, The Catholics won the battle of Dreux on 19 December 1562, capturing the prince de Condé.

9   *Dionysiacum*, battle of St Denis, 10 November 1567, at which Anne de Monmorency was killed.

13ff.   The third victory was Jarnac (13 March 1569) in which Henry d'Anjou defeated Condé, Coligny and D'Andelot. Charles' military role was negligible; in the earlier battles the duc de Guise had played a prominent part. Anjou's role was not well viewed by Charles, his brother.

26   William of Orange and the duke of Zweibrucken.

37   *Marcellus*, the conqueror of Syracuse.

41   *Fabius*, Cunctator, dictator of the second Punic War.

46   i.e. Charlemagne.

57   Another example of Dorat's numerological fancies.

78   Catherine was often styled Cybele by court poets, including Ronsard.

83   The duc d'Anjou campaigned successfully against English troops in the West.

85   Francois duc d'Alencon, later duc d'Anjou when the previous duke became Henry III.

89   Marguerite de Valois, later to marry Henry of Navarre, and the author of interesting Memoirs.

LXX   Petrarch, Francesco (1304–74). Born at Arezzo, he went early to Avignon, then to Montpellier and Bologna, and after completing his studies took holy orders. The famous first meeting with Laura took place in 1327. He spent much of his life travelling, sometimes on diplomatic missions, at others for scholarly reasons: he had several sojourns in Provence but moved about also in Italy. Though his fame rests in great measure on his vernacular poetry, he attached much importance to his Latin poem *Africa*; and certain other Latin works had immense impact, including the *De remediis* and the *Bucolicum carmen* (the eclogues). The experience of Rome in 1337 fixed his resolve to restore Latin studies and create a new Latinity.

See: E. H. Wilkins, *Life of Petrarch*, Chicago, 1961, as well as other monographs by the same author; U. Bosco, *Francesco Petrarca*, 2nd ed. 1961.

Source: *Bucolicum carmen ... in xii eglogis distinctum*, 1473, fol. 3r–4v; modern ed. by Tonino T. Mattucci, *Il Bucolicum carmen*, Pisa, 1970; see also *Laurea occidens. Bucolicum carmen*: testo trad. et commentato a cura di G. Martellotti, Rome, 1968.

This, the second eclogue, was one of those composed in 1346. It is a good example of the way in which contemporary events are shrouded in complex allegorical mode, a pattern that will recur in many court eclogues of the sixteenth century. Petrarch, with Vergil's fifth eclogue not far from his mind, celebrates the death of Robert of Anjou (Naples) his chief patron (19 January 1343). The key to the political allusions is to be found in a letter from the author to Barbato and Basili (*Epistolae variae*, No. 49). Andrew, the grand-nephew and married to Robert's grand-daughter Joan (1342) was designated as his successor, but was assassinated on 18 September 1345, a day or so before his intended coronation. The focus of the poem is the praise of Robert. The characters are as follows: Agrius = Robert; Idius = Barili; Pythias = Barbato Sulmoneo; Silvius = Petrarch.

5   *lenis somnus*, the peaceful state of the times.
6   *baculos*, reference to those who sought bishoprics and other ecclesiastical posts.
7–8 *fusca nubes*, death.
12–13 *altior . . . cupressus*, refers to the death of Robert.
24   According to *Epistolae variae*, No. 49, Petrarch chose the name Silvius in preference to Damon because of his love of woods and because this type of poetry came to him in his woodland solitude.
34   Jupiter, according to the legend, was suckled by Amalthea, daughter of Melissaeus. Early commentators believed that Christ, not Jupiter, was intended here.
42–5 the nobles showed hostility to the young king.
44   *Saturnum*, the Pope.
45   *Venerem*, Queen Joan 'quae Andream regem proterve respiciebat et mala intentione'.
47   *nebulas*, hangers-on of the queen.
48   *grues*, peace-loving men.
51   *Luna*, Robert's second wife, Sancha of Aragon, who entered a convent.
53   Reference to elder men prophesying these events.
89   *silva*, the realm here.   109 Variant: *artes* (skills).
113 *formosis . . . puellis*, the Muses.
122 *Sulmo*, where Barbato lived.
123 *silvas Etruscas*, Petrarch's region.
The elucidation of the Eclogues has been greatly helped

by various early commentaries; see Antonio Avena, *Il bucolicum carmen e suoi commenti inediti*, Padua, 1906. There is a modern English translation, *Petrarch's Bucolicum Carmen*, translated and annotated by Thomas G. Bergin, New Haven–London, 1974.

LXXI   Spagnuoli, Giovanni Battista (*c.* 1447–1516). Of partly Spanish descent, he was born in Mantua, where he studied under Tifernate and Georgius Merula. After further study at Padua he entered the Carmelite order of which he became Vicar-general in 1483. A prolific writer he wrote silvae, many poems of religious character (e.g. *Parthenicae*), but his fame rests mainly on his Eclogues (*Adolescentia*). The first eight were composed at Padua *c.* 1465, the other two in the 1480s. Late-medieval in inspiration, they are essentially didactic, but they have a wide range of tone and theme, and there is in Mantuan, as he is often known, a racy observer of the human scene. In spite of defects in Latinity and prosody, the eclogues established themselves in the school curriculum for some two centuries—often in the commented edition of Josse Bade. They were translated into the vernacular and left their mark on poets such as Alexander Barclay and Edmund Spenser. The satiric vein and the verbal vitality of these eclogues account for some of their popularity, and it is very likely that his rhetorical devices and linguistic habits influenced later writers. The seventh eclogue, quieter in tone than some of the others, has an evident autobiographical background.

See: *The Eclogues of Mantuan*, ed. W. P. Mustard, Baltimore, 1911.

Source: *Adolescentia in Aeglogas divisa*, Mantua, 1498, fol. Dvi*v*–eiii*v*. See also Mustard's edition. Transl.: *The Eglogs of the Poet B. Mantuan Carmelitan*, turned into English verse ... by George Turberville, Gent. anno 1567, London, fol. 65*v*–72*r*.

4   *bardocucullus*, a woollen coat of Gallic origin with a cowl; Mantuan uses the term to describe monastic garb.

9–56   Mustard sees this as the source for part of Alexander Barclay's fifth eclogue.

10   *Imber*, Gregorio Tifernate. Pollux is probably Mantuan himself.

14–31 Mustard sees echoes of these lines in Spenser's *July Aeglogue*, ll. 129–57.

25   *postea*, treated here as dactylic.

88 The choice of Hercules.

    Oreades, some early editions had *Orcades* (hence, English rendering).

172 *Baldo*, mountain near the Lago di Garda.

LXXII On Castiglione, see poem VI.

  Source: *Carmina quinque illustrium poetarum*, Venice, 1558, fol. 28*v*–31*r*. Composed in 1505 to the memory of Matteo Falcone, a friend from Castiglione's student days at Milan and later tutor to one of his younger brothers. This eclogue has left its mark on Milton's *Epitaphium Damonis*. Iolas is the author himself.

  See: T. P. Harrison, 'The Latin Pastorals of Milton and Castiglione', *PMLA* L (1935), pp. 480–93.

134 cf. Vergil, *Aeneid*, i, 409.

LXXIII On Sannazaro, see poem IX.

  Source: *Opera omnia*, Venice, Aldus, 1535, fol. 31*v*–33*r*. See also *The Piscatory Eclogues of Jacopo Sannazar*, ed. W. P. Mustard, Baltimore, 1914; Enrico Carrara, *La Poesia pastorale*, Milan, 1909; I. della Lunga, *Le Egloghe piscatorie di Jacopo Sannazaro*, Milan, 1909. The *editio princeps* appeared in 1526. These eclogues had an immense vogue and influenced poets right down to the eighteenth century. In England, Phineas Fletcher was particularly indebted to him, both in his Latin and vernacular verse. Transl.: *Select Translations* ... by Mr Rooke, London, 1726, 14–21.

5 J.–C. Scaliger quotes a version of this line which he had seen ten years before the first edition, with *rimantur* for *conlustrant*.

21 *Aenaria*, island of Ischia.

23 *Hyale*, Constanza d'Avalos, duchess of Francavilla, who in 1503 resisted for four months the French blockade of Ischia.

32 *Euploea*, island to the south-west of the Posilipo.

33 Scaliger's version read: *servat adhuc; totidem virides mihi Nesi echinos*.

42 *Melisaeus*, Pontano.

78 *Caietae*, Gaeta.

There is a modern translation of Sannazar's major works: *Arcadia and Piscatorial Eclogues*, translated with an introduction by Ralph Nash, Detroit, 1966.

LXXIV On Buchanan see poem XL.

  Source: *Opera omnia*, ed. Ruddiman–Burmann, Leiden,

1725, vol. II, 326–9. Transl.: *Select Translations* ... by Mr Rooke, London, 1726, 44–53.

P. de la Taste was a member of a well-known legal family in south-west France; Buchanan may have come to know him in Bordeaux, but at the time of the composition of the silva, his friend was studying law in Poitiers.

32   *Dordonides*, Ruddiman's correction of *Dardonidas*; this makes sense since the reference is to the Dordogne. The eighteenth-century translation interprets the word in a somewhat fanciful manner.

43   *Crotellae*, Croutelle, a little village south-west of Poitiers.